Sustainable Development Goals Series

The **Sustainable Development Goals Series** is Springer Nature's inaugural cross-imprint book series that addresses and supports the United Nations' seventeen Sustainable Development Goals. The series fosters comprehensive research focused on these global targets and endeavours to address some of society's greatest grand challenges. The SDGs are inherently multidisciplinary, and they bring people working across different fields together and working towards a common goal. In this spirit, the Sustainable Development Goals series is the first at Springer Nature to publish books under both the Springer and Palgrave Macmillan imprints, bringing the strengths of our imprints together.

The Sustainable Development Goals Series is organized into eighteen subseries: one subseries based around each of the seventeen respective Sustainable Development Goals, and an eighteenth subseries, "Connecting the Goals," which serves as a home for volumes addressing multiple goals or studying the SDGs as a whole. Each subseries is guided by an expert Subseries Advisor with years or decades of experience studying and addressing core components of their respective Goal.

The SDG Series has a remit as broad as the SDGs themselves, and contributions are welcome from scientists, academics, policymakers, and researchers working in fields related to any of the seventeen goals. If you are interested in contributing a monograph or curated volume to the series, please contact the Publishers: Zachary Romano [Springer; zachary.romano@springer.com] and Rachael Ballard [Palgrave Macmillan; rachael.ballard@palgrave.com].

Jan Servaes • Muhammad Jameel Yusha'u
Editors

SDG18 Communicaton for All, Volume 2

Regional Perspectives and Special Cases

palgrave
macmillan

Editors
Jan Servaes
KU Leuven
Leuven, Belgium

Muhammad Jameel Yusha'u
Harvard Kennedy School
Cambridge, MA, USA

ISSN 2523-3084 ISSN 2523-3092 (electronic)
Sustainable Development Goals Series
ISBN 978-3-031-19458-0 ISBN 978-3-031-19459-7 (eBook)
https://doi.org/10.1007/978-3-031-19459-7

This Palgrave Macmillan imprint is published by the registered company Springer Nature Switzerland AG.
The registered company address is: Gewerbestrasse 11, 6330 Cham, Switzerland

To the millions of people who strive for a sustainable future that is just and equitable, whilst living within the limits of supporting ecosystems.
To Patchanee, Fiona, Lisa, and extended families…
To Hauwa, Asma and Aishah for the blessing of having you as a family

Preface and Overview of the Books

Serendipity still exists. Even in corona times!

In September 2020 we were informed by Mala Sanghera-Warren, Commissioning Editor of Journalism, Media and Communication, and Molly Beck, coordinator of the advisory boards for Humanities subject areas at the Palgrave Macmillan office in London, that Palgrave was creating a new cross-disciplinary series dedicated to the Sustainable Development Goals (SDGs). The Palgrave Sustainable Development Goals series will span Palgrave's entire publishing portfolio, from Humanities subject areas (Media Studies, Cultural Studies, Literature, History, and Philosophy) to Politics, the Social Sciences, and Business and Finance.

They inquired whether I'd be interested in joining the advisory board for this new series. During the pursuing exchanges I did accept not only the board's membership but also the challenge to coordinate the editing of two volumes, of what we initially called "the missing SDG".

A Call for Chapters and Abstracts was distributed widely with a deadline set for 10 June 2021. Authors whose abstract met the high-quality criteria were contacted by 10 July 2021. Full chapters were expected by 1 November 2021. A total of 36 chapters were submitted. They all went through a two-tier peer-review process. This review and selection process was not always easy. We had to disappoint a number of people who were eager to contribute. After revisions, 21 manuscripts were selected for publication. They are split over the two volumes as follows:

Overview of Volume 2: Regional Perspectives and Special Cases

This volume contains ten chapters.

The introductory chapter by Jan Servaes and Muhammad Jameel Yusha'u summarizes the highlights from Volume 1 and elaborates on the Sustainable Competitiveness Framework.

In *Chap. 2*, Charles C. Okigbo and Jude Ogbodo start by noticing that the global landscape for development communication and social change has changed radically in the new millennium. Among the most significant of these changes is the international consensus on the importance of setting transnational targets for socio-economic developments across the globe. However, what was glaringly missing in this commitment was the recognition that communication is the catalyst and engine that drives positive socio-economic changes locally, regionally, and globally.

This has necessitated the call for "Communication for All" to stress the centrality and urgency of communication in serious development and social change enterprises.

The authors provide a short background on the MDGs and SDGs, as a backdrop for explaining Communication for All before arguing why it matters, especially in the African development context. They argue that Communication for All should have been the 18th SDG, but now that it is not the case, strategic communication deserves to be a clear component of all the 17 SDGs. The binding constraints of African development present perplexing and multifactorial challenges that deserve more attention than they get now from within the continent. More than any other world region, Africa needs "Communication for All" to pervade all aspects of human engagement on the continent.

Chapter 3, by Edgardo Luis Carniglia, argues that systematic, deep, and persistent inequalities are considered the main dilemma of development communication theory and practice in Latin America, the most unequal subcontinent in the twenty-first century.

Dilemmas related to social class, income, well-being, ethnicity, gender, and territory inequalities pose a serious threat for the future of development communication research and practice in a heterogeneous Latin American space, which at present is more vulnerable as a result of the COVID-19 pandemic.

Chapter 4, by Paul Clemens Murschetz, Franzisca Weder, Eduard Frantz, and Timo Meynhardt, explores the role of Public Service Media

(PSM) in supporting SDG18, from facilitating dialogue within the community to acting as a critical watchdog over business and government. They look to issues of public value theory and performance measurement with a view to strengthening PSM's role toward remaining strong arbiters of SDG18.

Critical debates into public value theory and performance management practice can help improve our understanding of the challenges of PSM trying to add value to programming output and service quality as perceived by audiences. In their view, the Public Value Scorecard (PVSC) model, which measures public value from an audience perspective, is an effective framework to generate valuable insights into the needs of increased audience engagement of public value creation for PSM.

In *Chap. 5*, Holly Randell-Moon focuses on First Nations voices in the Australian media landscape, as it has been well established that Australian news reporting has been harmful to First Nations. Misinformation about First Nations continues through deficit discourse and the framing of First Nations through statistics as deprived in comparison to non-Indigenous socio-economic standards. The sustainability of First Nations is inextricably connected to the accessibility, contestation, and creation of communication platforms that center First Nations information, perspectives, and goals.

An SDG18 Communication for All would not only support the important role of First Nations to the global communications environment; it would create a policy framework and information literacy imperative to ensure First Nations sovereign communication.

Chapter 6, by Bashir Sa'ad Abdullahi and Habeeb Idris Pindiga, compares traditional mass media to social media platforms from the perspective of educating the public about the SDGs and thereby help achieve social and behavioral changes needed to attain the goals.

This chapter tracks the major and recurring disinformation trends about SDGs on social media platforms and how COVID-19 exacerbated the trends of disinformation on SDGs. Studies have shown that development issues, in particular those pertaining to SDG3 (Health) and SDG13 (Climate action), are prone to disinformation. Using sampled social media posts from Twitter, along with insights from documented cases around the world, the chapter highlights the impact of disinformation on the attainment of the SDGs, arguing that such disinformation is undermining the implementation of the SDGs. The chapter further makes recommendations on how effective communication by all stakeholders can help tackle the damage disinformation is doing to the journey toward attaining the SDGs.

In *Chap. 7*, Sharynne McLeod, Sarah Verdon, and Kathryn Crowe contend that if SDG18 truly stands for "Communication for All", then we must listen to and advocate for people whose voices are rarely heard despite their right to "freedom of opinion and expression" being articulated as in the Universal Declaration of Human Rights and subsequent conventions and declarations.

This chapter focuses on three groups of people whose voices are particularly marginalized: (1) people with communication disabilities, (2) children, and (3) people who do not speak/understand/read/write the dominant language of their community. These three groups make up a large portion of the world's population but are unheard due to their invisible disability. The intersectionality between these three groups is a particular focus of this chapter leading to a call for multilingual children with communication disability to be supported to take their place as communicators in society, to fulfill their potential as multilingual speakers, and to realize their communication rights.

Chapter 8, by Satarupa Dasgupta, argues that women's equality is an integral aspect of inclusive and sustainable development. Therefore, the success of all SDGs depends on the achievement of Goal 5—the attainment of gender equality. Unfortunately, the targeted elimination of many of the structural barriers that restrict women's rights in private and public spheres has halted due to the COVID-19 pandemic.

Intimate partner violence (IPV) is of serious national concern that has the potential to be exacerbated in scope and impact by the COVID-19 pandemic. The chapter incorporates a conceptual framework of intersectionality, which recognizes that women of color experience life and negotiate a pandemic through multiple systems of oppression. The effects of the COVID-19 pandemic can reverse the limited progress made on gender equality and women's rights globally.

The chapter adds to research on a proposed SDG18 which will create a framework of accessible communication strategies for all. The proposed SDG18 can play an important role in overcoming barriers toward the attainment of Goal 5 among immigrant women (in the US), by highlighting on intersecting issues of displacement and marginalization during and after the pandemic.

In *Chap. 9*, Nurcan Törenli and Zafer Kıyan review the crisis communication model adopted by the Turkish Ministry of Health. The study argues that an effective crisis communication strategy, required during the COVID-19 pandemic, could not be adopted due to the communication problems across the social stakeholders in Turkey. This miscommunication stemmed from the Ministry of Health's flawed strategy and the value paradox due to the neglect of social reaction, demands, concerns, and requirements.

The Ministry of Health did not provide accurate, adequate, and timely information to its citizens, leading to the interruption of mutual and solidaristic communication between the ruler and the ruled. The Turkish COVID-19 experience presented in the study is a significant example that demonstrated how the provision of Sustainable Development Goals, especially the elimination of poverty (SGD1), hunger (SGD2), health and welfare (SGD3), and gender equality (SGD5), could be interrupted, and how the disruption of communication during the crisis could complicate normalization for social stakeholders in the absence of an accurate and realistic communication strategy.

A summary with conclusions is being presented in the concluding *Chap. 10.*

Overview of Volume 1: The Missing Link Between SDGs and Global Agendas

This volume contains 11 chapters.

In the introductory chapter, Jan Servaes and Muhammad Jameel Yusha'u position the need for an 18th Sustainable Development Goal—Communication for All.

Chapter 2, by Laurenzo Vargas and Philip Lee, explores the intersections between the United Nations Sustainable Development Goals (Agenda 2030) and communication and information issues. Taking a communication rights-based approach that emphasizes the need to address communication and information poverty in order to achieve sustainable development, the authors examine the four goals (5, 9, 16, and 17) where communication and information issues feature most prominently and make the case for the inclusion of an 18th goal—Communication for All—in order to address a range of communication and information deficits, such as digital exclusion and undemocratic media landscapes, that impede meaningful and transformational sustainable development.

Chapter 3, by Chi Kit Chan and Paul Siu Nam Lee, explicates the significance of communication to the promotion and practices of Sustainable Development Goals (SDGs). The chapter highlights how communication could contribute, and is indispensable, to the grand project of (re)setting global agendas for the sustainable goals.

In other words, communication is a much-needed jigsaw puzzle to complete the global momentum to (re)set SDGs as our universal goals. It plugs the strategic gap of shaping the world as well as local opinion, scrutinizes the cultural issues of introducing SDGs to different societies, and ushers in constructive and constitutive dialogues among various disciplines, contributing to social development for all.

In *Chap. 4*, Víctor M. Marí Sáez presents two primary theoretical challenges: the analysis of the basic characteristics of the current socio-political context of extractive capitalism and the ability to consider communication as an alternative post-capitalist horizon. He argues that a conception of (material and social) goods and communication as a commons implies a radically alternative worldview and political horizon. This approach includes a perspective of the economy, environment, and communication which encounters in the formulation of the commons a very useful theoretical template for constructing alternatives to extractive capitalism.

In *Chap. 5*, Andrea Ricci argues that six forces shape contemporary information and communication eco-systems. The first force is the logarithmic growth of information, particularly, but not only in the social media landscape. The second force is produced by the phenomena of the reflectivity of information and the impacts of reverb tails. The third force comes from the presumed recipients of information which have increasingly inconstant and insufficient attention. The fourth force is played by competition which disaggregates communities, including those of media and intelligence practitioners. The fifth force is brought by propaganda which dominates in a time erroneously considered as peaceful. The sixth force is introduced by oblivion and its growing black whole, the edges of which seem to start just after real-time experiences.

The six forces strike at the very core the metabolism of development: fostering the growth of cultures which hamper progress; limiting the understanding of "what works" to an elite of nomads with little capacity or willingness to coalesce; even endangering—with intelligence failures or ineffective risk analysis—the survival of individuals, companies, and State organizations. The sequence of strategic intelligence failures since 9/11, the incapacity to stop climate change, the unfolding of the COVID pandemic, the challenges brought by globalization and social media to companies' growth and individuals can all be analyzed under the lens of epistemic and cultural disservices induced by the influence of the six forces. The forces have in the past already challenged society. Today the energy behind the forces is dangerous: in stark contrast with the amount of information and communication at our disposal, basic certainties seem unknowable, weak, and questionable. Acts of governance are necessary to inverse the polarity at each of these six levels, truly supporting all other SDGs.

Chapter 6, by Naíde Müller, argues that strategic communication is a determining factor for social mobilization in the achievement of legitimacy and participatory and democratic adhesion. However, several areas of strategic communication, namely public relations, have long failed to recognize activism-related activities as an integral part of discipline and practice.

In this chapter, a case study which builds on an ethnographic approach at UMAR, a feminist NGO based in Portugal, and the consultation of communication experts is presented to illustrate the areas where public relations and activism intersect and to show how these intersections could be better understood and debated if SDG18 were included in the 2030 Agenda.

In *Chap. 7*, Valentina Bau discusses the importance of media literacy among groups who have experienced conflict, with particular focus on the youth. Drawing on the essential competencies of the digital and media literacy framework, the chapter analyzes the role that communication for development (C4D) projects implemented in conflict-affected realities can play when media literacy is placed at the center.

While discussing how these interventions can be built to have a positive impact on young people living in conflict-affected realities, this chapter reveals how targeting media literacy through a communication-specific goal is essential for development.

Chapter 8, by Jude William Genilo and Kamolrat Intaratat, investigated the initiatives and undertakings of the top ranked universities in the THE Impact Rankings 2021 toward Communicating the SDGs. The top ranked universities included (1) University of Manchester, (2) University of Sydney, (3) RMIT University, (4) La Trobe University, and (5) Queen's University. The findings indicated that these universities allocated a lot of time, energy, and resources in communicating the SDGs—through their teaching (degree programs); research (books, book chapters, and research papers); stewardship (websites, student-run media, and campus-based platforms); and community outreach (social media accounts, news articles, blogs, podcasts, video recordings, and opinion pieces). Based on their endeavors, the chapter recommends performance metrics and indicators for possible inclusion in future THE Impact Rankings.

Chapter 9, by Rachel E. Khan and Yvonne Chua, assesses disinformation or the so-called fake news which causes public confusion and risky behavior. They argue that misinformation undermines one of the underlying goals of communication for all: the formation of an informed and critical citizenry so essential to democracy and development.

Using the COVID-19 pandemic as a take-off point, this chapter discusses the ecology of false information and a scoping review of its effects on SDG goals. The chapter also discusses the processes by which disinformation is spread from the obscurity of the internet to the sphere of public and private communication platforms. As important, it explores multistakeholder efforts in countering fake news, and simple, appropriate tools and responses that citizens can use to safeguard spaces for communication.

In *Chap. 10*, Sol Sanguinetti-Cordero argues that the COVID pandemic presents us with a key opportunity to explore alternative ways in which the SDGs could be more inclusively applied. The first step should be to create a SDG18 in order to foster the realization of each of the 17 SDGs earlier agreed upon by the UN, thus promoting development and social change. Although the technology, knowhow, and all the necessary tools we need for a more developed, inclusive, healthy, and sustainable society already exist, SDG18 should be the means through which these reach the people who need them the most.

This chapter critically analyzes and explores what available routes of actions already exist and are not being exploited thoroughly, and which could be expeditiously developed or put to use in order to foster a more integrated communication system for development and social change within the SDG framework.

A summary with conclusions is being presented in the concluding *Chap. 11*.

Leuven, Belgium — Jan Servaes
Cambridge, MA, USA — Muhammad Jameel Yusha'u

Acknowledgments

We would like to acknowledge several people for their assistance in the preparation of these volumes.

In the first place, of course, all authors who contributed a chapter. Their expertise is self-evidenced across all contributions. We shouldn't forget other authors who expressed a sincere interest in the subject matter, some even submitted an abstract and chapter, but got selected out during the final review process.

The reviewers should be thanked for their assistance with the selection and peer review of the abstracts and manuscripts. The nature of their work requires that they remain anonymous.

At the publisher's level, apart from Mala Sanghera-Warren and Molly Beck, also Lauriane Piette, Associate Editor, and Arunaa Devi, the Book Project Coordinator and her production team, should be singled out.

Jan Servaes, Diest, Belgium

Muhammad Jameel Yusha'u, Jeddah, Saudi Arabia

21 May 2022, Eat more Fruits and Vegetables Day

Praise for *SDG18 Communicaton for All, Volume 2*

"This book has filled an important gap in communication for development. The country perspectives across different regions of the world have shown that communication is inevitable in addressing key development challenges such as poverty, hunger, climate change, peace and governance. The UN should consider SDG18 as a goal in the SDGs."

—Abdalla Uba Adamu, Professor, *Department of Information and Media Studies, Bayero University, Kano, Nigeria*

"This book thematizes the contradiction between the omnipresence of communication and the secondary role it is often attributed. The book's contributions unpack how communication has the ability to nourish the redistribution of power and open spaces for global dialogue."

—Nico Carpentier, President, *International Association for Media and Communication Research (IAMCR)*

Contents

Notes on Contributors

Edgardo Luis Carniglia a native and resident in Argentina, works at the Communication Department, School of Humanities, of the National University of Rio Cuarto. A complete undergraduate and postgraduate training and professional career in the Argentine public university, for more than three decades, reveal a systematic training and extensive research experience on communication for development from the convergence between social sciences and humanities. The theoretical-methodological work deepened the study of, among other problems, interpersonal, mediated, and digital communication in the relations between the countryside and the city crossed by social change. The permanent participation in research teams generated numerous publications in the form of books, chapters, articles, and technical assistance reports. The constant undergraduate and postgraduate teaching in thesis workshops for the social sciences and the supervision of thesis students provide feedback on this sustained trajectory of socio-scientific research. A prolonged participation in research associations projects the expertise accumulated in international academic scenarios such as IAMCR and ALAIC. Since February 2019, he is regular director of the ISTE—Institute of Social, Territorial and Educational Research, Universidad Nacional de Río Cuarto, Córdoba, Argentina (UNRC-CONICET).

He is author or co-author of books **such as** *Territorios latinoamericanos. Ciudades, ruralidades políticas de desarrollo* (UniRío, 2020), *Maestras y TIC en escuelas ruralizadas. Claves del acceso en la pampa cordobesa* (UniRío, 2019), *Un territorio desigual. Memorias y agendas de investigación para el sur de Córdoba* (UniRío, 2018), *Entre políticas, aulas y hogares. Dilemas de la* *informática educativa pública* (Dunken, 2013), *Políticas de desarrollo para los municipios del Gran Río Cuarto. Diagnósticos, agendas y proyectos 2011–2020* (UniRío, 2013), *De labradores y campos de papel. Recepción de prensa agraria por agricultores familiares* (EAE, 2012), etc.

Kathryn Crowe, PhD is a postdoctoral scholar at the University of Iceland and previous Fulbright Postdoctoral Scholar at the Center for Education Research Partnerships. She is a valued member of the International Expert Panel on Multilingual Children's Speech. Her research focuses on multimodalism and multilingualism, caregiver and professional decision-making, and speech and semantic skills in children and young adults with hearing loss.

Satarupa Dasgupta, PhD is Assistant Professor of Communication Arts (Applied Communication) at Ramapo College of New Jersey. Her research focuses on health communication, program development and evaluation, and social outreach, with experience spanning academia and not-for-profit sector. She has worked on violence prevention among commercial sex workers, prevention of sex trafficking, and rehabilitation of sex trafficking survivors in international settings, and also intimate partner violence support service provision among immigrant communities in the US. Other than being an academic, she has been a sexual assault advocate in her state of residence and has worked in the implementation of federally funded domestic violence and sexual assault support services programs among immigrant populations. She possesses extensive track record of producing peer-reviewed publications and grant writing. She has also served several national and international organizations as program chair and is on the editorial board for several journals.

Eduard Frantz, MA is a communication scientist and management researcher. Currently, he writes his doctoral thesis at the Dr. Arend Oetker Chair of Business Psychology and Leadership at HHL Leipzig Graduate School of Management, Germany, with the focus on issues of public value–oriented management and leadership, especially in the context of Public Service Media.

Zafer Kıyan, PhD is a research assistant at the Department of Journalism in the University of Ankara, since May 2009. He obtained his PhD from Ankara University in 2015. His research interests are the political economy of media and communication, information society studies, technology and culture, Internet and society, commodification of culture, social media, and protest movements studies.

Sharynne McLeod, PhD is a speech-language pathologist and Professor of Speech and Language Acquisition at Charles Sturt University, Australia. She has received Honors of the American Speech-Language-Hearing Association, is a Life Member of Speech Pathology Australia, and is a Fellow of the Royal Society of New South Wales. She has been an Australian Research Council Future Fellow, editor-in-chief of the *International Journal of Speech-Language Pathology*, and vice president of the International Clinical Linguistics and Phonetics Association. She has co-authored 11 books and over 230 peer-reviewed journal articles and chapters focusing on children's speech acquisition, speech sound disorders, and multilingualism. She has won Editors' Awards from *Journal of Speech, Language, and Hearing: Speech* (2018), *American Journal of Speech-Language Pathology* (2019), and *Topics in Language Disorders* (2020). She was named Australia's Research Field Leader in Audiology, Speech, and Language Pathology (2018, 2019, and 2020).

Timo Meynhardt, PhD is Professor of Business Psychology and Leadership at HHL Leipzig Graduate School of Management, Germany, and managing director of the Center for Leadership and Values in Society at the University of St. Gallen, Switzerland. He developed the Public Value Theory based on psychological needs and is editor of the *GemeinwohlAtlas*.

Paul Clemens Murschetz habil. Dr. MSc., is Lecturer in Media Management and Media Economics for HAW Hamburg. He currently works as senior researcher for Health Economics at the Paracelsus Medical University in Salzburg, Austria (Institute of Ecomedicine).

Jude N. Ogbodo, PhD teaches Mass Communication at Ebonyi State University, Abakaliki, Nigeria. He got his PhD in 2018 from the School of Journalism, Media and Performance, University of Central Lancashire, Preston, UK. He has published in different local and international journals in the areas of political communication, health communication, crisis communication, and alternative journalism. Outside his teaching time, Jude also writes for *Peio News* as a guest writer. He is a social entrepreneur, philanthropist, and advocate of equality and global peace.

Jude is a member of professional bodies such as African Council for Communication Education (ACCE) and Association of Communication Scholars and Professionals of Nigeria (ACSPN). He also belongs to some research groups and committees such as the Committee on Unbundling of Mass Communication in Nigeria, Ebonyi State University.

Charles C. Okigbo, PhD is a Professor Emeritus at North Dakota State University, where he taught advertising, public relations, strategic communication, action research, international communication, and social research methods. He is currently directing action research in election campaigns and strategic corporate communication. His other academic and professional interests are in mixed methods applications in studying social problems and executive education in fundraising and capital campaigns. His teaching experiences include full- or part-time positions at the University of Nigeria, the University of Lagos, the University of Nairobi, and Daystar University (Nairobi). He had been the Registrar of the Advertising Practitioners Council of Nigeria (APCON) and the Executive Coordinator of the African Council for Communication Education (ACCE) in Nairobi. His consulting experiences include work for UNESCO (Paris), UNICEF (East Africa), UNAIDS (Switzerland), and ORBICOM (Canada). His publications include *Development and Communication in Africa* (Rowman and Littlefield), *Development Communication Principles* (ACCE), and *Strategic Urban Health Communication* (Springer).

Habeeb Idris Pindiga is a doctoral candidate in Media and Communication at the University of Leicester, UK. His doctoral project investigates the factors shaping the content and journalistic practices of Nigerian newspapers. He currently works as Lead Knowledge Horizons Specialist at the Islamic Development Bank Institute (IsDBI), a role in which he leads a team responsible for communication, marketing and publications. Pindiga is a former editor of Nigeria's *Daily Trust* newspaper where he worked first as a reporter before rising through the ranks. He also served as an acting editor for the newspaper's weekend titles, *Weekly Trust and Sunday Trust.* He holds a master's degree in Communications, Media and Public Relations from the University of Leicester, UK, and attended the Executive Education Winter Course in Corporate Communication at Rotterdam School of Management, Netherlands, and The First 90 Days Executive Education Course at IMD Business School, Switzerland. He has co-authored a chapter on the nature of press coverage of the SDGs, published in the *Palgrave Handbook of International Communication and Sustainable Development*, and an article on the political implications of media framing of presidential illness, published in the *Journal of African Media Studies.* His areas of research interest include news production, development communication, political communication and media systems.

Holly Randell-Moon, PhD is a senior lecturer in the School of Indigenous Australian Studies, Charles Sturt University, Australia. She has published on cultural geography and digital infrastructure in *Media International Australia* and *Westminster Papers in Communication and Culture*. Along with Ryan Tippet, she is the editor of *Security, Race, Biopower: Essays on Technology and Corporeality* (Palgrave Macmillan, 2016). She is co-editor of the journal, *Somatechnics*.

Bashir Sa'ad Abdullahi is Doctoral Researcher in Media Studies at the Communications and Media Research Institute (CAMRI), University of Westminster, UK. Sa'ad Abdullahi's doctoral research focuses on disinformation ecosystems in Africa, with particular focus on "fake news" and its impact on journalism, governance, and coexistence in Nigeria. Bashir Sa'ad Abdullahi was a former editor of the BBC World Service's Abuja bureau in Nigeria. Bashir is the co-author of a chapter on 'Communicating Development: News Coverage of the SDGs in the Nigerian Press', published in the *Palgrave Handbook of International Communication and Sustainable Development*. His previous research focused on new media, development, and political communication. Bashir Sa'ad Abdullahi holds a master's degree in journalism and another master's degree in business administration.

Jan Servaes, PhD is Prof. Emeritus at KULeuven, Leuven, Belgium, and has been UNESCO Chair in Communication for Sustainable Social Change. He has taught International Communication and Communication for Social Change in Australia, Belgium, China, Hong Kong, the United States, the Netherlands, and Thailand, in addition to several teaching stints at about 120 universities in 55 countries. Servaes is editor of the Lexington Book Series *Communication, Globalization and Cultural Identity* (https://rowman.com/Action/SERIES/LEX/LEXCGC) and the Springer Book Series *Communication, Culture and Change in Asia* (http://www.springer.com/series/13565) and was editor-in-chief of the Elsevier journal *Telematics and Informatics: An Interdisciplinary Journal on the Social Impacts of New Technologies*.

Servaes has undertaken research, development, and advisory work around the world and is the author of more than 500 journal articles and 30 books on such topics as international and development communication, ICT and media policies, intercultural communication, participation and social change, and human rights and conflict management. He is known for his "multiplicity paradigm" in *Communication for Development. One World, Multiple Cultures* (1999).

Nurcan Törenli is a professor at the Faculty of Communication, Ankara University (Turkey). His research interests are crisis communication, social media, the political economy of new media, and information and communication technologies. Törenli has published several books, articles, and conference papers related to these topics.

Sarah Verdon, PhD is Associate Professor and head of Speech-Language Pathology at Charles Sturt University, Australia. Her research focuses on the development of a culturally responsive workforce and supporting the communication of children from diverse backgrounds. She is co-chair of the International Expert Panel on Multilingual Children's Speech and oversaw the development of the Speech Pathology Australia national position paper and clinical guidelines for "working in a culturally and linguistically diverse society".

Franzisca Weder is an associate professor, habil Dr., and a senior lecturer at the University of Queensland, Brisbane (Australia), and is researching, writing, and teaching in the areas of Organizational Communication and Public Relations with a specific focus on Sustainability Communication and Corporate Social Responsibility. She is chair of the Austrian Association of Communication Studies and chair of the International Environmental Communication Association (IECA).

Muhammad Jameel Yusha'u (PhD) is Editor-in-Chief of *Africa Policy Journal* and Edward S. Mason Fellow in Public Policy and Management, and Mid-Career candidate in the master program in Public Administration at John F. Kennedy School of Government, Harvard University. He works as the Division Manager for Outreach & Communication at the Islamic Development Bank. He is the author of *Regional Parallelism and Corruption Scandals in Nigeria* (2018) and co-editor of *The Palgrave Handbook of International Communication and Sustainable Development* (2021). He has worked as a journalist with the BBC World Service, London. During his stint at the BBC, he has contributed content/punditry to BBC World Today, BBC Focus on Africa, BBC World Have Your Say, BBC Arabic and more. He coordinated the first multimedia election desk and represented the Africa Service in reporting the royal wedding of the Duke and Duchess of Cambridge for the BBC. Prior to joining the

BBC, he was British Correspondent for Deutsche Welle (Hausa Service). He has served as Senior Lecturer in Media and Politics and Program Leader for the master's program in mass communication/business at Northumbria University, Newcastle upon Tyne, UK; Associate Lecturer in Global Journalism at the University of Sheffield; as well as a Lecturer in Mass Communication at Bayero University, Kano, Nigeria. He holds a PhD in Journalism Studies and MA in Political Communication from the University of Sheffield, UK, and an MBA from IE Business School, Madrid, Spain. Jameel is an alumnus of the Executive Education Program in Innovation and Entrepreneurship: Policy Considerations, JF Kennedy School of Government, Harvard University, and the Silicon Valley Executive Education Program in Innovation and Entrepreneurship, Haas School of Business, University of California, Berkeley. His research has been published in leading journals such as *Global Media and Communication*, *African Journalism Studies*, *Journal of African Media Studies* and the *Journal of Arab and Muslim Media Research*. He has published several book chapters on online journalism, corruption and the media, critical discourse analysis, and representation of Muslims in the media.

Abbreviations

ACCE	African Council for Communication Education
ACMC	Asian Congress for Media and Communication
AI	Artificial Intelligence
AIBD	Asian Institute for Broadcasting Development
AIDS	Acquired Immune Deficiency Syndrome
AMIC	Asian Media Information and Communication Centre
ASEAN	Association of Southeast Asian Nations
BCC	Behavior Change Communication
CCMS	Centre for Communication, Media and Society
CCSDG	Communication/Culture and the Sustainable Development Goals
CDSC	Communication for Development and Social Change
CfD or C4D	Communication for Development
CFPD	Communication for Participatory Development
CIA	Central Intelligence Agency
CIESPAL	International Center for Higher Communication Studies in Latin America
CODESRIA	Council for the Development of Social Science Research in Africa
CS	Corporate Sustainability
CSC	Communication for Social Change
CSD	Commission on Sustainable Development
CSO	Civil Society Organization
CSR	Corporate Social Responsibility
CSSC	Communication for Sustainable Social Change
CSSC&D	Communication for Sustainable Social Change and Development

CTCs	Community Technology Centers
DevCom	Development Communication
DSC	Development Support Communication
EC	European Commission
ECA	Ethnographic Content Analysis
EIA	Environmental Impact Assessment
EU	European Union
FAO	Food and Agriculture Organization
FGD	Focus Group Discussions
GAID	Global Alliance for ICT and Development
GATS	General Agreement on Trade in Services
GDI	Gender Development Index
GDP	Gross Domestic Product
GEM	Gender Equity Measure
GFATM	Global Fund to Fight AIDS, Tuberculosis, and Malaria
GLTB	Gay, Lesbian, Transgender, and Bisexual
GNH	Gross National Happiness
GNI	Gross National Income
GNP	Gross National Product
HDI	Human Development Index
HIV	Human Immunodeficiency Virus
HIV/AIDS	Human Immunodeficiency Virus/Acquired Immune Deficiency Syndrome
HPI	Human Poverty Index
IAMCR	International Association for Media and Communication Research
ICA	International Communication Association
ICT4D	ICTs for Development
ICTD	Information and Communication Technologies for Development
ICTs	Information and Communication Technologies
ILO	International Labour Organisation
IMF	International Monetary Fund
INEXSK	Infrastructure, Experience, Skills, Knowledge
IPDC	International Programme for the Development of Communication
IPS	Inter Press Service
ISCED	International Standard Classification of Education
IT	Information Technology
ITU	International Telecommunications Union
IUCN	International Union for Conservation of Nature
KAP	Knowledge, Attitude, and Behavior
LDCs	Least Developed Countries

M&E	Monitoring and Evaluation
MDGs	Millennium Development Goals
MOOCs	Massive Online Open Courses
NAM	Non-Aligned Movement
NGO	Non-Governmental Organization
NICTs	New Information and Communication Technologies
NITI	National Institution for Transforming India
NTIA	US National Telecommunications and Information Administration
NWICO	New World Information and Communication Order
OECD	Organisation for Economic Co-operation and Development
OPEC	Organization of Petroleum Exporting Countries
OU	Open University
PAR	Participatory Action Research
PBS	Public Broadcasting Service
PCR	Participatory Communication Research
PCRN	Participatory Communication Research Section/Network
PDR	People's Democratic Republic
PFA	Press Foundation of Asia
PPE	Personal protective equipment
PPP	Public-Private Partnership
PR	Public Relations
PSA	Public Service Advertisement
PSB	Public Service Broadcasting
PSM	Public Service Media
PV	Participatory Video
PVE	Perceived Value of Exchange
PVU	Perceived Value of Use
R&D	Research and Development
RME	Research, Monitoring, and Evaluation
RNTC	Radio Netherlands Training Center
RTC	Right to Communicate
SAARC	South Asian Association for Regional Cooperation
SD	Sustainable Development
SDGs	Sustainable Development Goals
SE	Sufficiency Economy
SEs	Social Enterprises
SEZ	Special Economic Zone
SITE	Satellite Instructional Television Experiment
SME	Small and Medium Enterprise
SMS	Short Message Service
STI	Sexually Transmitted Infections

TAM	Technology Acceptance Model
UDHR	Universal Declaration of Human Rights
UGC	User-generated content
UK	United Kingdom
UN	United Nations
UNAIDS	Joint United Nations Programme on HIV/AIDS
UNCDP	United Nations Capital Development Programme
UNCED	United Nations Conference on Environment and Development
UNCSD	United Nations Conference on Sustainable Development
UNCSTD	United Nations Commission on Science and Technology for Development
UNCTAD	United Nations Conference on Trade and Development
UNDG	UN Development Group
UNDP	United Nations Development Programme
UNEP	United Nations Environment Programme
UNESCO	United Nations Educational, Scientific, and Cultural Organization
UNFCCC	United Nations Framework Convention on Climate Change
UNFPA	United Nations Population Fund
UNICEF	United Nations Children's Fund
UNIFEM	United Nations Development Fund for Women
UNSC	United Nations Statistical Commission
US	United States
USAID	United States Agency for International Development
USSR	Union of Soviet Socialist Republics
WB	World Bank
WCC	World Council of Churches
WCED	World Commission on Environment and Development
WFTO	World Fair Trade Organization
WHO	World Health Organization
WMO	World Meteorological Organization
WSIS	World Summit on the Information Society
WTO	World Trade Organization
WWF	World Wildlife Fund

List of Figures

List of Tables

CHAPTER 1

Introduction: Sustainable Competitiveness in a Digital Age

Jan Servaes and Muhammad Jameel Yusha'u

Abstract This introductory chapter looks at new ways of assessing the methodologies used and impact of the SDGs at different societal levels. It analyses sustainable competitiveness for a nation-economy and identifies principles to promote communication for social justice in a digital age.

Keywords Social justice • Sustainable competitiveness • Digital age

Introduction

The 2030 Agenda for Development, also known as the Sustainable Development Goals (SDGs), is perhaps the most ambitious agenda collectively agreed by 193 countries in recent history. In 2015, the UN

J. Servaes (✉)
KU Leuven, Leuven, Belgium

M. J. Yusha'u
Operations Complex of the Islamic Development Bank (IsDB), Jeddah, Saudi Arabia

J. Servaes, M. J. Yusha'u (eds.), *SDG18 Communicaton for All, Volume 2*, Sustainable Development Goals Series,
https://doi.org/10.1007/978-3-031-19459-7_1

Member States adopted the 17 SDGs as a framework that would help address the challenges being faced by humanity. From eradicating poverty, ending hunger, providing universal access to healthcare and education, addressing climate change; to the partnering of individuals, philanthropists and nation states to achieve the global goals (UNDP, 2020).

Yet, the drafters of the 2030 agenda for development, comprising key stakeholders from all sectors of life, forgot to dedicate one goal to the role of communication and culture in achieving the SDGs.

In Volume 1 we have tried to correct this oversight, and we argued that it is nearly impossible to achieve the SDGs without the articulation and embrace of the role of communication for development. The challenge for us is to revisit and reposition the field of Sustainable Development and the SDGs and include communication and culture in it.

In this introduction to Volume 2, we will further problematize the challenges by looking at new ways of assessing the impact of sustainabilities, analysing sustainable competitiveness for a nation-economy and identifying p**rinciples to promote communication for social justice in a digital age.**

The SDGs Since COVID

Before the COVID-19 outbreak, the world was making progress towards the SDGs. Although no country was on track to achieve the SDGs, the evolution of the SDG Index scores (included in the Sustainable Development Reports) between 2010 and 2019 suggests some convergence, with regions and income groups that had lower SDG Index scores in 2010 progressing faster (Servaes & Yusha'u, 2021).

In particular, areas of the Global South, including sub-Saharan Africa, Latin America and the Caribbean, made significant progress during the MDGs period (2000–2015) and also showed progress during the early years of the SDGs. Of all UN regions, East and South Asia demonstrated the most progress on the SDGs (Salsiah et al., 2020).

Nevertheless, the reports also highlighted significant disparities in progress across the goals and countries. For example, Côte d'Ivoire, Burkina Faso and Cambodia improved the most on the SDGs, while Venezuela, Zimbabwe and the Republic of the Congo regressed the most (Sachs et al., 2020).

However, as argued by Samarajiva (2020), broad categorizations in geographic terms like "developed" world or the "industrialized" world or "advanced" nations make little sense. What does that mean?: "How developed are you if you don't have public health? How industrialized are you if you cannot distribute tests and PPE? How advanced are you if your people won't even wear a mask?" Furthermore, appealing to the individual social responsibility of citizens doesn't seem to work; notwithstanding economic or education levels. Hence, for instance, while in the East the wearing of masks was accepted by the population at large, in the West it was resisted by many with references to ambiguous 'freedom' calls.

Also the discussion about globalization (Servaes, 2015) emerged again with some arguing that "nation states" have remained important during the corona crisis. While globalization facilitates the rapid spread of viruses around the world, concerted national action by governments, the private sector, civil society and the scientific community has led to different solutions and strategies at national rather than supranational or global levels.

The current crisis, including hostilities among major powers like China versus the US, raises the *fear of global conflict instead of global cooperation*. Some do also see other trends emerging: "The traditional powers of the west are neither as strong economically, nor as confident of their social and organizational superiority" (Khan & Khan, 2020).

The magnitude of the COVID-19 pandemic has been forcing us to rethink our strategies and approaches, also with regard to the SDGs (Akufo-Addo & Solberg, 2020). The pandemic has drawn attention to the fact that, in order to support those who are hit hardest, our development interventions should be reassessed from a more multidimensional and local perspective (Horton, 2020). The social and human costs of this system evidenced at a micro level reveal the unequal nature of the current global economic system.

This is in clear contrast to the past when the transformation of the developmental state that became widespread after World War II and the decolonization period of the 1970s witnessed a series of state interventionist policies to promote economic growth, increase equality and encourage social cohesion.

Undoubtedly, some of these policies were controversial in many instances. For example, the economic interventionist and modernist approach proposed by foreign nations in developing nations with ultimate goal of discouraging the drive towards socialism that characterized the Cold War era. The rise of a modern form of capitalism epitomized by neoliberalism has become a predominant economic ideology that governs the world with repercussion on economic viability and social-cultural wellbeing.

The aggressive advancement of neoliberalism in the less developed countries by the "Washington Consensus" of the US government, the International Monetary Fund and the World Bank coupled with the adoption and transmission of this ideology into political platforms of developing nations played a major role in the shaping of the current global economy (Pollin, 2003).

The unequal benefits that accrue to nations due to neoliberalism create a pattern of winners and losers. The free trade policies and liberalization tendencies open many developing nations to foreign transnational corporations who set up 'sweatshops' for the manufacturing of products to be consumed in the developed countries. The poor in these less-developed nations are left with no choice but to participate in this process for a meagre income as handout to step out of abject poverty.

Questioning Methodologies and Impact Assessments

Already at an early stage, Jan Vandemoortele (2015), the "architect" of the MDGs, started raising questions on methodology and impact of the development goals. He started arguing that the global narrative—"mostly driven by global statistics and world maps for the MDGs"—needed to change radically. "The global assessment needs to pay more attention to how global targets make a difference at national and sub-national levels". And he elaborated further: "Despite their comprehensiveness and wordy nature, the SDGs lack sufficient specifics to qualify as a major reboot". To be valid, a target must contain three elements: (1) a numerical outcome, (2) a specific deadline and (3) a well-defined domain.

Item 3.1, for example, is a valid target: by 2030, reduce the global maternal mortality ratio to less than 70 per 100,000 live births.

On the other hand, item 17.2 does not contain a deadline: developed countries to implement fully their ODA commitments, including the commitment by many developed countries to achieve the target of 0.7% of ODA/GNI.

Item 16.5—substantially reduce corruption and bribery in all their forms—lacks all three elements.

The SDGs actually contain many such items as 16.5. The list is a mixture of ideals and norms, values and principles, generalities and oddities, and some repetitions; a few valid targets are sprinkled in. Indeed, the SDGs may contain 169 bullets, but actually fewer than 30 are concrete targets. "Not only does their complexity turn the SDGs into a difficult storyline, but also their fuzziness will create leeway and latitude for non-objective narratives" (Vandemoortele, 2016, see also Vandemoortele, 2017).

Also Lennie and Tacchi (2013) claim that standard indicators (which are widely applied by both academics and policymakers) are unable to capture complex realities and relationships:

> They can be useful ways of measuring change but not of capturing the reasons behind social change. In Communication for Development (C4D), and in particular the Communication for Social Change approach, indicators should be developed through dialogue and negotiation between key participants, so that they are chosen based on local assessments of what participants want to know and why, and they are more realistic and useful. While quantitative indicators are emphasized in mainstream Monitoring and Evaluation (ME) approaches, for C4D they often need to be qualitative to be most effective and appropriate. An alternative systems approach requires indicators that are flexible and encompass complexity, or, the use of alternatives to indicators such as stories of significant change and 'verifying assumptions'. (Lennie & Tacchi, 2013, p. 7)

In other words, the practical relevance of the SDGs requires that we dig deeper. Implementation needs to start with each country selecting and adapting those aspects of the SDGs that are most relevant to their national context. This is often dismissed as cherry-picking through a non-participatory process. However, in our opinion, besides government, such selection and adaptation need to include civil society, academics, think tanks, trade unions, employers' federations, and the people at large (Vandemoortele, 2018; Servaes, 2007, 2008, 2017). The question should also be how global targets make a difference at national and sub-national levels? Because, as Bali Swain and Yang-Wallentin argue: "Resources are limited and SDGs are fraught with trade-offs and inconsistencies. Therefore, strategic policy focus on socio-economic development in the developing countries may be a successful short-run policy to achieve sustainable development. Developed countries' results, however, suggest a greater propensity to achieve sustainable development by focus on the environmental and social factors" (Bali & Yang-Wallentin, 2020, p. 105).

Lie and Servaes (2000) adopted a convergent and integrated approach in studying the complex and intricate relations between globalization, consumption and identity. Such an approach would allow problems to converge at *key crossings* or nodal points. Researchers then are rid of the burden of studying linear processes in totality, for example, production and consumption of global products, and instead are allowed to focus on the nodal points where processes of in/equality intersect.

Several such nodal points were identified, including production, regulation, representation, consumption, action and local points of entry into the communications flow. The nodal points approach highlights the relevance of globalization as an area of research; however, it is also important to note that all these dimensions do rest on certain axial principles.

Social inequalities, human and environmental *sustainability* have become such central themes in global communication. Considerations and assessments of in/equality or sustainability are necessary to ensure a world worth living in for future generations. Besides political-economic approaches, *we also need socio-cultural approaches* to understand inequality or sustainability better. Moreover, it is essential to recognize that these problems are complex or *wicked*, and do not result in one single solution that is right or wrong, good or bad, or true or false. These are problems in which many stakeholders are involved, all of them framing the problems and issues in a different way.

Hence, we introduced *another way* of assessing the impact of inequality in communication by using "sustainability" as the main focus of analysis in a *matrix* for the study of social problems (such as in/equality) in media and communication (see Servaes et al., 2012; Servaes, 2013, 2014).

For each indicator we raised a set of questions designed to specifically measure the sustainability of a social change development communication project. We defined 'sustainability' by analysing whether the channels are compatible with both the capacity of the actors and the structural and conjunctural factors. If they are, the project will have a higher likelihood of being sustainable in the long run. We asked, to what extent was the process participatory and consistent with the cultural values of the community? Was the message developed by local actors in the community, and how was it understood? Our research showed, the more local and interactive the participation—in levels, communication approaches, channels, processes and methods—the more sustainable the project would be, and hence it would contribute to less inequality.

We didn't claim that the indicators we presented are the only ones available. For sure, other contextual indicators—such as financial structures, levels of professionalism and/or governance mechanisms—could also be considered and developed further.

One of the key aspects in this matrix is the issue of participation. Participation is essential not only in understanding inequality in media and communication, but equally in addressing inequities. Participation forces us to confront positionality of power and the marginality of groups in society.

As evidenced by the contributions in the two volumes on social inequalities, media and communication (Servaes, 2016; Servaes & Oyedemi, 2016a, 2016b), positionality of power and marginality push to the forefront of social inquiry the issue of empowerment. As a result scholars in these two volumes ask critical questions about how the social constructions of history, gender, economy, race and class define who can (not) shape narratives about people and how such narrative in the media shape lived-experiences.

Communication for Social Justice in a Digital Age

In addition to these methodological and epistemological questions, we need to highlight two more specific issues which have come to the foreground recently: the challenges for communication for social justice in the digital age, and the new innovative ways to assess sustainable competitiveness for nation states.

At a Symposium of the World Council of Churches (WCC) on 21 September 2021, the following specific challenges were identified for Communication for Social Justice in today's Digital Age (**https://www.oikoumene.org/resources/documents/manifesto-of-the-symposium-communication-for-social-justice-in-a-digital-age**):

- We face various *digital divides*: economic, geographic, racial, educational, class, gender, age, cultural, technological and global. There are also digitally caused divides.

These digital divides point to both the complexity of social justice in a digital age and the need for intersectional reflection. Digital justice requires, at the same time, gender justice, climate justice, economic justice, racial justice and so much more.

- ***Accessibility:*** The primary concern is often seen as access to the digital space itself, emphasizing the difference between lower-, middle- and higher-income economies, and also in-country differences. Meaningful access includes access to basic communication infrastructure such as stable electricity and internet connections, tech devices, access to various digital tools, data, programming and content from the local cultural context, but also the legal frameworks and economic resources to access and invest in them.

Access affects power relations and distribution of resources, and as such, access to digital technologies is both a cause and a result of divides.

- ***Public space:*** This is the space where states and the public interact, where people, including the media, can express thoughts and feelings and participate democratically. Digitalization creates the opportunity for expanding this space, but the restriction of digital freedom can also cause this space to shrink.
- ***Inequity:*** Control, use and analysis of data gathered due to digitalization are heavily vested in a few corporations and in specific geographic regions. Governments may also be heavily implicated in data control and manipulation.
- ***Education:*** Digital education, including in questioning and critical examination of information and sources, is vital for all people. Access to this education is often sharply divided based on age, academic background, language, gender, geographical location and societal gender roles.
- ***Gender justice:*** Women benefit from digitalization in the personal, educational and economic arena, and active participation in the digital space can contribute to full participation in all domains of life. However, pervasive gender power inequities restrict this access.

Increased digitalization has also led to greater exposure of girls and women to sexualized harassment, surveillance, trolling and online hate, which may also lead to physical violence. The impact of online violence is silencing women, forcing them to disengage from the digital space.

- ***Privacy and security:*** The universal challenges of the use of data and loss of privacy are compounded by arbitrary government control, national digital laws and guidelines that are vague and fraught with loopholes, internet blackouts that clamp down on online dissent and unwarranted state surveillance.
- ***Militarization:*** There is military investment in digital technologies, and the technologies are in turn militarized—increasing risk in situations of war and conflict.

Similar trends and concerns can be found in other reports, such as WEF's *Global Risks Report 2022*: "Along with labour market imbalances, protectionist policies and widening disparities in education and skills, the economic fallout from the pandemic risks splitting the world into divergent trajectories".

The Five Pillars of Sustainable Competitiveness for a Nation-Economy

Published since 2012 by the sustainable intelligence think tank and consultancy SolAbility (https://solability.com/), the *Global Sustainable Competitiveness Index (GSCI)* is the most comprehensive ranking of countries currently available. *Sustainable Competitiveness means 'the ability of a country to meet the needs and basic requirements of current generations while sustaining or growing the national and individual wealth into the future without depleting natural and social capital'.*

The *GSCI* measures competitiveness of countries based on 131 measurable, quantitative indicators derived from reliable sources, such as the World Bank, the IMF and various UN agencies.

The 131 Indicators are grouped into the five pillars of a nation-economy: Natural Capital; Social Capital; Resource Efficiency; Intensity, Intellectual Capital & Innovation; plus, Governance Efficiency. As a whole they contribute to an understanding of the Sustainable Competitiveness needed to assess the relevance and impact of the SDGs (Fig. 1.1).

- *National Capital*: the given natural environment, including the availability of resources, and the level of the depletion of those resources—the Natural Capital Index 2021—is topped by Laos, followed by Colombia, Paraguay and Bolivia.
- *Social Capital*: health, freedom, security, equality and life satisfaction within a country, contributing to social cohesion—the Social Capital Index is topped by Iceland, followed by the other Scandinavian nations.
- *Resource Efficiency & Intensity*: efficiency as a measure of operational competitiveness in a resource-constrained world, calculated per capita and per economic output—the Resource Efficiency Index is topped by Malawi, followed by Kenya and El Salvador.

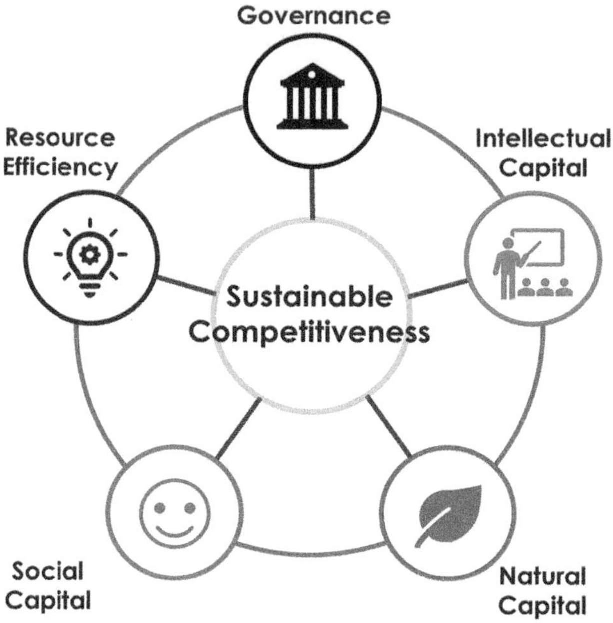

Fig. 1.1 Sustainable Competitiveness Framework

- *Intellectual Capital & Innovation:* the capability to generate wealth and jobs through education, innovation and value-added industries in the globalized markets—North-Eastern Asian nations (South Korea, China, Japan and Singapore), plus Scandinavian nations (Sweden and Denmark) dominate the Intellectual Capital Index of the GSCI.
- *Governance Efficiency*: the results of core state areas and investments, for such as infrastructure, market and employment structure, provision of a framework for sustained and sustainable wealth generation, plus resource allocation, corruption and fiscal considerations—the Governance Index is topped by Estonia, followed by Ireland, the Czech Republic and Finland.

For more details, see https://sustmeme.com/2021/10/07/beyond-gdp-global-sustainable-competitiveness-index-2021

In addition to the full integration of sustainability performance data, the sustainable competitiveness index also analyses and incorporates the data trends over time to allow for a better expression of the future development potential. The results aim at serving as an alternative to the GDP and to be used to analyse future development prospects of nations.

For instance, focusing on the *Intellectual Capital* pillar one can elaborate further on education and innovation. Countries with a high score in this ranking are more likely than others to develop (or sustain) successful economies through research and knowledge-driven industries, that is, high-value added industries, and therefore achieve higher growth rates.

The global average in the Intellectual Capital Index is 40—the gap to a perfect World 60 (https://solability.com/the-global-sustainable-competitiveness-index/the-index/intellectual-capital). The difference between low-performing countries (lowest: 15) and the highest score (78) is striking and reflects—even stronger than a GNI comparison—the North-South dimension. A high score in the Intellectual Capital Index is the basis for future innovation and therefore economic success. Unfortunately, poor countries also score poorly in Intellectual Capital, raising the fear that large parts of Africa will remain trapped in poverty.

On a positive note, nearly 60% of all indicators show positive development globally. However, most of the improvements seem to be originating in Europe, Far & South-East Asia and Americas (excluding Central America).

The *Intellectual Capital Index Ranking 2021* shows that:

- North-Eastern Asian nations (S. Korea, China, Japan, Singapore) and the Scandinavian Nations (Sweden, Denmark) dominate the intellectual capital sub-index of the GSCI.
- North-East Asia trend show a faster development than their counterparts in 'The West'.
- The innovation and competitiveness ranking continue to be topped by South Korea—by a considerable margin.
- The UK is ranked 6th, the US 8 and Germany 11.
- Eastern European countries and the Baltic States rank fairly high.
- Of the BRICS countries, China ranked 2nd, Russia 16, Brazil 28, South Africa 65 and India 103.
- The highest ranked South American Nations are Chile (51) and Brazil (52) and Costa Rica (58).
- Africa is unfortunately still underperforming in the global comparison, raising fear of prolonged entrapment in poverty.

Principles to Promote Communication for Social Justice in a Digital Age

No matter the issue—violence against women, abuse of children, poverty, conflict resolution, self-determination, racism, migration, labour rights, Indigenous rights, health, land, climate—little can be done without effective communication.

For this, we need a holistic, inclusive approach to create digital technologies that promote life, dignity and justice rather than undermine it.

We need principles that allow all people to engage in transparent, informed and democratic debate, where people have unfettered access to the information and knowledge essential to peaceful coexistence, empowerment, responsible civic engagement and mutual accountability.

Rooted in the history of communication rights, these principles provide for a world in which:

- Everyone is entitled to communicate, to inform and to share knowledge. This requires equitable access to communication infrastructures and the right to free expression.
- Everyone is entitled to participate in the information and communication society with particular consideration for minority and vulnerable groups. This requires inclusive and participatory governance of media infrastructures and digital platforms.
- Everyone is entitled to fair and unbiased public communication. This requires ethical norms, accountability and redress for misrepresentation.
- Everyone is entitled to dignity and respect. This requires transparency and accountability of media and digital platforms.
- Everyone is entitled to privacy and control of their information, including deleting their data, provided they are not engaged in human rights abuses or criminal activity. This should be inherent and intrinsic to each person's digital identity and requires legal frameworks that balance the right to privacy and the protection of human rights.
- Everyone is entitled to their own cultural and linguistic identity. This requires spaces for linguistic and cultural diversity, and access to ownership and control of media.

- Everyone is entitled to communication skills and media literacy. This requires culturally appropriate training and building dialogue, conversation, listening, openness and critical thinking skills.
- Everyone has access to sustainable power sources to enable their digital or electronic media. This requires access to technologies such as solar or wind power.
- Everyone is entitled to affordable devices or public access to devices in safe spaces. This requires economic resources as well as the 'right to repair'.

Achieving Sustainable Competitiveness

Solability claims that a more sustainable ***and*** more prosperous economy is not a utopia (https://solability.com/global-sustainable-competitiveness-index/12-policies-for-more-sustainable-and-more-competitive-socities). It can be achieved—technically, not politically—fairly simple through 12 policies for more sustainable and more competitive societies:

1. ***A global climate tax.*** Climate change is a gigantic market failure. We need a global climate tax—introduced in phases, paid back to the people in cash and reinvested in a renewable energy infrastructure—to avoid disaster. Now.
2. ***More democracy.*** In the twenty-first century, it is not possible that individuals decide over whole countries. The people need to be consulted on policy and law changes through mandatory referenda, and the possibility to induce issues on the governing agenda. And—it is not possible that people have to stand in line to vote in the twenty-first century.
3. ***Better governance.*** It's silly to assign responsibility for an entity as complex a country to a single individual, and winner-takes-it-all-systems allow minorities to govern. Ministries should be assigned according to national voter share, cabinet meetings are chaired by one of the ministers, in turns. The same applies in the corporate world: we don't need presidents and we don't need CEOs; we need teams of decision makers.
4. ***Real market economy.*** Markets only work when all costs are incorporated. The environmental costs of substances, materials and processes have to be integrated in the market price—based on a globally agreed level. The taxes generated need to be fiscally neutral (cash-back and/or used to offset the environmental cost).

5. ***Quality education for all.*** We need quality education, equal for all; taxed and re-distributed at the national level, so the same resources are available to each student.
6. ***Working financial markets.*** We need financial markets that support the real economy, and not vice versa. This can be achieved through a transaction tax on, and/or a minimal holding periods for all financial instruments.
7. ***Health care and social security for all.*** We need affordable basic health care for all—paid for as percentage of income, directly deducted, with the choice of additional insurance for more luxurious health care.
8. ***Impartial and efficient justice system accessible to all.*** The justice system has to work fast, efficient, accessible to all while minimizing abuse. Judges need to be completely impartial, appointed through a process that is safeguarded from any political influence.
9. ***Unitary Taxing.*** We need a global approach to tax multinational corporations (e.g. by a combination of revenues/employees/sourcing per country), as well as private tax. These are not normal times. A wealth tax on the rich, maybe for a limited time, needs to be seriously considered.
10. ***Fact-based, impartial information.*** We need impartial, science- and fact-based information, not opinions. Financed through taxes, but safeguarded against any control attempts by governments/politicians.
11. ***Freedom for, and from, religion.*** Faith is a choice. Science is not. Everybody is free to practice their faith, and nobody has their freedom impaired by other people's faith. We need a total separation of state governance and religion.
12. ***Total equality.*** It is a shame that this has to be mentioned in the twenty-first century—but we need total equality. Between genders, races, regions, wealth.

Conclusion

In the light of the 2030 Agenda for Sustainable Development, and in order to achieve the goals set within, the global community can no longer participate in a system that highlights division and inequality. All cultures contribute to sustainable development, which is in itself a reflection of the progress made since the implementation of the MDGs. We need to accelerate joint learning and help to overcome the compartmentalization of technical and policy work by promoting integrated approaches to the interconnected economic, social and environmental challenges confronting the world.

As Ian Gouch (2017) and others convincingly argued, the pursuit of wellbeing and social justice is inadequate if it is at the expense of the biosphere and future generations. At the same time, the pursuit of social justice within planetary limits is inadequate if justice is understood solely in procedural terms, such as greater civic rights and Western democracy, while ignoring more material aspects of wellbeing.

Therefore, we need a revolution in policy mind-set and practice. Sustainable lifestyle concepts that are grounded in a mechanistic paradigm are no longer useful and are preventing an effective response to our complex and dynamic world. "Lifestyles then are not only concerned with individual behavior but instead are a manifestation of identified patterns of thinking, being, and acting that are embedded in today's 'socioecological' realities. We acknowledge that it will take some time to recognize the benefits, as we are all immersed in the current social paradigm. However, it is a starting point that may help to ignite a new discourse. It can thus contribute to the transformation of lifestyles, which is required for a just socioecological transition towards a caring and flourishing society" (Böhme et al., 2022) (see also Horton, 2020). Consequently, "rather than abandoning goals that reflect basic human rights and ignoring the need to respect Earth's planetary boundaries, experts should uphold the SDGs and speak truth to power about what is needed to achieve them" (Sachs et al., 2020, p. 344).

References

Akufo-Addo, N., & Solberg, E. (2020). *Amid coronavirus pandemic, SDGs are even more relevant etoday than ever before*. Retrieved June 20, 2020, from http://www.ipsnews.net/2020/04/amid-coronavirus-pandemic-sdgs-even-relevant-today-ever/?utm_source=English+-+SDGs&utm_campaign=2852368cb8-EMAIL_CAMPAIGN_2020_04_21_01_32&utm_medium=email&utm_term=0_08b3cf317b-2852368cb8-4622673

Bali, S. R., & Yang-Wallentin, F. (2020). Achieving sustainable development goals: Predicaments and strategies, international journal of Sustainable Development & World. *Ecology, 27*(2), 96–106. https://doi.org/10.1080/13504509.2019.1692316

Böhme, J., Walsh, Z., & Wamsler, C. (2022). Sustainable lifestyles: Towards a relational approach. *Sustainability Science*. https://doi.org/10.1007/s11625-022-01117-y

Gouch, I. (2017). *Heat, Greed and Human Need. Climate change, capitalism and sustainable wellbeing*. Elgar.

Horton, R. (2020). *The COVID-19 catastrophe. What's gone wrong and how to stop it happening again* (p. 133). Polity Press.

Khan, D., & Khan, L. Y. (2020). *Will COVID-19 change the global blance o power?*, IPSnews. http://www.ipsnews.net/2020/10/will-covid-19-change-global-balance-power/?utm_source=English+-+SDGs&utm_campaign=0a2c7878c2-EMAIL_CAMPAIGN_2020_10_05_08_29_COPY_01&utm_medium=email&utm_term=0_08b3cf317b-0a2c7878c2-4622673

Lennie, J., & Tacchi, J. (2013). *Evaluating communication for development. A framework for social change*. Routledge Earthscan.

Lie, R., & Servaes, J. (2000). Globalization: Consumption and identity. Towards researching nodal points. In G. Wang, J. Servaes, & A. Goonasekera (Eds.), *The new communications landscape. Demystifying media globalization* (pp. 307–332). Routledge.

Pollin, R. (2003). *Contours of descent: U.S. economic fractures and the landscape of global austerity*. Verso.

Sachs, J., Schmidt-Traub, G., & Lafortune, G. (2020). SDGs: Affordable and more essential now. *Nature, 584*, 344.

Salsiah, A. A., Wignaraja, K., & Susantono, B. (2020). *Fast-tracking the SDGs: Driving Asia pacific transformations, United Nations (ESCAP), the Asian Development Bank (ADB) and the United Nations Development Programme (UNDP)*. https://doi.org/10.22617/SPR200149-2

Samarajiva, I. (2020). *The overwhelming racism of COVID coverage. Western media cannot write western failure*. https://medium.com/indica/the-overwhelming-racism-of-covid-coverage-78e37e4ce6e8

Servaes, J. (Ed.). (2007). *Communication for development. Making a difference, background paper for the world congress on communication for development*. October 25–27, 2006.

Servaes, J. (Ed.). (2013). *Sustainability, participation and culture in communication. Theory and praxis*. Intellect-University of Chicago Press.

Servaes, J. (Ed.). (2014). *Technological determinism and social change. Communication in a Techn-mad world*. Lexington.

Servaes, J. (2015). Studying the global from within the local. *Communication Research and Practice, 1*(3), 242–250.

Servaes, J. (Ed.). (2017). *The sustainable development goals in an Asian context* (p. 174). Springer. http://www.springer.com/in/book/9789811028144

Servaes, J., Polk, E., Shi, S., Reilly, D., & Yakupitijage, T. (2012). Towards a framework of sustainability indicators for 'communication for development and social change' projects. *The International Communication Gazette (Sage), 74*(2), 99–123.

Servaes, J., & Yusha'u, M. J. (2021, July 30). *Are UN's Sustainable Development Goals in the Doldrums Due to the Corona Virus?* IPS News and Views from the Global South. http://www.ipsnews.net/2021/07/uns-sustainable-development-goals-doldrums-due-corona-virus/

Servaes, J. (2008). Confusion about MDGs and participatory diffusion. *Global Journal Communication for Development and Social Change, 2*(3).

Servaes, J. (2016). Studying complex inequalities. In J. Servaes & T. Oyedemi (Eds.), *The praxis of social inequality in media: A global perspective* (Vol. 2, pp. 243–258). Lexington Books, Rowman and Littlefield.

Servaes, J., & Oyedemi, T. (Eds.). (2016a). *The praxis of social inequality in media: A global perspective* (Vol. 2, pp. 243–258). Lexington Books, Rowman and Littlefield.

Servaes, J., & Oyedemi, T. (Eds.). (2016b). *Social inequalities, media, and communication: Theory and roots* (Vol. 1, p. 272). Lexington Books, Rowman and Littefield.

UNDP. (2020). *What are the sustainable development goals?* Retrieved July 7, 2020, from https://www.undp.org/content/undp/en/home/sustainable-development-goals.html

Vandemoortele, J. (2016). *SDGs: The tyranny of an acronym?* https://impakter.com/sdgs-tyranny-acronym/

Vandemoortele, J. (2015). *Are the SDGs a major reboot or a sequel to the MDGs?* https://oecd-development-matters.org/2015/12/08/are-the-sdgs-a-major-reboot-or-a-sequel-to-the-mdgs/

Vandemoortele, J. (2017). From MDGs to SDGs: critical reflections on global targets and their measurement. In *Sustainable development goals and income inequality*. Edward Elgar Publishing. https://doi.org/10.4337/9781788110280.00007

Vandemoortele, J. (2018). From simple-minded MDGs to muddle-headed SDGs. *Development Studies Research, 5*(1), 83–89. https://doi.org/10.1080/21665095.2018.1479647

CHAPTER 2

Communication for All in Africa: The Complexities of Development and Communication

Charles C. Okigbo and Jude N. Ogbodo

Abstract The global landscape for development communication and social change has changed radically in the new millennium. Among the most significant of these changes is the international consensus on the importance of setting transnational targets for socio-economic developments across the globe, as expressed in the eight objectives that constitute the Millennium Development Goals (MDGs). In 2000, the global coalition of 193 leaders committed to focus their concerted energies on addressing poverty, primary education, gender equality, child mortality, maternal health, HIV/AIDS and other diseases, environmental sustainability, and global partnerships. What was glaringly missing in this commitment was the recognition that communication is the catalyst and

C. C. Okigbo (✉)
North Dakota State University, Fargo, ND, USA
e-mail: charles.okigbo@ndus.edu

J. N. Ogbodo
Mass Communication, Ebonyi State University, Abakaliki, Nigeria

J. Servaes, M. J. Yusha'u (eds.), *SDG18 Communicaton for All, Volume 2*, Sustainable Development Goals Series,
https://doi.org/10.1007/978-3-031-19459-7_2

engine that drives positive socio-economic changes locally, regionally, and globally. In 2015, we witnessed the formulation of the 17 successor Sustainable Development Goals (SDGs) through a more inclusive process that involved multiple stakeholders, but communication was still left out of the lofty focal goals. This has necessitated the call for "Communication for All" to stress the centrality and urgency of communication in serious development and social change enterprises. In this chapter, we provide a short background on the MDGs and SDGs, as a backdrop for explaining Communication for All before we argue why it matters, especially in the African development context. We argue that Communication for All could have been the 18th SDG, but now that it is not the case, strategic communication deserves to be a clear component of all the 17 SDGs. The binding constraints of African development present perplexing and multifactorial challenges that deserve more attention than they get now from within the continent. More than any other world region, Africa needs "Communication for All" to pervade all aspects of human engagement on the continent.

Keywords SDGs • Communication for all • Africa • African development • Communication for development

Introduction

The omission of communication as one of the millennium and sustainable development goals has attracted the deserved attention of media and communication scholars, policymakers and analysts, journalists, and development professionals who understand the centrality of communication in social development. It is presumptuous to expect the planners and implementers of specific activities involved in the development enterprises associated with the Millennium Development Goals (MDGs) and the Sustainable Development Goals (SDGs) to engage strategic communication unconsciously and intuitively in addressing their extant development preoccupations and activities. The MDGs were a revolutionary approach to provide a clear sense of direction to propelling global development of all world regions by focusing on eight pivotal objectives relating to eradicating poverty, achieving universal primary education, promoting gender equality, reducing child mortality, improving maternal health, combating HIV/AIDs, and ensuring environmental sustainability. Clearly, communication could have been one of the goals because of the centrality of messages, media, and persuasion in addressing human behavior, which is at the root of each goal.

Not having communication as one of the eight MDGs, it would have been appropriate to have it as one of the 17 SDGs, hence the argument now that Communication for All should have been SDG 18 to clearly show how communication should be used strategically to address each of the sustainable development goals. This is more desirable in the industrializing regions, especially Africa, which is in dire need of both emergent and strategic communication approaches in redressing its multiple challenges and binding constraints which had contributed to a less than stellar performance with the MDGs. Although remarkable progress was made in Africa's socio-economic development, the continent was close to attaining only three of the eight MDGs, namely Goal 2 on achieving universal primary education, Goal 3 on promoting gender equality and empowering women, and Goal 6 on combating HIV/AIDS and other diseases (ECA et al., 2015). Communication for All has different interpretations all of which apply to the expectations of the roles for communication in African development, specifically in the context of the SDGs, and more broadly in the overall improvement of the human condition on the continent. What do we mean by Communication for All? Why does it matter in dealing with the SDGs, particularly regarding African development communication?

Communication for All

Effective communication is so fundamental and necessary in people's lives as individuals and in the lives of organizations and nations that success is bound to be severely limited by an inability to communicate optimally. Communication for All is the principle that all individuals need relevant information and messages to attain optimal performance as sources, channels, and subjects in their various roles in community. Every person, regardless of their abilities, can take advantage of extant communication situations to achieve their goals. This is the sense in which the Association for Persons with Severe Handicaps (TASH) created the "Communication for All" campaign, which is aimed at promoting effective communication for people with disabilities. It is based on the conviction that all peoples can benefit from proper uses of communication. The TASH campaign is aimed at promoting personal and group development through awareness, professional development, access to communication technologies, instruction, and support (TASH, 2021).

Like TASH, the World Association for Christian Communication (WACC) has adopted a "Communication-for-All" framework in all its work for promoting individual and organizational development, as evident in its characterization and branding statement which is "WACC—communication for all" (WACC, 2021). Communication for All underlines WACC's belief that "everyone has the right to communicate and to be in communication, in the same way that they have the right to food, shelter, and security" (WACC, 2021, np). WACC's publication *Communication for All: New World Information and Communication Order* (Lee, 1986) analyzes the information and communication imbalance between industrialized and industrializing nations, as well as the response to the calls for a new order of greater balance for all, following the historic UNESCO 1977 Report on alternative communication systems.

The UNESCO Report, better known as the MacBride Commission's *Many Voices, One World* (MacBride, 1980), showed the need for more balanced scenarios for global communication to provide less industrialized countries with more autonomy that would obviate the domination by the advanced economies. Communication for All should lead all world regions toward "a new more just, and more efficient world information and communication order" (MacBride, 2004). The idea that communication should be for all has had many iterations among which are many voices, one world; one world, multiple cultures; and many worlds, one voice (Servaes, 1999; Ayish, 2005; Thussu, 2015). The genesis of these iterations is the 16-member MacBride Commission which gave impetus to the calls for "Communication for All" more than four decades ago. Although Africa provided 4 of the 16 representatives on the MacBride Commission (Ekonzo, Zaire; Masmoudi, Tunisia; Omu, Nigeria; and el Oteifi, Egypt), the continent has not fared any better because of the work of the Commission.

Communication for All is important in the global enterprise of promoting social change and development communication, particularly in Africa. In addition to providing that everybody be accommodated in the communication enterprise for social change and development, Communication for All is invoked also in the designs that every aspect of human engagement be accorded communicative significance. It is in this sense that strategic communication was expected to be mainstreamed into the 17 SDGs, or better still that Communication for All should have been SDG 18.

The omission of Communication in the MDGs and SDGs exacts a negative toll on developing countries. The greatest of this toll is felt in Africa, which is still one of the worst theaters of slow development. Africa, a continent of 1.3 billion people, is third in global demographic significance after China (1.4 billion) and India (1.37 billion). Therefore, it deserves unreserved attention in the discourse of global development goals. African development requires an astute interpretation of "Communication for All" to understand the complexities of the apparent failures of development goals and plans on the continent. Development is a cross-cutting subject that necessitates the mainstreaming of multiple dimensions such as the respective 17 SDGs into local, regional, national, and global planning frameworks. Having Communication for All as the 18th SDG would have made it easier to avoid a silo approach that focuses on one or a few dimensions instead of the integrated approach that sustainable development requires. African development is problematic and mainstreaming communication is imperative for the successful implementation of the SDGs. Why does Communication for All matter in Africa?

Why Communication for All Matters in Africa?

Communication for All is applicable in multiple contexts beyond the traditional domains that UNESCO envisaged in the New World Information and Communication Order (Servaes, 2007). In Africa, we can expect its application in at least four areas which are in the concerns for addressing Africa's peculiar development problems, the management of the tension between traditional and modern communication, the peculiar roles of African governments, and fashioning new roles for education and communication in the future of African development. The most important of these four roles for Communication for All in Africa is in the urgency for using total communication in addressing the peculiar development challenges of the 54 countries on the continent. Africa's development challenges are legion and include persistent and pervasive problems of low-yielding agriculture, slowly developing industrialization, burgeoning population, low skills development, unstable political development, and the negative effects of past colonial misadventures, among many others. Communication is one of the common elements in the solutions proffered for all these challenges, but it is not just any form of communication. Ideally, it should be communication that is both strategic and comprehensive; ideally, strategic Communication for All, which is meant the totality of the essential communication aspects of sources, messages, media, and audiences. Piecemeal approaches have not worked in Africa, starting from the Indirect Rule of the British Colonial Governments to the Assimilation policies of their French counterparts, both of which have had no appreciable recognition for the value of traditional communication, out of spite for indigenous African culture and intelligence.

Traditional communication in Africa has served only as a footnote in the propositions for sustainable African development, and it has not attracted the deserved attention in African communication scholarship (Hachten, 1971; Mutua et al., 2022). It is currently facing some challenges in the recent expansions of modern mass communication with increasing penetration of high-speed internet and mobile telecommunication penetration, which is a common feature in every nook and corner of the African continent (GSMA, 2021). By the end of 2020, GSMA, a global organization that unifies mobile ecosystem, reported that cell phone penetration in Sub-Saharan Africa stood at 495 million. This new development in telecommunication expansion is leading to an inevitable combat between old and new communication tools which have given rise to interesting new possibilities for strategically combining the best of the old and new to achieve new realities of the beneficial confluence of rural, urban, national, and global communication scenarios that are complimenting and competing at the same time (Essoungou, 2010).

These new developments have important consequences for Communication for All in Africa because of the need to employ all aspects and techniques of traditional and modern communication in strategic and participatory manners instead of delimiting the applications. The true sense of Communication for All calls for recognizing traditional and modern communication as complementary, and not denigrate indigenous and old while accentuating the foreign and the modern. In the wide range of exciting possibilities for deploying communication in all its aspects for sustainable African development, African governments have singular roles to play.

Governments in Africa play central roles in the lives of the people, their communities, and all other actors that participate in the public arena. Starting from the colonial era of governments being perceived as "the alpha and omega," contemporary African governments control almost all the levers for production and distribution, including the uses of communication infrastructure. According to Nwozor, Okidu, and Adedire (2021) the state and its administrative system are the key requirements and critical pathways to achieving sustainable development in Africa. The African state plays key role in enhancing the capabilities for delivering the collective development dividends for health, education, industries, and infrastructural facilities for sustainable development (Evans, 2010, Guseh & Oritsejafor, 2019). Communication for All contributes to socio-political and economic development. This is true especially following the historical waves of democratization and media privatization (Karikari, 2010) which opened the communication media space in Africa for more varied ownership structures that include both private and community entrepreneurship.

However, there is a growing private sector energization in public communication, not only in the sense of media ownership but also in citizen communication which underlines the value of Communication for All in Africa. Governments are still powerful, but so are the other forces outside government such as corporations, conglomerates, communities, religious organizations, and the expanding non-profit sector. These indicate new expectations that suggest that going forward, Communication for All in Africa must embrace alliances between the state and non-state actors in the areas of communication messages, strategies, and tactics. The “All” must include multiple actors and channels, bearing on the problems of development and communication. In these new realities, formal education as well as continuing education must get pride of place.

Communication education in Africa must be part of the Communication for All discourse because the future of the continent is to be determined not so much by the quantum of the natural resources as by the quality of the human resources which significantly impacts the overall development of the continent. The abundant natural resources in many African countries have turned out to be curses rather than blessings. The most naturally endowed states have turned out to be the most wracked, troubled, crises-ridden, and lacking in political leadership. The five poorest countries in Africa as of November 2021 were Angola, Benin, Burkina Faso, Central African Republic, and Chad (UNCDP, 2021).

On the other hand, the most promising African countries are Mauritius, Seychelles, Algeria, Tunisia, Botswana, Libya, South Africa, Egypt, Gabon, and Morocco. The best prospects for African development suggest that peace, conviviality, and stable leadership are more important than natural resource endowments in themselves. So, Communication for All is essential in Africa because of the need for using communication to address the continent’s myriad of development challenges, the value of combining traditional and modern communication, the necessity of intersectoral alliances that encourage private, public, and non-profit collaborations, and the central place of communication and education in the sustainable development of African countries. Above all, the demographic significance of 1.3 billion people in Africa, who make up about 20% of the world population, cannot be denied. The proper use of communication in all spheres of social development is not intuitive; it should not be arbitrary. It requires strategic designing and careful planning, which are two of the valued hallmarks in developing the SDGs as a guide to national, continental, and global development. Africa is a major beneficiary of the SDG designs, which were formulated to obviate some of the underperformance of the MDGs.

African Development: The Challenges and Promises of the SDGs

Africa is unique in its development challenges and promises more than any other region of the world. Once thought of as the "dark continent" on account of its impenetrability, it has been undergoing a period of renaissance, although signs of political turmoil, internal conflicts, and economic recession are not far to see. The much-publicized African renaissance is leading to a new scramble for favor by China and Western countries, which are poised to take advantage of the continent's evolving economic opportunities and the vast mineral resources. According to D'Alessandro and Zulu (2017, p. 2) "Africa, particularly Sub-Saharan Africa (SSA), is increasingly seen as the new frontier for development in the twenty-first century," particularly in the post-MDG era. The euphoria about positive change and development in the horizon can be short-lived as is the situation with Ethiopia, which showed great promise for urban transformation, industrialization, and internal peace, which earned the Nobel Prize for the Prime Minister, Abiy Ahmed in 2019. Only a few years later, all the gains were reversed, and it has now become one of the worst cases of fractured relations and internal warfare (BBC, 2021).

Other parts of Africa have been witnessing various development challenges many of which were responsible for the poor performance on the MDGs (UNECA et al., 2015). The transition from the MDGs to the SDGs marks an important turning point for African development with new challenges and opportunities. The SDGs are not only more numerous than the MDGs, but they are also selected with a clear focus on the strategies and means of implementing them with respect to countries and regions that had severe gaps in their MDGs performance. The key constraints of African development are addressed by the SDGs, focusing on poverty, hunger, good health and well-being, quality education, gender equality, clean water and sanitation, affordable and clean energy, decent work and economic growth, industry, innovation, and infrastructure. The others are reduced inequalities, sustainable cities, responsible consumption, climate action, life below water, life on land, peace, and partnerships. No doubt, there was a serious effort to touch on all the key development challenges to create a new landscape for Africa's 2030 agenda for planned and sustainable growth.

Africa's underperformance with the 8 MDGs (with 18 time-bound targets and more than 60 measurement indicators, 48 of which were quantitative) could be repeated with the 17 SDGs and their 169 indicators. It is to improve on the opportunities for better results that the new Africa Agenda (Agenda 2063) has been produced to align with the targets of the SDGs. From the MDGs to the SDGs and the new Africa Agenda (Agenda 2063), which outlines the continent's long-term goals for the next half century (*The Africa We Want*, African Union Commission, 2016), Communication for All is imperative, in the context of requiring not only that all African peoples be involved but also that every development goal deserves a clear articulation of the place of strategic communication in its implementation.

The SDGs have notably addressed some of the lapses that were inherent in the "deeply inadequate MDGs" (Donald, 2015). This has led to the SDGs being seen as "a major departure that differs not just in the number of goals and targets, but in their very purpose, conception, and the political process that drove their elaboration" (Fukuda-Parr, 2016, p. 44). A striking feature of the SDGs is the inclusive nature of their formulation and the deliberate emphasis on inclusiveness. According to UNGA (2015), the declaration and goals of the SDGs comprise 40 mentions of the term "inclusive", which even though it is undefined in declaration, in most cases, it appears to suggest "all"—all people who have the right to access the opportunities outlined in the goals. This means that the Global South stands to benefit from the MDGs as much as the Global North. Communication for All should have no boundaries and the use of communication in social change and development should apply to all theaters and subjects of social development.

As articulated, the SDGs were designed to be more comprehensive and far-reaching in their impacts on the constituencies for sustainable development. They not only succinctly defined the new broader and yet more specific scope of coverage, but also remained the most inclusive development goals in addition to their aspirations for universal concerns. These concerns addressed both variegated and specific concerns such as widening cases of inequality, climate change, agricultural subsidies, social protection, and responsive and inclusive decision-making at all spheres (Razavi, 2016). Moreover, the SDGs represent a contemporary vision designed for global transformation, building upon the limited successes and significant failures of the MDGs.

In the past two decades of the original MDGs and their successor SDGs, African countries have gained a measure of experience in terms of implementing various development agendas albeit with uninspiring results. Attaining these goals and targets has been hampered by various challenges. Indeed, the Economic Commission for Africa ([ECA], 2011) identified the following as some of the nagging problems standing between Africa and the realization of the new development agenda:

> the adverse impact of climate change, increasing water scarcity, biodiversity and ecosystem loss, desertification, low resilience to natural disasters … energy crisis, food crisis, limited benefits from globalization, health security, the global financial crisis, trafficking and piracy, low penetration of ICT services, urbanization, need to develop better disaster response mechanisms, genetically modified crops in relation to food security and technology transfer among others. (n.p.)

No doubt, these challenges, problems, and binding constraints have significantly impacted the continent's development trajectory in the past and will continue to become significant hindrances for achieving the new SDGs. Whether we see Africa's development glass as half full or half empty, the challenges of sustainable development are real on the continent and require strategic interventions that can benefit from a clear focus on Communication for All. One of the most worrisome aspects is the apparent ignorance of many Africans about the SDGs, and the poor state of using communication, indeed Communication for All to address each of the SDGs. The absence of communication as MDG 18 (Communication for All) makes the realization of the 17 MDGs the more problematic in Africa. How can African peoples be engaged strategically to play more active roles in the African development process? The imperative of communication to this development process cannot be over-emphasized. African development is largely unachievable without a robust deployment of communication in all aspects of planned social change in a context that involves the people as active participants and not passive receptors.

African Development Communication Today

Communication is an important lubricant for oiling the wheel of development. Without adequate and effective communication strategy, even the most promising development goals may not be achieved. Thus, the process of helping people to understand and recognize the developmental interventions can only be guaranteed through an effective communication strategy that defines what the project is all about and how the people might benefit from it. As Okigbo succinctly observed, "communication is one of the key factors of positive change and it is expected to be a channel for transmitting new ideas, a catalyst for the adoption of new ways, and a symbol of modernization" (2021, p. 193). Effective communication serves the purpose of galvanizing support for development projects and giving ordinary people a sense of belonging and the interest in participating actively as stakeholders and not passive observers.

In Africa's pluralistic and multi-ethnic societies, it is important that development agendas such as the SDGs are communicated in cultural contexts that ordinary people can identify with. Anything short of that will make interventions unpopular and difficult to actualize. Indeed, Bussotti (2015) has argued that communication is one of the most important tools for implementing development strategies, and that many lofty initiatives or programs have failed as a result of lack of or ineffectual communication between international organizations, national elites and the common masses who are often the target of such programs. The interface between development and communication in Africa deserves more attention than it gets now. The continent has a long history of scholarly and practical engagements with communication for development, some of which are being transformed into contemporary evaluations of the relationship between communication and social change. Such evaluation stands to benefit from applications of Communication for All in the MDGs and SDGs, especially in the context of traditional and modern communication. There are multiple scenarios for the passing of traditional African societies into the modernization that comes from information technology, new farming techniques, new ways of learning and trade, and imperceptible changes in everyday behavior as urbanization becomes a fact of modern life in every African country. All these present theaters for Communication for All applications in development.

Development communication today in Africa has become inseparable from all those planned interventions involving the uses of messages, people, and media to bring about positive change in society, much in the sense that McAnany (2012) referred to as "saving the world." In this case, it is saving the continent. The SDGs bring into sharp focus the different areas where communication should be used to bring about development. Unfortunately, no specific SDG was reserved for communication alone, but rather communication is expected to be mainstreamed in all the SDGs. The nearest we came to having one SDG on communication was SDG 17—(the means of implementation), which stresses the need for partnerships and working across the other goals. This cross-cutting SDG resembles MDG 8—(Global Partnership for Development), which had suffered from neglect in the MDG era. It is important therefore to incorporate communication in future development goals, because of the innate value of communication in development planning and implementation. Communication is a basic human need, which should be treated as a vital development factor, without which neither Africa nor the entire world can be saved.

The appraisal of the SDGs in connection with how communication can be used to accelerate the achievement of the development goals in Africa is therefore important. This is aimed at charting the continent's development trajectories within the tenets of social change and how the goals and targets of the SDGs can be achieved. The development communication that African countries need today is not perfunctory but strategic communication that places due emphasis on planning, research, implementations, and evaluation processes, all geared toward achieving predetermined development goals, as expressed in the SDGs. It is not just about any type of communication. Okigbo (2021) notes that such communication must be strategic enough if the goals of social change and development are to be realized. Not being perfunctory, the new development communication in Africa should ideally take strategic campaign approaches to minimize chances for failure. Many communication campaigns fail due to poor planning and lack of research acumen. As Okigbo (2021, p. 198) has argued, "communication and social change campaigns fail due to wrong choice of targets and segments, or misconceptions about their demographic, psychographic and life-style characteristics or their media use habits."

Modernization, saving the world and Africa, strategic communication campaign approaches, and the uses of relevant communication research methods—these are all components of the new development communication in Africa, which can be mainstreamed in the SDGs to usher in a new era of social change and development on the continent. Despite the poor performances with the MDGs, many believe that "the SDGs are potential game changers of regional development prospects" (Smith, 2015, p. 44). We could be at the threshold of a new African century. But at the same time, without proper attention to the goals for national, regional, and continental development, the next 50 years may be only a mirror of the last 50. The challenges and constraints are real, not imagined, but so are the potentials for sustainable development that is built on the SDGs and the New Africa Agenda 2063.

Agenda 2063 and the SDGs

The 54 countries that make up the African continent face common development challenges that have necessitated the setting up of common development objectives and targets that when achieved would lead to the desired new realities that are envisaged in the original MDGs of 2000 and the subsequent SDGs of 2015. Africa still remains one of the poorest continents whereas the dreams of successive African governments since independence have been to transform the largely developing, agrarian, and subsistence-dependent economies to industrializing and self-sustaining countries. The Organization of African Unity (OAU), which was established to promote economic and industrial development as well as political independence on a platter of positive Afrocentric values, had an ambitious charter that emphasized non-alignment, autonomy, and economic self-sufficiency (OAU, 1963).

The African Union (AU) became a successor to the OAU, and it is both an admission of the failures of the OAU and an affirmation of the need for continued strategic planning at the continental level for sustainable African development. On the one hand, the progression from the OAU to the African Union (AU) and the New Partnership for African Development (NEPAD) shows abiding interests in continual searches for plans of action that promote positive social change. But on the other hand, the minuscule results from these efforts indicate that not much can be shown for these efforts. The latest effort is the new Africa Agenda 2063 which is based on the conviction that 100 years after the OAU's 1963 Charter, "the new Africa" would have been created from systematic and programmed development, as elaborately expressed in the Africa Agenda 2063 Strategic Plan, launched by the African Union in 2013. Africa Agenda 2063 is a call for action to all segments of African society to collaborate successfully to build a united and prosperous Africa. Looking much further ahead to a distant date 2063 which is 100 years from the founding of the OAU, Africa Agenda 2063 provides an unusually long development planning horizon, which will be rolled out in the initial 10 years, following 25 years, and various short-term action plans.

Africa Agenda 2063 is an ambitious continental strategic plan which emphasizes endogenous activities that would position Africa focusing on seven strategic aspirations which are inclusive of growth, integrative Pan-Africanism, good governance/democracy, peace/security, cultural identity/heritage, people-driven development, and competitive/active partnership. As strategic plans go, Africa Agenda 2063 lays out not only the strategic aspirations but also identifies the strategic impact areas (wealth creation, shared prosperity, sustainable environment, and transformative capacity). It also provides the performance indicators that will be used in evaluating the implementation and performance. These have contributed to the many positive views of the plan. However, there are enough reasons for doubt and skepticism considering that many of Africa's problems have remained unredressed since the launching of the continent-wide strategic plan in 2013. The review of Africa Agenda 2063 achievements for the first decade will be due in 2023, and this will show how well the implementation has gone in the face of some unflattering shared themes in African socio-economic development. African development is paradoxical in the sense that many resource-rich countries are "characterized by disappointing growth rates, high inequality, widespread impoverishment, bad governance, and an increased risk of civil violence" (Ayee, 2014, pp. 15–16).

Conditions for Sustainable African Development: Two Binding Constraints

Once referred to as the "dark continent," originally by Henry Stanley (1878) who remarked then that it was poorly known, and later by various others, based on the impenetrable coastlines, poor coverage in the media, and underrepresentation in scholarly research areas (Bassil, 2011, Pimm,

2007). Africa presents as an intriguing subject not least because of the unflattering characteristics and development challenges in the face of huge natural endowments and potentials for significant demographic dividends. Two binding constraints that have imperiled African development are the prevalent misfortunes of the natural environment and the pervasive poor governance that started with colonialism and has persisted to the present. The scale of natural and human-made disasters has escalated in recent years owing to increased rates of urbanization, deforestation, and environmental degradation including sand harvesting for building houses in some areas. Intensifying climate variables such as higher temperatures, flooding, erosion, and desertification pose serious problems in many African countries. Environmentally related diseases, even before the COVID-19 pandemic, contributed to compromising the productivity of African communities, thereby making it more difficult to generate needed revenue and resources to address the environmental problems.

In addition to the natural disasters that are ever pressing different African countries, there is the human-made problem of poor governance which often leads to armed conflicts as is the case in South Sudan, Democratic Republic of Congo, Mali, Cameroon, and Nigeria. In addition to internal strife within respective countries, there is an increasing incidence of pan-regional terrorism and Jihadist attacks. Large-scale corruption and government inefficiencies are both causes and effects of poor governance problems of many African countries. The combination of natural disasters and human-made poor governance issues jeopardizes the chances for sustainable development of Africa, even with the well-articulated goals of the SDGs and Agenda 2063. Many African countries are still reeling from the ravages of their colonial past, and ironically, they are now being sucked into neo-colonial subjugation at the instance of China, which is systematically becoming the new creditor for development projects of questionable value to African development.

China and African Development: The Debt Burden

Africa has enormous [natural] resources to be self-sufficient but leadership failures and endemic corruption among other factors have kept the continent on the peripheries of development. It is the reason why a continent with the population of over 1.3 billion remains a burden to the world as developed economies, especially China exploits the untapped potentials of the continent to bolster their well-being. This has been the bane of development in African countries which depend on the loans from powerful countries to fund their ["white elephant"] projects. The Sino-Africa relationship is one that has remained dramatic and evolving in the context of African development. It has elicited mixed reactions from analysts and scholars alike.

To put it mildly, the analytical framing of the relationship between Africa and China is replete with various "specialists" or those who claim to know Africa more than Africans. Indeed, according to Steven Chan, the

> views of China in Africa are often constructed by Sinologists who are not Africanists, or Africanists who are not Sinologists, or by Africanists and Sinologists who are not experts in international relations or international political economy, or international relations scholars who know nothing about either China or Africa. (Chan, 2013, p. 3)

Some admirers argue that the new corporation between Africa and China is important as it affords the Asian powerhouse and Africa who share common historical affinities of struggles against Western imperialism and humanistic aspirations an opportunity to foster a mutual alliance for development. On the other hand, critics contend that the relationship re-enacts the era of European colonization of Africa a century ago, when the continent was a ground for sourcing cheap labor and raw materials. Africa is thus seen as a lucrative continent where cheap substandard goods are exported in exchange for the huge loans with complex payback mechanisms. In this context, China is viewed by critics as Africa's biggest development challenge due to its perceived exploitative growth and insatiable quest to dominate the global markets, a move that further jeopardizes Africa's quest for independence, development, and competitiveness (Zeleza, 2014).

Admittedly, the truth about Afro-Sino relationship remains even more complex and contradictory. One way to interpret this complexity is that it is a relationship rooted in a long history that has undergone several phases. Second, it is a multifaceted partnership that stretches through economic, political, cultural, social, and strategic dimensions. As no African country is anywhere near the economic and numerical strength of China, this relationship also underscores the unequal power relations in the context of the bilateral relations with Africa. This is no doubt added to the unnerving development challenges facing many African countries which are aggravated by poverty, wars, political instability, brain drain, and high population growth, among others. In the context of the SDGs, these factors also constitute some of the constraints in the way of achieving these goals.

Also worrisome is Africa's unsustainable debt profile which has steadily been on the rise. Some of the loans, particularly that of China to African countries, have been described as booby traps, and they pose unsurmountable challenges that will derail the continent's aspirations for sustainable development. This will be a throwback to an earlier period of African misadventure with foreign debts. Indeed, Nwozor et al. (2021, p. 701) note that "Africa's experience in the 1990s with debt peonage was responsible for its stagnation during that period. Debt burden undermined the capacity of the continent to develop as debt servicing obligations gulped the funds that could have been deployed for infrastructural development." This recurring cycle of foreign debts has landed many African countries in a tragic cycle of borrowing more now to fund their past and existing indebtedness, leading to a situation of "debt slavery or servitude" that inevitably leads to economic stagnation and perennial underdevelopment.

Consequently, the debt profile of many African countries has remained unsustainably high, jeopardizing the prospects for economic growth. In fact, a greater number of African countries are heavily indebted to international financial institutions and foreign countries. Current estimates show that the cumulative value of Africa's Eurobond debt passed US$100 billion in 2019 (Nwozor et al., 2021). Indeed, many African countries such as Angola, The Gambia, Eritrea, Sao Tome and Principe, Somalia, South Sudan, and Sudan have not been able to meet many of their debt obligations (Shelton, 2019). Since money is one of the drivers of the development strides Africa is yearning for, the future is more bleak than optimistic in the context of what lies ahead of the continent. As the World Bank (2020, p. 7) reported, Africa recorded the fastest accrual of external debt stock in 2019 with an average increase in the region of 9.4%. The report further suggests that Africa's total external debt stocks amounted to US$625 billion in 2019. Angola, Nigeria, Egypt, and South Africa account for the greater percentage of Africa's accumulated external debt profile (World Bank, 2020). Although other Western countries and monetary organizations such as the IMF and World Bank give loans to African countries, a substantial portion of current debt profile of Africa is owed to China. Indeed, World Bank (2022) has noted that China is the largest creditor to Africa. The situation is both perplexing and suggestive of a modern equivalent of financial enslavement.

With the hydra-headed effect of corruption in the continent, a large portion of the money borrowed by African countries are often deposited abroad or embezzled by the leaders. Much of it is used for white elephant projects. As such, African countries have often been branded as countries "at high risk of debt distress or in debt distress" (Nwozor et al., 2021; Brautigam et al., 2020). Some of the African countries which are in debt distress include Eritrea, The Gambia, Mozambique, the Republic of Congo, Sao Tomé and Principe, South Sudan, and Zimbabwe. Others are Burundi, Cape Verde, Cameroon, Central African Republic, Chad, Djibouti, Ethiopia, Ghana, Kenya, Mauritania, Sierra Leone, Sudan, and Zambia (see Brautigam et al., 2020). The insatiable appetite to keep borrowing has made Africa an easy target for Chinese loans which are often for projects that would be contracted to Chinese firms such as roads, railways, sea ports, and airports. The governance gaps—corruption, reckless borrowing, and misappropriation of the loans—add to the debt burden plaguing the continent. In fact, there is no doubt that the inability of African countries to pay back their loans from China would eventually result in seizure of such projects or properties by the Chinese government (Broadman, 2020).

The discourse around Sino-African economic relations usually relapses into the conversant narrative of foreign "aid" or "assistance" and even "charity". This also strains credulity about the dominant narratives among Western scholars, and some African skeptics that China is using its questionable donations or loans to deepen its largely opportunistic and selfish economic strategies in Africa. Although such narratives place Africa as "a passive pawn of China" (Power & Mohan, 2011, p. 44), the reality is more intricate and complex. African countries are not necessarily as hapless and helpless as they appear. They enter into the loan arrangements voluntarily and accept the conditions that accord to their expectations knowing that there are other alternatives to the Chinese loans. The case for African development is not an entirely hopeless one, as there are some countries that show there are prospects for growth even in the face of widespread despair.

The Ten Most Developed African Countries

Development is measured by many indicators such as Human Development Index (HDI), Gross National Product (GDP), Gross Domestic Product, birth rate and death rates, infant mortality rate, literacy rate, life expectancy, etc. These indicators are rated varyingly according to countries and rating organizations. As such, a developed country is expected to have an improved economy a stable and efficient leadership/government, a robust infrastructural development, a functional educational system, and requisite job opportunities in addition to inclusive health and social services, as well a high level of personal freedom. Countries that are close to maintaining such indicators are categorized as developing countries, while those that fall far short of these standards are called the least developed countries. These countries can benefit from certain United Nations support programs designated to cushion the effects of underdevelopment. The most universally recognized development index is predicated on the United Nations Human Development Index (HDI). The HDI is a United Nations indicator used to track other indicators such as the literacy rate among adult populations, life expectancy, and income inequality. This is compiled on the basis of low human development (0–0.55), medium human development (0.55–0.70), high human development (0.70–0.80), and very high human development (0.80–1.0) (HDR, 2020).

Africa remains the least developed continent in the world. Several continent dynamics such as high rate of poverty, high-scale corruption, political instability, and armed conflicts have contributed in no small way to retard the continent and relegate it to the background. Out of 54 countries, only 1 African country—Mauritius—was rated as having "very high human development" in 2020 (HDR, 2020). Some African countries have made positive gains in the human development index. For instance, the most recent HDI ranking shows that eight African countries have demonstrated "high human development" and are on the verge of reaching the "very high" plateau in the nearest future.

With HDI of 0.804 which clears the "very high" threshold as the above Table 2.1 indicates, Mauritius, an island African country, is ranked as the most developed on the continent. The country of 1.266 million also has a highlife expectancy of 75 years with a 91.3% literacy rate buoyed by its developed economy and free healthcare and education. On the global scale, Africa still lags the rest of the world. Although Mauritius ranks first in Africa, it is only 66th out of 189 countries used for the ranking. This demonstrates the widening gap between Africa and the other continents. Nonetheless, this shows a sense of promise.

Trailing behind Mauritius in a second position is Seychelles which has a "high" HDI of 0.796 as the above table demonstrates. Seychelles has a viable economy driven mainly by tourism. Part of this improved rating can

Table 2.1 The ten most developed African countries

Country	*Point*	*Remark*
1. Mauritius	0.804	Very high
2. Seychelles	0.796	High
3. Algeria	0.748	High
4. Tunisia	0.740	High
5. Botswana	0.735	High
6. Libya	0.724	High
7. South Africa	0.709	High
8. Egypt	0.707	High
9. Garbon	0.703	High
10. Morocco	0.686	Medium

Source: HDR (2020)

be attributed to the size of the country which now stands at little over 98,000. As the above details show, the fewer the population, the more equitable resources can get to the masses. In large countries like Nigeria, the reverse is the case. Development in Africa is complex and perplexing. Island nations, countries in North Africa, Southern Africa, and Central Africa, largely without less population are better disposed to development than some of the bigger countries such as Nigeria and Ethiopia. These best prospects for development stand good chances for improved performance if Communication for All is applied to the strategies for the SDGs and Africa Agenda 2063. The same will apply also to the lesser developed countries.

Three Least Developed African Countries

Generally, the least developed countries (LDC) find themselves at a disadvantaged position in the comity of nations. This has been worsened since the uncertainties caused by the ongoing COVID-19 pandemic. Yet the United Nations Conference on Trade and Development ([UNCTAD], 2021) encourages countries categorized as LDCs to find alternative means of survival by diversifying their streams of internally generated revenues rather than their usual reliance on foreign aid and loans. Faced by the scale of issues affecting them, LDCs also contend with means of funding the SDGs. Globally, 46 countries are categorized as LDCs. Out of these, Africa accounts for about 33. This highlights the enormity of the development strides expected of the continent. The expectation is that meeting the targets of the SDGs and the Agenda 2063 will transform many African countries and ensure better economic and social conditions for most of their citizens.

Based on the UNCTAD (2021) report, the three least developed African countries are Angola, Benin, and Burkina Faso. Countries are rated as underdeveloped when there is high birth rate, high rate of infant mortality, low degree of life expectancy, high rate of unemployment, low per capita GDP, low literacy rate. These indicators may not be comprehensive, but they give insight into how development is measured on the flipside. Angola is a southern African country that has a huge deposit of various mineral resources such as diamond, iron ore, gold, copper, and phosphate among others. Yet endemic corruption has led to low development in the country as the available resources are not put into effective use that would benefit the 33 million citizens of the country.

Similarly, in 2019, the World Bank reported that Benin, a country of about 12 million people, has a fertility rate of 5.7 children per woman. This is in addition to a life expectancy of 61.2 years while poverty rate was at 38.5%. Although unemployment rate was at 2.4%, underemployment rate was 72%.

In Burkina Faso, political instability, armed conflicts in addition to corruption have plunged the country into underdevelopment. These indices show the enormity of development challenges facing African countries. The conditions have made Africa an easy prey for kick-back loans from China and the rest of the world.

The Complexities of Communication and Development

It is mainly by efficiently sharing information, as well as by motivating and committing the masses to it that development programs reach their full potential. In other words, there is no amount of development goals that will bring about enduring changes in people's living standards unless the people are co-opted into it as the driving force. As such, in many respects, communication is essential to development. It allows policymakers to consult with the masses when identifying and formulating development programs. Doing this is necessary since it considers people's needs, attitudes, and aspirations. Through effective communication strategies, the beneficiaries of any development initiatives such as the ones enshrined in the

SDGs will be the primary actors working toward the success of such initiatives. By implication, providing communication support to the masses helps them to recognize key issues and identify common ground for shared responsibility and action toward development.

Furthermore, development necessitates change and giving the people a voice in the development initiative not only allows the people to feel a sense of belonging, but also helps in steering such development agenda. The media, including the vernacular channels, can be used to make people believe in the development initiatives as well as contribute to the realization of such goals. Vernacular channels are particularly important to carry the illiterate populations along. If the goals are clearly communicated to the people, achieving them becomes easier since the people can voice their support or concerns or even make choices in terms of the goals to prioritize.

In this era of proliferation of communication channels, the world can no longer undermine the apparent impact of communication in development. In today's new context of societal change, communication can play a significant role in supporting development (Mehta, 1987). Conditions are becoming increasingly favorable for those that use effective communication for development. The need for galvanizing public support and participation in development programs is also being stressed across the literature. At the moment, development agendas are often drafted without mapping out the means through which communication can be used to help in the success of the programs. The failure of MDGs in most African countries and other developing countries failed to convince global leaders to look inward and integrate communication into the development programs that followed—that is, SDGs. Effective communication deployed through the media, participation and mobilization of the masses, and increased awareness can steer the programs to success in the continent.

The human factor is central to most contemporary development discourses. The idea is that the success or failure of development can only be determined by the people involved more than by natural resources or other factors of production. True sustainable development, even in the age of artificial intelligence and automation, is about people. Machines, mechanization, finances, and other contributions to development come after the human factor of people as communicators and intelligent actors. People, their degree of awareness, and participation will dictate the future shape, pace, sustainability, and ultimate direction of positive social change and development. Without a simultaneous investment in the "communication capital"—aimed at enlightening people, opening up spaces for them to establish consensus for action, and developing the knowledge and skills required to put material assets to the greatest possible use—scientific and material inputs will yield no meaningful results.

In the context of development, communication is a recurring theme. Communication is the common thread that connects development agendum and its success. As such, at any period of societal change, communication in the form of dialogue and debate occurs naturally. In recent years, developments in the global political framework have coincided with growing freedom of expression. On the other hand, communication contains the most intriguing prospects as an intentional intervention to effect social and economic transformation. A communication-based development method can uncover people's underlying attitudes and conventional wisdom, assist them in adapting their perspectives and learning new abilities, and promote new societal norms.

Communication does not necessarily depend on the availability of media channels, as large as the mass media may loom in society. To be optimally effective, human communication needs careful planning that takes into cognizance the essential elements of sources, channels, messages, noise, feedback, and the social context. Of great importance is the work of communication planners and implementers in taking advantage of extant situations, guided by strategic designs. Communication has been used strategically in various social contexts to drive desirable change by individuals and groups. The belief in Communication for All is founded on the innumerable experiences of successful uses of communication to achieve predetermined goals, such as the MDGs, the SDGs, and Africa Agenda 2063, as well as in commercial and political campaign situations. The value of audience or target market involvement and participation is not lost on the best practitioners of effective strategic communication.

Indeed, lessons from the expired MDGs have shown that any development initiative that only considers the masses as beneficiaries rather than active participants in the process of change is not likely to succeed. Better results are usually realized when the people (as project beneficiaries) are consulted and actively involved in making decisions that will impact them in the long run. Communication research and the steps in communication planning contribute immensely to creating an environment for successful communication interventions. The use of self-evaluation, for instance, can assist a community in developing realistic recommendations for new development efforts, as well as generating a lot of enthusiasm for them to succeed. In rural African settings for instance, people's perspectives can also help to steer future work plans and keep them from going in the wrong path. Stakeholders and practitioners can therefore interact through systematic communication mechanisms. While there is no guarantee of successful outcomes in social communication activities, the chances for achieving desirable outcomes increase with better planning in the contexts of comprehensive communication with people as beneficiaries and agents of change. Consultations based on genuine appreciation for the value of the people's contribution yield better outcomes. Before drafting a development program, due attention needs to be paid to people's views, capabilities, and requirements as they see them. These are some of the gaps observed in the design and implementation of the MGDs. Although the successor SDGs addressed these in their inclusiveness, there was still the failure to accord pride of place to Communication for All. Social change and sustainable development programs require clear recognition of the centrality of comprehensive and strategic communication in all the relevant theaters of social action.

Conclusion

Communication is such a fundamental human process; it is not surprising, therefore, that it is a human right which is accorded to all people, regardless of their capacity or ability. This is one of the principles undergirding Communication for All. Communication for All applies to people as sources and audiences, and also to subjects or topics, as well as the affairs of people such as poverty, hunger, health and well-being, quality education, clean energy, societal inequalities, and partnerships, among other human interests. Understanding Communication for All to apply to all peoples of the world and their various endeavors for development, we expected that communication would have been one of the MDGs, instead of being mainstreamed in all of them. That was not to be. Similarly, we had expected that since the SDGs were designed to close some of the gaps in the MDGs, communication should have been a separate stand-alone goal. Not having communication as a stand-alone MDG and SDG has denied humanity an important tool that should have been given deserved autonomous standing because of its centrality in the affairs of people, especially regarding development and positive social change. Communication is more than media, messages, and men/women. It is the fundamental human process that deserves to be accorded full status as a full-fledged MDG and SDG.

The unfortunate omission of communication and Communication for All in the MDGs and SDGs exerts its greatest toll on Africa because of the continent's peculiar needs for strategic and accelerated socio-economic, political, and technological development. African economies still suffer from the deleterious consequences of colonialism, many of which have carried into the contemporary social milieu. Although Africa is largely one contiguous landmass and territory, there are 54 independent countries, all different from each other in significant respects such as language, traditions, and political practices. The MDGs did not make a significant dent in Africa's development outlook, an unfortunate scenario that the SDGs were formulated to redress. However, the perennial binding constraints and challenges in Africa can prove to be insurmountable obstacles unless there are strategic designs from within and outside Africa to bring sustainable development to the fore in all African countries. Saving Africa requires looking at the continent with old and new eyes, intent on making the best of modernization, urbanization, economic growth, total human development, and balanced growth, which is not at the expense of future generations or our cultural values and mores. Development is not Westernization nor is it necessarily modernization.

The SDGs are a body of lofty development goals that hold strong promises of catapulting Africa and the rest of the world out of the abyss of poverty, hunger, poor health, and well-being to relative prosperity. As we blame the missed opportunity of integrating Communication for All into the goals of the SDGs, its non-inclusion should not be an excuse for the low level of performance we had with the MDGs. To chart the development trajectory, world leaders, especially those of African extraction, can begin the process of interpreting these goals and their inherent benefits in the languages that are indigenous to the people so as to actively involve them in the development process. This is in recognition of the role of communication in driving socio-economic development. Through this measure, the SDGs (even without Communication for All) can be truly people-oriented and thus more easily achievable. Without galvanizing public support through strategic Communication for All, Africa may end up not achieving any of the lofty goals.

And as we say in Africa, "until the rotten tooth is removed, the mouth must chew with caution." It is therefore important to not only recognize the place of strategic communication in driving development home, but also effectively use it to mobilize the masses using the language they clearly understand and presenting development as truly native to the people. This is just one way of making the SDGs more easily realizable. The SDGs represent global targets while Africa Agenda 2063 encapsulates the specific targets that African countries have set for themselves to close the development gaps between the continent and the rest of the developed world. Adopting Communication for All as a mantra and guiding framework toward achieving the targets set by Africa Agenda 2063 will provide a Univision and focal point for varied strategically planned interventions and initiatives.

Recommendations

Although Communication for All is not SDG 18, as we would have liked, we need not throw away the baby with the bath water. Thus, we recommend that African policymakers and development professionals adopt inclusive and sustainable structural transformation agendas that take integrative approaches, even in the absence of a communication SDG. Such approaches would help prevent seeing respective SDGs as silos. A silo's approach would lead to focusing on one or a few dimensions at the expense of others, thereby yielding a less than optimal impact on transformation, social change, and development. Unfortunately, many African governments and countries have weak communication structures and inadequate human resources which make mainstreaming communication across the SDGs a tall order. Strengthening the human capital and capacities for communication use across all SDGs is imperative, and so is the use of reliable data which can be improved through executive education programs and the closing of ranks between governments and academic institutions. Working across the SDGs is facilitated by our communication infrastructure including the new information and communication technologies.

Across the continent, African professionals are making interesting new advances in the adaptation of the new information and communication technologies to traditional African settings in new ways that encourage synergistic relationships. According to D'Alessandro and Zulu (2017, p. 9), "the adoption and use of cell phone technology in Africa is nothing short of a revolution, which has brought improvements to many sectors of life." One such innovation is the *Ushahidi* (meaning testimony or witness in KiSwahili), which is an open-source platform for grassroots activism and citizen journalism that was developed to report on post-election political violence in Kenya in 2008 (Grant, 2015). It has now yielded a lot of benefits including improved transparency, information democratization, monitoring of elections, and distribution of medicines. Such new transformational uses of new information and communication technologies are called for so that Africa can as well export its new inventions to other world regions, thereby shoring up the confidence of its peoples in the evolving new landscape for sustainable development. Africa needs to play a more active role in global development discourse. This is the goal of Africa's Agenda 2065.

Any objective analysis of Africa's place in the realization of the MDGs and SDGs shows that there are gaps in performance which are attributable to the general and broad nature of the goals which are designed to apply to all countries and world regions, but not specifically and exclusively to Africa. To carve out its Africa-specific development targets, the Africa Union Commission (2014) created Africa's Agenda 2063, which put Africa squarely in focus by recommending that African countries and governments aspire for "a prosperous Africa based on inclusive growth and sustainable development; and an integrated continent, politically united and based on the ideals of Pan-Africanism and the vision of Africa's Renaissance." We recommend that Africa's Agenda 2063 be the subject of vigorous continent-wide strategic communication campaigns to make the ideas household words in every African country.

The final picture that emerges from this excursion into the appropriateness of Communication for All in the SDGs against a backdrop of African development and communication shows that communication is an essential human characteristic which is fundamental in the discourse of change and development. In the peculiar case of Africa, with its complexities of development and communication, Communication for All would have served the continent well in addressing the various facets of development from poverty alleviation, to fighting hunger, providing quality education, and reducing inequalities, among the other 17 SDGs. Communication for All in Africa would afford desired inclusivity with nobody left out, regardless of their personal abilities. In the final analysis, Africa stands to benefit immensely from the use of strategic communication to address social change and development.

References

Ayee, J. (2014). The status of natural resource management in Africa: Capacity development challenges and opportunities. In K. T. Hanson, C. D'Alessandro, & F. Owusu (Eds.), *Managing Africa's natural resources: Capacities for development* (pp. 15–38). Palgrave Macmillan.

Ayish, M. (2005). From 'Many Voices, One World' to 'Many Worlds, One Voice' reflections on international communication realities in the age of globalisation. *Javnost-The Public, 12*(3), 13–30.

Bassil, N. R. (2011). The roots of Afropessimism: The British invention of the 'dark continent'. *Critical Arts, 25*(3), 377–396.

BBC. (2021). Ethiopia's Abiy Ahmed: The Nobel Prize winner who went to war. Retrieved November 15, 2021, from https://www.bbc.com/news/world-africa-43567007

Brautigam, D., Huang, Y., & Acker, K. (2020). Risky business: New data on Chinese loans and Africa's debt problem. *Briefing Paper* No. 3. https://static1.squarespace.com/static/5652847de4b033f56d2bdc29/t/6033fadb7ba591794b0a9dff/1614019291794/BP+3++Brautigam%2C+Huang%2C+Acker++Chinese+Loans+African+Debt.pdf

Broadman, H. G. (2020, October 31). Africa's governing elite share the blame for China's 'belt, road' debt crisis. *Forbes*. https://www.forbes.com/sites/harrybroadman/2020/10/31/africas-governing-elite-share-the-blame-for-chinas-beltroad-debt-crisis/?sh=1354b3bd783c

Bussotti, L. (2015). Short reflections on the history of African communication. *Short Reflections on the History of African Communication, 20*(1), 205–222.

Chan, S. (2013). The middle kingdom and the dark continent: An essay on China, Africa and many fault lines. In S. Chan (Ed.), *The morality of China in Africa: The middle kingdom and the dark continent*. Zed Books.

D'Alessandro, C., & Zulu, L. C. (2017). From the Millennium Development Goals (MDGs) to the Sustainable Development Goals (SDGs): Africa in the post-2015 development agenda. *A geographical perspective. African Geographical Review, 36*(1), 1–18.

Donald, K. (2015). Strong commitments to human rights survive in final SDG text despite sordid final compromises. Retrieved October 27, 2021, from http://www.cesr.org/article.php?id=1758

Economic Commission for Africa [ECA]. (2011). New and emerging challenges in Africa. Summary Report. Retrieved October 27, 2021, from https://sustainabledevelopment.un.org/index.php?page=view&type=400&nr=502&menu=1515

Essoungou, A. (2010). A social media boom begins in Africa. https://www.un.org/africarenewal/magazine/december-2010/social-media-boom-begins-africa

Evans, P. B. (2010). Constructing the 21st century developmental state: Potentialities and pitfalls. In O. Edigheji (Ed.), *Constructing a democratic developmental state in South Africa: Potentials and challenges* (pp. 37–58). HSRC Press.

Fukuda-Parr, S. (2016). From the millennium development goals to the sustainable development goals: Shifts in purpose, concept, and politics of global goal setting for development. *Gender & Development, 24*(1), 43–52.

Grant, R. (2015). *Africa: Geographies of change.* Oxford University Press.

GSMA. (2021). The mobile economy Sub-Saharan Africa 2021. http://www.gsma.com/mobileeconomy/sub-saharan-africa/

Guseh, J. S., & Oritsejafor, E. O. (2019). Governance and democracy in Africa: Regional and continental perspectives. .

Hachten, W. (1971). *Muffled drums: The news media in Africa.* Iowa State University Press.

Human Development Report. (2020). Human Development Report Office of the United Nations Development Programme (pp. 343–346). hdr.undp.org.

Karikari, K. (2010). African media breaks 'culture of silence'. *Africa Renewal, 24*(2), 23–25.

Lee, P. (1986). *Communication for all: New world information and communication order.* New York: Mary Knoll, Orbis Books.

MacBride, S. (1980). *Many voices, one world. Report by the international commission for the study of communication problems.* Unipub.

MacBride, S. (2004). *Many voices, one world: Towards a new, more just, and more efficient world information and communication order.* Rowman & Littlefield.

McAnany, E. G. (2012). *Saving the world: A brief history of communication for development.* Chicago: University of Illinois Press.

Mehta, S. R. (1987). Communication and development: Concepts and methods. *Sociological Bulletin, 36*(1), 1–19.

Mutua, E. M., Musa, B. A., & Okigbo, C. C. (2022). (Re) visiting African communication scholarship: Critical perspectives on research and theory. *Review of Communication, 22*(1), 76–92.

Nwozor, A., Okidu, O., & Adedire, S. (2021). Agenda 2063 and the feasibility of sustainable development in Africa: Any silver bullet? *Journal of Black Studies, 52*(7), 688–715.

Okigbo, C. (2021). Rethinking social change and development communication in Africa. In *Learning from communicators in social change* (pp. 191–209). Springer.

Organization of African Unity (OAU). (1963, May 25). *Charter of the organization of African Unity.* Retrieved March 14, 2022, from https://www.refworld.org/docid/3ae6b36024.html

Pimm, S. L. (2007). Africa: Still the 'Dark Continent'. *Conservation Biology, 21*(3), 567–569.

Power, M., & Mohan, G. (2011). China and the geo-political imagination of African 'development'. In C. M. Dent (Ed.), *China and Africa development relations*. Routledge.

Razavi, S. (2016). The 2030 agenda: Challenges of implementation to attain gender equality and women's rights. *Gender & Development, 24*(1), 25–41.

Reddy, S. G., & Kvangraven, I. H. (2015). Global Development goals. *If at all, why, when and how?* https://papers.ssrn.com

Servaes, J. (1999). *Communication for development. One world, multiple cultures*. Hampton Press.

Servaes, J. (2007). Communication for development approaches of some governmental and non-governmental agencies. In J. Servaes (Ed.), *Communication for development and social change* (pp. 201–218). SAGE Publications India.

Shelton, J. (2019, April 03). *Global debt on the rise, Africa hit hardest*. Deutsche Welle. https://www.dw.com/en/global-debt-on-the-rise-africa-hit-hardest/a-48190068

Smith, R. (2015). *The Caribbean and the post-2015 development agenda*. United Nations.

TASH. (2021). The Association of Persons with Severe Handicaps. https://tash.org.

Thussu, D. K. (2015). Reinventing 'many voices': MacBride and a digital new world information and communication order. *Javnost-The Public, 22*(3), 252–263.

Transparency International. (2021). Corruption perception index 2020—Sub-Saharan Africa. Retrieved October 27, 2021, from https://images.transparencycdn.org/images/CPI2020_Report_EN_0802-WEB-1_2021-02-08-103053.pdf

United Nations Committee for Development Policy. (2021). https://www.un.org/development/desa/dpad/wpcontent/uploads/sites/45/publication/ldc_list.pdf

United Nations Conference on Trade and Development. (2021). The least developed countries in the post-COVID world: Learning from 50 years of experience. The least developed countries report 2021. https://unctad.org/webflyer/least-developed-countries-report-2021

United Nations Economic Commission for Africa, African Union, African Development Bank & United Nations Development Programme. (2015). MDG report 2015. Lessons learned in implementing the MDGs: Assessing progress in Africa towards the Millennium Development Goals. https://reliefweb.int/sites/reliefweb.int/files/resources/MDG%20Report%202015_ENG.pdf

United Nations General Assembly. (2015). Transforming our world: The 2030 agenda for sustainable development. Retrieved October 27, 2021, from https://sustainabledevelopment.un.org/content/documents/21252030%20Agenda%20for%20Sustainable%20Development%20web.pdf

WACC. (2021). World Association of Christian Communication. https://wacglobal.org

World Bank. (2020). *International debt statistics 2021*. World Bank. https://openknowledge.worldbank.org/bitstream/handle/10986/34588/9781464816109.pdf

World Bank. (2022). Global Economic Prospects: Slowing growth, rising risks. https://www.worldbank.org.en/publication/global-economic-prospects

Zeleza, P. T. (2014). The Africa-China relationship: challenges and opportunities. *Canadian Journal of African Studies, 48*(1), 145–169. https://doi.org/10.1080/00083968.2014.946298

CHAPTER 3

Communication for All in the Twenty-First Century. Inequalities as Dilemmas in Latin America

Edgardo Luis Carniglia

Abstract This chapter addresses the problem of systematic, deep, and persistent inequalities in Latin America with a meta-theoretical approach based on empirical-critical theories of communication and development. The history of development communication shows strengths in its research and action capabilities together with a thorough assessment of the ideas proposed in its wide, open, and dynamic field of knowledge, which includes the analytical capacity, the understanding ambition, and the normative perspective about the modes, media, and genres of social communication. Given the renewed sensitivity of the current public agenda in the face of social inequality, particularly concerned about reducing and eventually overcoming it, systematic, deep, and persistent inequalities are considered the main dilemma of development communication theory and

E. L. Carniglia (✉)
Communication Department, School of Humanities, National University of Rio Cuarto, Córdoba, Argentina
e-mail: ecarniglia@hum.unrc.edu.ar

J. Servaes, M. J. Yusha'u (eds.), *SDG18 Communicaton for All, Volume 2*, Sustainable Development Goals Series,
https://doi.org/10.1007/978-3-031-19459-7_3

practice in Latin America, the most unequal subcontinent of the twenty-first century.

From this reasoning: (1) the changes and continuities of development communication are recognized as key factors in the field of research and practice, (2) renewed critical approaches about inequality in different areas of the public agenda are summarized, (3) the extended reproduction of inequality in Latin America is thematized, and (4) some dilemmas that social class, income, well-being, ethnicity, gender, and territory inequalities pose for the future of development communication research and practice of a heterogeneous Latin American territory, which at present is more vulnerable as a result of the COVID-19 pandemic, are identified. This is an important debate as the current sanitary and social emergency highlights in an unprecedented way that development is a communication issue, and communication is a matter of development, as it is shown in our and other studies about the digital gaps and other info-communicational asymmetries in the rural areas of Argentina.

Keywords Communication • Development • Inequality • Sustainability • Latin America

Introduction

A particular emphasis of the highly visible 2030 Sustainable Development Goals (SDG) on the global issue of inequality demands an assessment of the pertinence, history, and scopes of their relations with development communication during the next years from a perspective on systematic, deep, and persistent inequalities in Latin America. This chapter addresses this problem with a meta-theoretical approach based on empirical-critical theories of communication and development.

Systematic, deep, and persistent social inequality, more precisely inequalities in its plural form, constitutes a classic and renewed social theory issue, among other areas of the public agenda, almost without an explicit and systematic treatment in development communication theory and practice.

One of the recent papers which relate to this is Cees Hamelink's (2014) essay pointing out, from the international political agenda debate, that the prevailing inequality condition in the world poses a basic threat to human survival. Hamelink's analysis of the current international agenda regarding communication inequality transcends the highly visible digital gap, just one type of inequality, from a social communication perspective that includes the dignity, power, and resources dimensions: "The communication rights that the members of the human family can all equally claim are freedom rights, cultural rights and protection rights" (Hamelink, 2014, p. 85).

Hamelink (2014) concludes that the current international system about human rights cannot provide a solid theoretical and normative framework for distributive justice because it lacks a genuine cosmopolitan foundation.

Also, in another well-known paper, Néstor García Canclini (2005) criticizes the fact that the history of social sciences treats differences, inequalities, and disconnections as isolated objects of study. However, he highlights that a consistent theory about interculturality in times of neoliberal globalization must work on the three processes that make up the intercultural forms and dynamics together, since such modes of existence are complementary and each form of deprivation is also associated with ways of belonging, possession, and participation.

Furthermore, the social, political, and academic agendas of the twenty-first century recognize, from different perspectives, the multiple causes, processes, modes, consequences, and contexts of the various systematic, deep, and persistent inequalities. These agendas also discuss the modes and mechanisms to reduce and eventually overcome the different asymmetries in the current economic, social, political, and cultural developments of the different Latin American societies (Benza & Kessler, 2021).

As a result, given this renewed sensitivity of the current political agenda in the face of the deep and persistent inequalities, social inequality can be considered the main theory and practice dilemma about the modes, media, and genres of development communication in Latin America, the most unequal continent of the twenty-first century.

Development Communication Changes and Continuities

The proximity of socio-scientific analysis to moral discourse (Craig & Muller, 2007) underlies development communication theory and practice which often includes the analytic perspective (how it is) with an understanding of ambition (why) and a normative sensitivity (what for) in its wide, open, and dynamic field of knowledge.

The path of development communication is, in more than one sense, equivalent to the general dynamics of development theory in the Western world. The idea of progress is consolidated in the nineteenth century; the classic theories about social change accompany the institutionalization of the social sciences since said century; the economic growth associated with industrialization predominated between 1945 and 1965; the Latin American thinking about development arises from the 60s with diverse structuralist and dependence ideas and from 1976, approximately, arise the sustainable, human development, and territorial issues in a wide range together with the question of post-development (Carniglia, 2015).

In turn, a history of almost seven decades of communication for development shows significant strengths in its research and action capabilities together with a thorough assessment of the proposed ideas within said field of knowledge that, as it was said before, articulates the analytic capacity, the understanding ambition, and the normative perspective.

Many assessments in the field of development communication support this preliminary diagnosis. On the one hand, Robert White recognized toward the end of the twentieth century that "approximately every 10 or 15 years the field of development communication has been marked by agonizing reevaluations and the inadequacy of the proposed issues has been publicly admitted" (1992, p. 42). At the same time, Luis Beltrán (2005), for example, explores the different development communication research and practice stages in Latin America during the twentieth century showing that diversity in unity is one of its possibility conditions. On the other hand, Jan Servaes (2000) and Silvio Waisbord (2009) recognize the validity of two particular models of social communication in the twentieth century, focusing on diffusion or participation, with eventual points of convergence between them that generate a diverse toolbox, specific for research and action in development communication.

In this sense, it can be said that the continuities and changes in the development communication path are related, like in other socio-scientific fields of knowledge (Jelin et al., 2020), to each discipline's internal developments, but also with the debates about the policies in national and especially international entities, and with the challenges that the real-world trends and experiences pose in different regions of the world.

This premise shows, among other aspects, a two-way relationship between development communication and the different areas of the public agenda. On the one hand, as Robert White (1992) points out, development communication shows a permanently renewed sensitivity to build a public sphere of national scope at least: "Even though communication and development perspectives have changed significantly in the last forty years, as communication theorists and political experts in developing countries became more committed, the debate continued focusing on the role of communication in the public eye" (White, 1992, p. 45).

On the other hand, the state, the market, and the civil society, among other definition areas of the dynamic and open public agenda, show the field of development communication some classic and new issues of the socio-cultural dynamics with different specialized theory and intervention demands. So, for example, the recently deceased Jesus Martín Barbero stated that: "The formulation of communication and culture demands by the civil society involves a double task: research them, we do not know them and those we know are highly influenced by the media, and legitimize them with the modest but effective support which in the long term may grant the legitimacy that the university has in our countries" (Martín Barbero, 1990, p. 74).

Inequalities, a Key Issue of Three Contemporary Agendas

An increasing renewed sensitivity for systematic, deep, and persistent inequalities has emerged in different social, political, and academic agendas in the twenty-first century as a demand, among others, to update development communication theory and practice.

Systematic, Deep, and Persistent Inequalities: A Journey Through Recent Critical Theory

Inequality is a foundational topic of the modern social sciences which also goes through its theoretical path from the study of social classes, for example. In this sense, Jakobsson et al. (2021) highlight social classes as a persistent and questioned concept, but also key to current research about the media in an increasingly unequal world. His perspective emphasizes, on the one hand, the mediation of structures, interests, and class conflicts, particularly in journalism and, on the other hand, how individuals with different social statuses move in a media contemporary panorama, more complex due to cultural, technological, and socio-economic changes. Busso and Messina (2020), for example, show that inequality limits access to sanitary information in Latin America during the COVID-19 pandemic, since basic knowledge about the symptoms, diffusion, and prevention of the virus is less precise in the lower parts of people's income distribution.

Systematic, deep, and persistent inequalities also constitute a permanent concern of social theory in Latin America. On the one hand, as Jelin et al. (2020) point out, the different inequalities are usually codified in terms of the social class dynamics and structure in the countryside and in the cities of the subcontinent (Kessler, 2016; Benza & Kessler, 2021). On the other hand, Cristobal Kay (1990) identifies the debate about social marginalization, one of the processes and consequences of inequality, as one of the five Latin American contributions to development theory during the twentieth century.

However, during the last quarter of the century, research about systematic and persistent inequalities was renewed in its epistemological, theoretical, methodological, and empirical aspects, by responding to diverse questions, like the following:

1. Inequality of what? (Income, well-being, social status, gender, ethnicity, race, and territory)
2. Inequality between whom?
3. How are the different inequalities articulated?
4. When and where can inequalities be observed?
5. How are inequalities empirical references recorded?
6. How are inequalities explained?
7. How are inequalities overcome?

Our initial standpoint in this debate articulates the functional, structural, and historical dimensions from a particular emergent perspective about inequalities as illegitimate asymmetries: the dynamic expanded reproduction of deep and persistent inequalities (history) crystallizes in a heterogeneous social structure (system) with diverse asymmetries (functions) under a predominant development form (neoliberalism) in Latin America in the last decades.

The renewed social theory about deep and persistent inequalities is generally supported by a multidimensional critique of the conceptual, methodological, empirical, and ideological aspects of some current approaches about this social issue. All the critical theories presented next also share the premise that the reduction and eventual overcoming of systematic and persistent inequalities find their relative conditions of possibility in collective political projects.

Particularly, the predominating inequality perspective in the public agenda of the Latin American region is associated with the theory about poverty and focuses on income inequality among people, measured by the Gini coefficient developed using quantitative information provided by home surveys. Poverty measurement also includes the complementary or alternative method of unsatisfied basic needs, for example education and housing. Also, income inequality measurement at a national level sometimes calculates functional distribution of income between capital and work.

In this sense, Juan Pérez Sáinz (2016, 2020) summarizes four of the current critiques of the approaches about poverty that focus on the home as an observation unit. This sociologist points out that these perspectives concentrate on the redistribution of wealth without taking into consideration the previous primary distribution generated in some markets of a society; they do not consider the causes of inequality because the family income, in its different working and non-working ways, is just the result of a distribution process; they give privilege to the individuals relativizing or ignoring the influence of other collective individuals like social classes; and its research method, home survey, does not capture the elite members who hoard power in the social distribution of income. Thus, the author concludes that an imaginary about inequalities alternative to the one imposed by the neoliberal order is necessary in Latin America because the current conception depoliticizes the social question in the subcontinent.

Charles Tilly and the theory about persistent categorical inequalities. All social relations imply temporary and fluctuant inequalities. However, the causal explanation of this American sociologist emphasizes the persistent categorical inequalities, those that remain during a career, life, or organizational history. The main argument of his book is that big and significant inequalities in the advantages human beings have are mainly due to categorical differences like black/white, male/female, and citizen/non-citizen, among others, more than individual differences in relation to attributes, tendencies, or performances.

According to this author, persistent inequality among categories arises when people who control valuable production resources set, with or without being aware of their action, certain social closure, exclusion, and control systems to solve important organizational problems by means of categorical divides. Therefore, various historical situations analyzed by

C. Tilly show how the classifications of black, woman, and indigenous are associated with the lowest positions in the socio-economic and power statuses within diverse contexts.

The organizational forms and processes of persistent categorical inequality are repeated in a great variety of contexts because the four inequality generation mechanisms—exploitation, opportunity hoarding, emulation, and adaptation—work together and present a tendency to self-reproduction:

1. Exploitation reproduces itself when providing surplus to the resource-controlling elites; these use part of this surplus to reward crucial collaborators and, also, to regulate the distribution of resources.
2. Opportunity hoarding selectively feeds the rewards in segregated networks and recruits substitutes in less favorable areas within them. It also includes emphatically the deliberate transmission of wealth and other benefits to children and other recognized heirs.
3. Emulation not only reduces organizational division costs, established below their theoretical alternatives, but also gives the impression of ubiquity and, therefore, inevitability.
4. Adaptation articulates unequal organizational devices with adjacent and overlapped valued social routines, in a way that the election costs of theoretically available alternatives increase in a way that makes them prohibitive (Tilly, 2016, p. 201).

In this sense, it is worth recognizing the role that social communication plays in the reproduction of persistent categorical inequalities given that the different communication modes, media, and genres contribute to the social (de) construction of the relationships and discourses associated with the four-generation mechanisms of categorical inequalities.

Kari Karppinen and Outi Puukko (2020), for example, recognize four discourses of digital rights: the protection of negative liberties, state obligations, informational justice, and affordances provided by platforms. Table 3.1 shows that those discourses differ in their definition about subjects of rights, objectives, limitations, and ways of government, but they share, according to these authors, an anthropocentric orientation that ignores the environmental footprint of the new digital technologies or the planet borders that can limit the permanent expansion of equipment, programs, and connections.

Table 3.1 Discourses about digital rights

Discourse	*Subjects of rights*	*Objectives*	*Limitations*	*Governance framework*
Digital rights as protection of negative liberties	Private individuals (corporations)	Freedom of expression, individual choice	State intervention, centralized control, censorship	Fundamental personal and property rights; limits on state power
Positive rights and state obligations	Individuals as citizens, citizens collectively	Active citizenship, equal access, effective capability to communicate	Social inequalities, market power	Regulation, public politics
Right as a vehicle of "informational justice"	Individuals, social groups, and communities	Distributive justice, protection of vulnerable groups	Discrimination, structural inequalities, state and corporate concentration of power	Regulation, public politics, social practices, and norms
Affordances provided by platforms	Users of specific services	Technological opportunities	State regulation; arbitrary, non-transparent corporate policies	Self-regulation, corporate social responsibility, terms of use

Source: Karppinen and Puukko (2020, p. 312)

Theory and Method of Income Inequality: Thomas Piketty

At least three contributions summarize those of the international research team about income inequalities coordinated by this French economist. Two of his contributions are related to the methodologic strategy and the third one has to do with the theoretical dimension.

The documented book *Capital in the Twenty-first Century* (Piketty, 2014), an authentic bestseller of recent social theory, is based on two types of very relevant data sources, but very little used by economists, historians, and other social scientists to study wealth distribution dynamics with a very long-term comparative perspective. A group of sources, tax returns, relate to income and distribution inequality; the other sources, personal property and family succession documents, focus on property, its distribution and relationship with income.

The first conclusion of this comparative research study with a really long-term approach shows that from the eighteenth-century income distribution dynamics in central or North Atlantic countries, and eventually some peripherical countries like Australia and Argentina with less documented processes, unfold powerful convergent mechanisms, that is, reduction of income differences, and divergent mechanisms, that is increase of income differences. In particular, the main strength or extended reproduction mechanism of income inequality is summarized in the formula $r > g$ which records the regressive tendency, noticeable in the last decades, for which the annual rate of return on capital (benefits, dividends, interests, rents, and others) is higher than the production and income annual growth rate in a society.

A later book by this economist (Piketty, 2019) centers the transnational research interest in inequality on the evolution of unequal ideologies and deals with this issue from a wider temporal, spatial, and comparative perspective. This study includes the old slave and trifunctional societies to modern postcolonial and hyper-capitalist societies. The author says that the current history of the justification and structure systems of social inequality shows that: "every human society must justify its inequalities. Reasons must be found because, without them, the whole political and social edifice is in danger of collapsing" (Piketty, 2019, p. 11).

Piketty (2019) proposes the concept "inequality regime," which encompasses the political regime and the property regime of every society. In this way, the author recognizes that the progresses made in relation to health, education, and purchase power have hidden immense increasing inequalities and weaknesses in most countries and regions of the planet from the 1980s. The greatest inequalities are expressed, for example, in the increase of the percentage of participation in the total rent of ten percent of the population with higher income.

Dynamics of Global Intertwined Inequalities

This perspective, as a social theory in progress based on comparative international research, arises toward the end of the twentieth century in a renewed socio-territorial context at a local, national, transnational, and global scale. This new scenario involves, on the one hand, a critical analysis of global capitalism and a review of the effects of neoliberal policies that subordinate the role of the state in the distribution and redistribution of the different resources and, on the other hand, the emergence of new struggles for the distribution of socially produced wealth (Jelin et al., 2020).

The perspective of intertwined global inequalities renews research considering at the same time inequalities in the plural form, like an expression of multiple asymmetries, but also in the singular form as the different inequalities are inserted within capitalism like a unique global social structure (Motta et al., 2020). This emergent theory consists of four changes in research about social inequalities: a more integral understanding of the problem that transcends the exclusive interest in the socio-economic inequalities to focus on the power, existential, environmental, and symbolic or subjective dimensions; the focus of analysis removes the nation as an observation unit to consider the pluri-local and transnational spaces; the new approach integrates multiple categorizations, apart from social classes, in the configuration of the current statuses as it records the articulation between horizontal categories like gender, race, and ethnicity; and the change in methodological orientation emphasizes the qualitative and quantitative register of political and symbolical issues before the collection of data about social structures.

Research about global intertwined inequalities contributes to understanding the structures, categories, and dynamics of inequalities at a global level and in Latin America in particular (Costa et al., 2020). A first finding shows the historical persistence of inequalities in countries and the continuity of the inequality structure in each country. A second contribution broadens the perspective to include, apart from income inequality, the asymmetries in terms of power, well-being, and environmental resources. A third contribution highlights the historical and political condition of inequalities, whose paths show changes and continuity over time within specific social contexts. See Busso and Messina (2020) for an updated and wide panorama with diverse quantitative and qualitative indicators about various dimensions of inequality in Latin America and the Caribbean.

These three renewed theoretical perspectives about the deep and persistent inequalities call us, in their similarities and differences from a critical view, to think about the communication correlates about the deep social asymmetries that affect Latin America during the twenty-first century. In this sense, Jesus Martín Barbero (2011) asks about the ways of collective belonging in the fragmented societies of Latin America, where most of the people do not find meaning in their lives at work and in politics. His answer supports, as central thesis, that culture in society changes when technological mediation of communication stops being merely instrumental to become structural mediation as its novelty does not lie in the devices but on the ways of perception and language, in the new sensitivities and writings.

Inequality and Political Agenda: The 2030 Agenda, a Global Consensus About the Pending Development

Persistent inequalities and other social asymmetries severely damage rights, in general, and communication and information rights, in particular. These rights are recognized from the national and international political agendas, the norms like national constitutions, specific laws, the policies at different levels, and territorial scope and the practices of social subjects who demand the continuation of the validity of different legitimized rights and/or the legitimacy of new rights.

In this context, the United Nations Development Program (UNDP) has been from some decades one of the intergovernmental areas of permanent agreed definition of the goals for development with a relative capacity to influence the specific definitions of the political, social, and even academic agenda of different countries.

In this sense, the 2030 SDG (Sustainable Development Goals), approved by the United Nations in the Sustainable Development Summit of September 2015, represents an arising discourse from the UNDP with wide circulation in the political, social, and academic agendas about the desired social change for the next decades of the twenty-first century. Given their wide international visibility, these goals demand an assessment of the pertinence, history, and scopes of their relations with development communication during the next years from a systematic, deep, and persistent inequalities perspective.

The 172,030 SDGs set the following goals for future development:

- End poverty in all its form everywhere.
- End hunger, achieve food security and improved nutrition, and promote sustainable agriculture.
- Ensure healthy lives and promote well-being for all at all ages.
- Ensure an inclusive and equitable quality education and promote lifelong learning opportunities for all.
- Achieve gender equality and empower all women and girls.

- Ensure availability and sustainable management of water and sanitation for all.
- Ensure access to affordable, reliable, sustainable, and modern energy for all.
- Promote sustained, inclusive and sustainable economic growth, full and productive employment, and decent work for all.
- Build resilient infrastructure, promote inclusive and sustainable industrialization, and foster innovation.
- Reduce inequality within and among countries.
- Make cities and human settlements inclusive, safe, resilient, and sustainable.
- Ensure sustainable consumption and production patterns.
- Take urgent action to combat climate change and its impacts.
- Conserve and sustainably use oceans, seas, and sea resources for sustainable development.
- Protect, restore, and promote sustainable use of terrestrial ecosystems, sustainably manage forests, combat desertification, and fight against and reverse land degradation and stop biodiversity loss.
- Promote peaceful and inclusive societies for sustainable development, provide access to justice for all, and build efficient, accountable, and inclusive institutions at all levels.
- Strengthen the means of implementation and revitalize the world alliance for sustainable development (PNUD, 2017; CEPAL, 2018a).

These renewed SDGs highlight, among other characteristics, a sensitivity for the different deep and persistent inequalities that outstand in the first part of the twenty-first century like a social phenomenon, a research object, and a matter of political intervention in the local, national, and global scenarios. In particular, the lexicon of these development goals includes two explicit references to (in)equality, the mentioning of two inequality dimensions like well-being and gender, and other two specific allusions to material aspects of well-being like access to water and energy. Furthermore, the adjective "inclusive," one of the most repeated words of the text with six mentions in its singular or plural forms, stands out like an active politics orientation closely related to the issue of inequalities.

However, the 2030 SDGs do not explicitly recognize social communication as a particular field of the collective imagination about the desired development for the next decade. Such a significant omission is debatable from three premises of development communication in Latin America: (1) the relational, symbolic, and material conditions of social communication that constitute all structures and development processes (Servaes, 2000; Waisbord, 2009; Carniglia, 2015); (2) the historical, systematic, and functional dimensions of development communication valid for around eight decades (White, 1992; Beltrán, 2005); and (3) the modes, media, and genres of communication that provide a toolbox renewed by the transformation of the communicational ecosystem associated to the changes caused by the digitalization of life, work, and consumption (Lupač, 2018).

Resistance to Inequalities from Social Movements

How do marginalized people who want to improve their condition behave toward marginalization, nowadays due to capitalism and globalization? This question crosses, as it has been said, the social theory in Latin America, from its arousal in the second half of the twentieth century, as a key question of the debates about social development focused on, for example, research about the lifestyles of marginalized people (Kay, 1990).

Pérez Sáinz (2019) updates this question in his study about the responses to surviving extreme inequalities in the Latin American subcontinent. The different answers of marginalized people include, among other ways, the disruption of violence, resistance to marginalization, refuge in religion, and the collective search of transformations by means of social movements. In this sense, the author summarizes in the table below the empowering dynamics of three current social movements in other countries of Latin America: the Landless Workers' Movement (Brazil), the indigenous people of Neozapatism (Mexico), and the unemployed picketers (Argentina) (Table 3.2).

In this sense, this systematization identifies some communicational characteristics of collective action in the three social movements with social transformation purposes. In this way, some communicational practices, like assemblies, can be seen, communication interlocutors for social change are highlighted, and some emerging meanings for collective action are recognized. However, development communication research studies are still missing which, for example from the emerging incidence perspective (Carlosena et al., 2020), dig deeply into the knowledge about these

Table 3.2 Empowering dynamics of social movements in Latin America

Dimension	*Landless movement*	*Neozapatism*	*Picketers*
Struggle method	Camping and unused land occupation	Armed uprising National and global display Territorial control	Pickets, assemblies, and riots
Empowerment achievements of subaltern sectors	Settlement and productive use of land Overcoming of social exclusion Democratization of local life	Access to land and indigenous autonomy Vindication of indigenous dignity Women's empowerment	State help and overcoming of unemployment stigmatization
Tensions	Bases heterogeneity. Women's limited leadership	Intracommunity and intercommunity disputes Emigration impact	Intracommunity disputes Picketers vs. beneficiaries Women's limited leadership
Relation with the state	Resistance and negotiation	Resistance and self-exclusion	Resistance, negotiation, and cooperation
Contributions to society	Keep the agricultural reform in force	Visibility of indigenous rights, democratic openness, and state presence	Exit from the accumulation model based on financial valuation Keeping a job as a central social inclusion mechanism
Symbolic impact in the regional, national, and global areas	Direct questioning of the neoliberal order Practice of experiences with a strong utopian content ("another world is possible")		

Source: Pérez Sáinz (2019, p. 208)

and other conditions of the specific action at the same time they suggest communication strategies for the internal and external work of these organizations, focusing on the expansion and sustainability of the empowerment processes in progress.

Social Inequalities in Latin America. From Persistence to Extended Reproduction

As it has been said, our critical perspective articulates the historical, structural, and functional dimensions about the social asymmetries that severely damage the validity of the different human rights: the dynamic extended reproduction of deep and persistent inequalities (history) crystalizes in a heterogeneous social structure (system) with diverse asymmetries (functions) under a development mode (neoliberalism) predominating in Latin American in the last decades.

Inequalities and development modes: processes and moments. The renovation of critical theory about different social asymmetries includes various studies about multiple causes, processes, frameworks, consequences, and contexts of deep and persistent inequalities in Latin America.

In this sense, Juan Pérez Sáinz's (2016) research stands out from a radical view about one of the main negative conditions of the development frameworks that constitute the history of the subcontinent. This author's premises take the issue of power to understand inequalities as processes of (dis)empowerment, move the view from the redistribution sphere toward the distribution space, focus on the basic markets (work, capitals, land, and knowledge) of the surplus asymmetries, pluralize the conceptualization of social subjects because they incorporate to the social classes in the surplus struggle, and incorporate the problems of gender, ethnicity, race, and territory differences to explain their conversion in inequalities.

In this regard, Pérez Sáinz (2016) identifies four generating processes of deep inequality that allow us to understand the persistence of the different asymmetries in Latin America. Two of the dynamics correspond to the processes of (un) empowerment by surplus distribution across social classes while the remaining ones belong to the individualization processes and the recognition of differences in a society. First, the labor markets tend to generate work, instead of employment as work with non-market rights, with great asymmetry in favor of capital. Second, in the other markets (capitals, land, and knowledge) opening and closing mechanisms work in a way that when any of these markets is closed by the concentration of property in just a few, they favor asymmetric situations that generate deep inequalities. Third, when access to a minimum of social citizenship is restricted (education, health, pension, and care) individualization processes do not relativize both class dynamics of the classic markets. Fourth, the process of making someone inferior denies differences favoring the formation of gender, ethnicity, race, and territory asymmetries, among others, also added to the social class dynamics.

These four processes came into being in three periods during the development of capitalism in Latin America, with their corresponding stages and transitions. During the oligarchy stage, between mid-nineteenth century and 1929, the two fields of surplus inequalities were founded, which marked the subsequent development. The national modernization stage, between the 1929 crisis and the beginning of the 1980s, gave great importance to the state in the transformation of surplus inequalities as well as in the process of social citizenship and the recognition of categorical pairs, although other asymmetries continued, for example, rural areas remained, in general, outside these inclusive processes. The time of globalized modernization, from the 1980s to the present, implies, under different circumstances, the formal employment crisis based on an accumulation model with industrialization oriented toward the internal market.

In relation to this, it is the job of development communication to face a double intellectual and political challenge: on the one hand, to systematize the previous and current studies of the communicational field, making them interact with these socio-historical findings about the processes of persistent and deep inequality in Latin America and, on the other hand, to foster new research studies in the areas of knowledge vacancy and specific intervention.

The ECLAC and a Contemporary Critical Condition of the Region

The Economic Commission for Latin America and the Caribbean (ECLAC) has been for some decades a key referent of the theory on Latin American development styles. Some of their ideas, for example, the center-periphery theory (Kay, 1990), represent and identify key for research about the social and economic processes as they provide the normative framework, concepts, diagnosis, and strategic orientations.

The ECLAC has also shown an acute sensitivity about the issue of inequality that affects all Latin America. In this sense, an early document (CEPAL-IIDH, 1997), written in the middle of the neoliberal transformation of the Latin American economies, highlighted the importance of giving privilege to a really wide perspective of social and cultural rights in the processes of economic and social development.

What is more, some recent documents of this intergovernmental organization consider equality as a central value of development. In particular, the report *The inefficiency of inequality* (CEPAL, 2018b) goes deep into the normative aspects, the consequences, costs and policies of systematic and persistent inequalities:

> The Latin American region and the Caribbean face a scenario of opportunities, but also of global uncertainties in times when their economies require deep and urgent transformations. Moving towards a path of greater equality is not only an ethical imperative in a region with social gaps that are expressed in different areas; it is also a necessary condition to accelerate productivity growth, internalize and disseminate digital revolution, move towards environmental sustainability and provide an institutional framework that allows us to act in a world where big imbalances are combined with huge possibilities. (CEPAL, 2018b, p. 13)

This document, as well as others, highlights Latin America and the Caribbean as the most unequal region in the world, in terms of income distribution and other socio-economic indicators, and, at the same time, more violent, according to the homicide rate every 100.000 inhabitants, excluding war areas or armed conflicts. The text also presents other indicators of the current territorial, ethnic, gender gaps or lacks in this region distinguishing between vertical inequalities (income) and horizontal inequalities (gender, ethnicity, race).

In particular, this United Nations organization concludes that inequality is inefficient and unsustainable for the region because the education and health gaps limit the economy and people's capabilities, income inequality prevents intergenerational social mobility, income inequality is positively associated with informal employment, gender inequality causes discrimination in the labor market and the lack of social protection and care affect economic growth and employment.

Scope of Recent Policies: A Closed Debate Due to the Pandemic?

From the first decade of the twenty-first century, there was an unusual context of economic growth based on a major increase of the price of raw materials or commodities (agricultural, mineral or hydrocarbon products, among others) exported by Latin America; many countries of the region improved their well-being indicators by implementing public policies to make up some growing and persistent inequalities, for example, the conditioned transfers of income to the homes related to their members' participation in health and education services.

This and other redistribution policies caused a sustained intellectual and political debate about the relevance, scopes, and consequences of the measures implemented by the State. One of the aspects of the debate is about whether these policies correspond to a new development model, characterized alternatively as "post-neoliberalism" (Pérez Sáinz, 2016) or "progressive neo-developmentalism" (Svampa, 2012), or if they imply adjustments within the neoliberal model in force from the last decades of the twentieth century or transitions toward other ways of development. Another key of this controversy highlights the contradictions, at least apparent, among these policies that, for example, in the case of Argentina (Kessler, 2014), recognize health rights which facilitate access to assisted fertilization techniques to just a few citizens while thousands of people are not treated for the Chagas disease transmitted by Triatomine bugs.

The globalized pandemic due to COVID-19 arises in this context, from the beginning of 2020 in the Latin American region as a complex, dynamic, and uncertain social and sanitary configuration with very damaging effects regarding deaths, social isolation, destruction of the economies and an extended reproduction of persistent inequalities and other social asymmetries. In Argentina, one of the most affected countries by the pandemic, until July 2021 ten percent of the population contracted the virus, more than 100.000 died, around 6.000 companies abandoned the economic activity, most of them medium and small companies, and around 120.000 people lost their jobs (*Puntal*, various editions).

Thus, some recent well-documented studies, for example, Benza and Kessler (2021), anticipate that a new deepening phase of illegitimate social inequalities might have started in Latin America of a still uncertain magnitude, but it already registers a general deterioration of the living conditions and a setback of historical and recent improvements in income, employment quality, health, and education.

In this sense, review of the regional development communication experiences in this new critical context of the twenty-first century would be relevant to differentiate the scopes and limitations in terms of people's access to culture, communication, and digital rights. It is important to go deep, for example, into the comparative research about the contribution of arising communication policies in Latin America (Mastrini & Carboni, 2012) to reduce inequality to access communication infrastructure, equipment, services and content. Another research area belongs to the ways of connection between the different persistent and illegitimate inequalities and the specific gaps or lacks in the communication modes, media, and genres.

Development Communication Dilemmas: Inequalities, Rurality, and Digital Gaps

Carniglia et al. (2013) remind us that the word dilemma comes from the Greek term *dilemma*, formed by di, two, and lemma, premise or proposition. This term is used to identify a group or class of reasoning with two or more disjunctions. Philosophers call polylemma, in general terms, these arguments with two or more disjunctive members.

The dilemmatic reasoning has originally been a rhetorical device used in polemic controversies to persuade, confuse, or exhaust the rival or opponent to make them silent. In this way, in everyday use the word dilemma refers to a situation in which each available action alternative leads to an inappropriate or unpleasant consequence. Also, in a general way, disjunctive syllogism is also called dilemma, that is, the opposition of two theses, therefore, if any one of them is true, the other one can be considered false or vice versa.

Nevertheless, from traditional logic first and sequential logic later, it is believed that disjunctive syllogism must not be confused with dilemma in its strictness sense. Under this reasoning, the speaker or writer uses all members of the disjunctive proposition to conclude or infer something that makes the dichotomic or excluding mind of their interlocutor uncomfortable, although the dilemma does not necessarily present a totally unsatisfactory or undesired conclusion.

In this sense, from a development communication perspective subject to deep and persistent inequalities, an example of a dilemma says the following:

Different governments project communication public policies for development that they implement or do not implement.

If they implement these policies, governments incur significant costs to the public funds and are responsible in the face of the citizens.

If public policies are not implemented, governments cause significant social costs and are responsible in the face of the citizens.

Therefore, whether policies are implemented or not, governments are responsible in the face of their citizens.

The Emerging Digital Gap in Ruralities and Development Dilemmas

Petr Lupač (2018) points out that updated research about the structure and dynamics of the digital gap, aligned to the growing relevance of the digital networks for participating in society, also helps to understand material infrastructures of the society and the recognition of how these infrastructures are related to social inequality, social change, and social structure.

In this sense, our research in progress about the integration of digital technologies in the work of teachers in rural public elementary schools (Tamargo & Carniglia, 2019) provides various preliminary signs of the interpenetration between rural development processes, social communication dynamics, and the emergence of deep and persistent inequalities. The following reasoning highlights five conditions of a current situation of the articulation among the income, gender, territory, and digital inequalities recognized by recent studies (Tamargo & Carniglia, 2019; Cimadevilla, 2021).

First, elementary school in the countryside is an invisible institution in the academic, social, and political discourses, whose path is influenced by the structures and processes of the different Argentinean ruralities. This school context, particularly in the pampa region more integrated to global agriculture under the agribusiness model, recognizes a productive expansion process with technical change, socio-economic concentration, farm depopulation, and environmental vulnerability from approximately 1970.

Second, in this renewed agricultural context the pluri-grade or multi-grade system as a pedagogical framework and some infrastructure (buildings and roads) and services (tap water, phone lines, transportation, and broadband connectivity) shortages are kept permanent in ruralized schools, while they present significant changes in the students' sociodemographic condition. The number of students nowadays tends to be reduced and unstable, and it consists of children who come from dependent rural workers' homes who sometimes migrate from and to other Argentinean regions.

Third, women, in general without specific pedagogical training for the pluri-grade system and the ruralities, predominate in the school work as the only teachers in elementary public schools with three different educational roles (principal, teacher, and assistant teacher) which also include other activities which take place between the country and the city.

Fourth, teachers participate in three not-necessarily excluding ways of Communication and Information Technologies (ICT) training sessions to face the serious shortage in this area (Carniglia & Tamargo, 2021). The most frequent way of informal literacy includes the training of rural teachers in the use of digital technologies by their own means without the intervention of any state, private, or community educational institution. A basic and formal way of digital literacy includes teachers in the rural areas who take part in institutionalized educational proposals of general training to use information equipment, programs, and services. A smaller group of teachers take part in the intermittent official training in digital technologies that emphasize on the integration of info-communicational resources into the school planning, thus providing strategies, materials, and documents that can be used during their lessons in rural schools.

Fifth, given these systematic, institutional, and individual limitations for the integration of the ambivalent ICTs in elementary public schools of the Cordoba pampa areas, teachers from the south of the province of Cordoba (Argentina), mediators between urban and rural areas, bring computers, digital networks, and cell phones to the pedagogical, organizational, administrative, and community teaching work in an outlying and unequal way.

This particular articulation between income, gender, territorial, and digital inequalities require from development communication, on the one hand, other research studies about the scope of the info-communication asymmetries in the very risky new conditions imposed during the COVID-19 pandemic and, on the other hand, urgent interventions to deal with the socio-educational conditions of a reproducing problem of the nineteenth century, illiteracy in its various ways, in the knowledge and information society of the twenty-first century.

Futures of Communication for Development Theory and Practice

Deep and persistent inequalities are present in Latin American societies like a permanent social condition in their historical, structural, and functional dimensions. Socio-historical studies reveal an interpenetration between diverse inequalities whose scope has deepened in the last decades at the same time that the social structure crystalizes, in different positions, a sustained network of relationships among different social groups that are useful, for example, to reproduce some power asymmetries in a particular way of excluding development in Latin America.

In this sense, Néstor García Canclini (2005) maintains that in all Latin American societies it is possible to imagine transformations toward a fairer intercultural citizenship regime with policies which communicate those who are different according to their ethnicity, gender, and territory; amend inequalities arising from unequal distributions of resources and connect with the information and the cultural, health, and well-being repertoires globally expanded.

Furthermore, Jesús Martín Barbero (2000, 2002) highlights the need of communication policies that include cultural diversity within the nation to build the Latin American cultural space, integrate into wider cultural policies, reach the public and private areas of the mass media, and project over the education system, institutions, and actors.

Therefore, a result of our previous understanding is the need of some renovation of the complex, dynamic, and open field of development communication. This introduction of a new key in the unity of specific thinking and action derives from the growing visibility that the issue of diverse deep and persistent inequalities gains in the academic, political, and social agenda of the twenty-first century.

The expansion proposed in the theory and practice of development communication implies an internal movement in the field of research and practice, in terms of ideas and strategies, as well as an external movement, with social legitimation purposes in different areas of the public agenda.

Some corollaries, among other relevant ones, of our reasoning highlight some possibility conditions for a transformation of development communication theory and practice for the twenty-first century, subject to the interpenetration among the different inequalities in the Latin American region:

- The multiple paths of social theory and thinking about development in general have at least five non-consecutive stages.
- The specific history of development communication in Latin America also recognizes the important continuities and changes throughout its almost eight decades.
- The diffusion and participation arise as alternatives, as paradigms or at least as conflicting models, in development communication research and practice in Latin America.
- The relative consolidation of both paradigms and models enables, in their converging points, a common toolbox for development communication specialists.
- Contemporary socio-cultural transformations of communicational experiences imply a more than incipient interpenetration among oral, written, and visual cultures.
- The growing digitalization of the media communication experience sets a new media ecology with dynamic connections among the traditional communication media and the digital media and platforms.
- The different social communication genres—from the letter to the scientific paper, from the news story to the soap opera, from radio drama to podcasts, from the Argentine improvised folk verse *payada* to rap, in an almost endless list—are also influenced by the transformation of relational, symbolic, and material conditions of the modes and media of communication.
- The reproduction of a wide range of systematic and persistent inequalities—of class, income, well-being, gender, ethnicity, race, and territory—represents a renewed dilemma for development communication theory and practice in Latin America.
- The cultural, communicational, and digital gaps constitute the most specific communicational demonstration of the systematic, persistent, and deep inequalities in the Latin American territory.
- The integral communication policies and other equivalent collective actions are now facing more than ever the challenge of overcoming the persistent and systematic inequalities that, like a dilemma from the past, affect the Latin American region during the twenty-first century with a renewed threat for the future of human cohabitation.

References

Beltrán, L. (2005). *La comunicación para el desarrollo en América Latina: Un recuento de medio siglo*. Buenos Aires.

Benza, G., & Kessler, G. (2021). *La ¿nueva? estructura social de América Latina*. Buenos Aires.

Busso, M., & Messina, J. (Eds.). (2020). *La crisis de la desigualdad: América Latina y el Caribe en la encrucijada*. Washington.

Carlosena, M., Kenbel, C. A., Yañez, P. C., & Pugliese Solivellas, V. L. (2020). Comunicación para la incidencia pública: un abordaje posible desde las organizaciones para el cambio social. *Revista Latinoamericana de Ciencias de la Comunicación. Año XIX*(33), Enero-abril, pp. 1–11. http://revista.pubalaic.org/index.php/alaic/article/view/1562

Carniglia, E. (2015). *La teoría del desarrollo en el siglo XXI. Algunas tesis sobre cambio sociocultural y comunicación, Río Cuarto*. UNRC-FCH-DCC, Curso Teoría del Desarrollo.

Carniglia, E., Macchiarola, V., & Busso, G. (2013). *Entre políticas, aulas y hogares. Dilemas de la informática educativa pública*. Buenos Aires, Dunken.

Carniglia, E., & Tamargo, C. (2021, July 11–15). *In lack of policies: rural teachers and modes of digital literacy. IAMCR 2021 Online conference, communication policy and technology section.*

CEPAL. (2018a). *La Agenda 2030 y los Objetivos de Desarrollo Sostenible. Una oportunidad para América Latina y el Caribe*. Santiago de Chile, Naciones Unidas.

CEPAL. (2018b). *La ineficiencia de la desigualdad*. Santiago de Chile.

CEPAL/IIDH. (1997). *La igualdad de los modernos. Reflexiones acerca de la realización de los derechos económicos, sociales y culturales en América Latina*. Cepal, IIDH.

Cimadevilla, G. (2021). Rurbanidad y TIC, un rompecabezas de pocas piezas. In M. Poggi & X. Carreras (Eds.), *Usos y representaciones de las TIC en el agro argentino: repensar el espacio desde la virtualidad* (pp. 49–76). Buenos Aires.

Costa, S., et al. (2020). Reflexiones finales. In E. Jelin (Ed.), *Repensar las desigualdades* (pp. 319–324). Siglo XXX.

Craig, R., & Muller, H. (Eds.). (2007). *Theorizing communication. Reading across traditions*. Sage.

García Canclini, N. (2005). *Diferentes, desiguales y desconectados. Mapas de la interculturalidad*. Gedisa.

Hamelink, C. (2014). Equality and human rights. In K. Wilkins (Ed.), *The handbook of development communication and social change* (pp. 72–91). Wiley.

Jakobsson, P., Lindell, J., & Stiernstedt, F. (2021). Introduction. Class in/and the media: On the importance of class in media and communication studies. *Nordicom Review*, 1–19.

Jelin, E., Motta, R., & Costa, S. (Eds.). (2020). *Repensar las desigualdades.* Siglo XXI.

Karppinen, K., & Puukko, O. (2020). Four discourses of digital rights: Promises and problems of right-based politics. *Journal of Information Policy, 10,* 304–328.

Kay, C. (1990). *The Latin American contribution to development theory.* Working Papers Institute of Social Studies, Holanda, N° 82.

Kessler, G. (2014). *Controversias sobre la desigualdad. Argentina, 2003–2013.* FCE.

Kessler, G. (Comp.). 2016. *La sociedad argentina hoy. Radiografía de una nueva estructura.* Siglo XXI-OSDE.

Lupač, P. (2018). *Beyond the digital divide: Contextualizing the information society.* Emerald.

Martín Barbero, J. (1990). Teoría, investigación y producción en la enseñanza de la comunicación. *DIA-LOGOS, 30,* 71–76.

Martín Barbero, J. (2000). Nuevos mapas culturales de la integración y el desarrollo. In B. Klisberg, & L. Tomassini (Comps.), *Capital social y cultura: claves estratégicas para el desarrollo* (pp. 335–354). FCE.

Martín Barbero, J. (2002). De las políticas de comunicación a la reimaginación de la política. *Nueva sociedad,* 70–84.

Martín Barbero, J. (2011). La pertenencia en el horizonte de las nuevas tecnologías y de la sociedad de la comunicación. In M. Hopenhayn, & A. Sojo (Comps.). *Sentido de pertenencia en sociedades fragmentadas* (pp. 105–126). Siglo XXI.

Mastrini, G., & Carboni, O. (Comps.). (2012). *Siete debates nacionales en políticas de comunicación. Actores, convergencia y tecnología.* Universidad nacional de Quilmes.

Motta, R., et al. (2020). Introducción. In E. Jelin (Ed.). *Repensar las desigualdades* (pp. 11–36). Siglo XXX.

Pérez Sáinz, J. (2016). *Una historia de la desigualdad en América latina.* Siglo XXI.

Pérez Sáinz, J. (2019). *La rebelión de los que nadie quiere ver.* Buenos Aires.

Pérez Sáinz, J. (2020). El imaginario de las desigualdades en América Latina. ¿Es necesaria otra mirada? In E. Jelin et al. (Eds.), *Repensar las desigualdades* (pp. 137–154). Siglo XXI.

Piketty, T. (2014). *El capital en el siglo XXI.* México.

Piketty, T. (2019). *Capital e ideología.* Buenos Aires.

PNUD. (2017). *Transformar nuestro mundo: la agenda 2030 para el desarrollo sostenible.* Buenos Aires.

Servaes, J. (2000). Comunicación para el desarrollo: Tres paradigmas, dos modelos, Temas y Problemas de Comunicación. *Año, 8*(10), 5–27.

Svampa, M. (2012). Pensar el desarrollo desde América Latina. In G. Massuh (Ed.), *Renunciar al bien común. Extractivismo y (pos)desarrollo en América Latina* (pp. 17–58). Mar Dulce.

Tamargo, C., & Carniglia, E. (2019). *Maestras y TIC en escuelas ruralizadas. Claves del acceso en la pampa cordobesa*. UniRío.

Tilly, C. (2016). *La desigualdad persistente*. Buenos Aires.

Waisbord, S. (2009). *Family tree of theories, methodologies and strategies in development communication*. Rockefeller Foundation, mimeo.

White, R. (1992). Análisis cultural en la comunicación para el desarrollo. *Dia-Logos, 34*, 42–57.

CHAPTER 4

Public Service Media and Sustainability? A Critical Debate of the Value of Public Service Media in Supporting the SDG18 (Communication for All)

Paul Clemens Murschetz, Franzisca Weder, Eduard Frantz, and Timo Meynhardt

Abstract

Purpose and Argumentation
The purpose of this study is to explore the role of Public Service Media (PSM) in supporting the Sustainable Development Goals 18 (Communication for All), from facilitating dialogue within the

P. C. Murschetz (✉)
Institute of Ecomedicine, Paracelsus Medical University, Salzburg, Austria
e-mail: paul.murschetz@pmu.ac.at

F. Weder
University of Queensland, Brisbane, QLD, Australia
e-mail: f.weder@uq.edu.au

E. Frantz • T. Meynhardt
HHL Leipzig Graduate School of Management, Leipzig, Germany
e-mail: eduard.frantz@hhl.de; Timo.meynhardt@hhl.de

J. Servaes, M. J. Yusha'u (eds.), *SDG18 Communicaton for All, Volume 2*, Sustainable Development Goals Series,
https://doi.org/10.1007/978-3-031-19459-7_4

community to acting as a critical watchdog over business and government. We look to issues of public value theory and performance measurement with a view to strengthening PSM's role toward remaining strong arbiters of SDG18. We view the lineages of the curent debate on public value for PSM as a useful exercise for answering questions surrounding the fundamental change in the news media industry and independent journalism, the challenges that PSM are currently facing under the impact of sustainability, and the grounding public value theory and performance management thinking offers for PSM research and practice in understanding the breadth and complexity of these challenges. We argue that PSM benefit from improving the efficacy of their public value remit by exploring the Public Value Scorecard (PVSC) model which measures public value from an audience perspective. If PSM output and services are to improve the public value for audiences, it needs to consider criteria such as improving the well-being of individuals and communities across a wide range of dimensions.

Findings

We find that critical debates into public value theory and performance management practice can help improve our understanding of the challenges of PSM trying to add value to programming output and service quality as perceived by audiences. In our view, the PVSC is an effective framework to generate valuable insights into the needs of increased audience engagement of public value creation for PSM. Measuring public value outcome on multiple dimensions comes as a defining moment of PSM wishing to improve outcomes for media audiences and stakeholders toward meeting SDG18 objectives, given the need that PSM becomes measurably more efficient and accountable.

Originality/Value

This study critically examines the public value concept and empirically proves both economic value and societal welfare of PSM offerings. It adds value to discussions about the fitness of PSM and their role as guarantors of public value for society in meeting the SDG18 goals.

Keywords Public service media • Public value • Sustainability • Public value scorecard • SDG18 (Communication for All)

Introduction

Public Service Media (PSM), which is mainly "legacy" public broadcasting, of which the British Broadcasting Corporation (BBC) is the best-known example, have a legal remit and commitment to inform, entertain, and educate the public who pay for them. But in doing so they must also protect their independence and ensure accountability.

In countries where the theme of information as a public good is taken seriously, governments are supporting media in the public interest—ideally without wielding editorial influence. However, challenged by the pressures of diminishing public funds, the growth of commercial media, new technologies, and globalization, PSM no longer enjoys the dominant—even, in some countries, monopolistic—position that it once held.

Problem Background

Digitization and emergent technologies are changing media use rapidly, with private streaming services and online platforms are gaining in importance and making it harder for legacy PSM to hold their ground. PSM are today bound to deliver more and better services despite diminishing public resources and financial support (Gransow, 2020; Lowe et al., 2018; Donders, 2021; Serong, 2017).

Worse yet, news media around the world have continued to face enormous challenges such as restrictions on press freedom ushered in and expanded under the cover of COVID-19, concerns around fake news and misinformation, a sense of mistrust and alienation from younger audiences and their migration to social media or the loss of revenue through the decline of long-established business models (CMPF, 2021; Horowitz et al., 2021; Murdock, 2021; Newman, 2021).

However, right now, supporting the role of trustworthy, anti-partisan quality news journalism and news media in a democratic society—primarily taking the form of license-fee funding or tax contributions for PSM but also as direct grants and indirect support to private media incumbents—seems ever more important (Murschetz, 2020).

And yet, despite public support for PSM being common across Europe and beyond, it remains a contested matter, stricken with many challenges and threats to all stakeholders involved. Some examples may illustrate this. While Austria, for example, provides grants for institutions training journalists, France has shelved income tax allowances for journalists, a surprising move that could exacerbate the existing lack of diversity of opinion in the country's media. In Poland, a reform of public service media took place in 2016, putting public television and radio under the direct control of the government and restricting the constitutional role of the existing media regulator.

Now, if we assume that critical journalism is synonymous with *independent* public interest journalism, according to which publishing facts and opinions about what matters to society, and covers topics that are vital for democracy and its citizens to make informed decisions and choices, we may then suggest that governments are well-advised to care for both political protection and financial support for these media and journalists in ways that work to monitor and hold accountable the institutions of government, commerce, and civic life.

National peculiarities apart, questions concerning public service broadcasting can be reduced to the following question: What social and cultural goals that are attributed to broadcasting require a specially mandated, noncommercially driven organization that is publicly owned, publicly funded, and publicly accountable? Broadcasters, politicians, media professionals, creative people, community activists, and scholars worldwide are wrestling with this question.

However, when society increasingly requests that the common good becomes a priority but no longer trusts news media to do so, what flexibility do PSM have? How can public media value be safeguarded and strengthened and how can PSM performance in supporting the SDGs best be measured?

Rationale

The purpose of this study is to explore the role of Public Service Media (PSM) in supporting the Sustainable Development Goals 18 (Communication for All), from facilitating dialogue within the community to acting as a critical watchdog over business and government. We look to issues of public value theory and performance measurement with a view to strengthening PSM's role toward remaining strong arbiters of SDG18.

We view the lineages of the current public value debate for PSM as a useful exercise for answering questions surrounding the fundamental change in the news media industry and independent journalism, the challenges that PSM and are currently facing under the impact of sustainability, and the grounding public value theory and performance management thinking offers for PSM research and practice in understanding the breadth and complexity of these challenges. We argue that PSM benefit from improving the efficacy of their public value remit by exploring the Public Value Scorecard (PVSC) model. If PSM output and services are to improve the public value for audiences, it needs to consider criteria such as improving the well-being of individuals and communities across a wide range of dimensions.

Propositions

To answer the questions raised above, we discuss the following three propositions:

Proposition 1: "PSM must rethink their public value" Firstly, we re-enter the debate of "public value" and present some current dominant scholarly debates around the concept's use, practicality, and validity surrounding questions related to the role of PSM in times of transformational change.

Based on the above introduction, we posit that it is necessary to rethink the role of media organizations in general and PSM in a more fragmented society more particularly. On the one hand, this involves refining the societal contribution of public service. Starting from the notion that PSM should, as McQuail (2010, p. 178) put it, "serve the public interest by meeting the important communication needs of society and its citizens," these needs (e.g., contribution to democratic governance and culture, production of information and knowledge, cohesion and integration, or progress) and the ways PSM can address these needs in unique ways must not be ignored. We argue that PSM need to rethink their public value engagement and explore new performance measurement tools and public value reporting strategies. To be truly effective, PSM values need to be based on the Public Value Scorecard model which defines public value both more broadly and narrowly at the same time. More broadly in mission and vision, and more narrowly in measurable impact.

Proposition 2: "PSM must endorse new performance measurement approaches" Secondly, we support the notion that PSM need to endorse new performance measurement approaches that help them deal with the "new realities" in the management and wider social impacts of media today, that is, sustainability. In this context, we discuss the Public Value

Scorecard (PVSC) model as an alternative performance measurement and reporting tool. To be truly effective, we argue that public value for PSM needs to be based on performance measurement and reporting models such as the PVSC which defines public value both more broadly and narrowly at the same time. More broadly in mission and vision, and more narrowly in measured impact.

Proposition 3: "PSM are dedicated arbiters of SDG18" Thirdly, the issue of "sustainability" in media and communications comes as a further emergent challenge for public value theory and PSM practice. Sustainability is called into question by institutional and intellectual transformations that push inexorably toward changing current governance and regulation policies to support news media and safeguard independent journalism. Clearly, however, media and communication can play an important role in raising awareness about the Sustainable Development Goals (SDGs), from facilitating dialogue within the community to acting as a critical watchdog over business and government, media can excel its capacity in advancing Sustainable Development Goals (SDGs).

Methods Used

Methodologically, we shall draw literature from various academic fields such as media policy, journalism, and media management studies, and thereby systematize, link, and extend familiar definitions, characteristics, types, and dimensions of these perspectives on sustainable communication from extant literature in these fields. By delineating the central properties of public value for news media and independent journalism, we attempt to make strides toward building a conceptual bridge between public value for news media and the notion of SDG18 (Communication for All).

PSM and the Public Value Debate Revisited

The European Broadcasting Union (EBU) is the world's leading alliance of public service media. Well-known as the producer of the annual Eurovision Song Contest, the EBU has 115 member organizations in 56 countries, and there are an additional 31 Associate Members in Asia, Africa, Australasia, and the Americas. EBU members operate nearly 2000 television, radio, and online channels and services, and together they reach an audience of more than 1 billion people around the world, broadcasting in more than 160 languages.

At the Union's 2012 General Assembly, EBU members from Europe and abroad unanimously adopted six core values that define why PSM are indispensable in truly democratic societies.

These are (EBU, 2012, 2020):

- Universality ("to reach everyone, everywhere with our content");
- Independence ("to be trusted program makers, independent of political, commercial and other influences");
- Excellence ("to act with the highest standards of integrity and professionalism and set benchmarks within the creative industries");
- Diversity ("to be diverse and pluralistic in our programming, the views we express and the people who work with us");
- Accountability ("to be open and listen to audiences and engage in meaningful debate");
- Innovation ("to be a driving force for innovation and creativity and enrich the media environment of the countries we work in., i.e., intensive promotion of new formats, new technologies and new ways to connect with the audience");

To achieve these core values, however, they must be properly operationalized and effectively measured. To do this, key figures of PSM as value-driven media organizations must first be identified, which are then combined in a meaningful way in the scorecard model.

The public value of PSM is thus multi-dimensional. As such, it can thus become subject to testing various hypotheses based on relations between the variables involved.

For example, a recent study by the Austrian Academy of Sciences has raised the question as to whether government financing of public service media would directly influence audience success. Hence, "broadcasters with higher public funding achieve higher market shares, greater relevance as a trustful source of information and higher levels of trust in independence from external influences" (Eberwein et al., 2019, p. 143).

Based on the above core values, the EBU has launched peer-to-peer reviews to provide its members with dedicated, professional-standard analysis at an international level of how they are complying with their public service remits. These peer-to-peer reviews highlight best practices while offering comparisons and suggestions for improvements based on the experiences of other public service media organizations.

The academic debate about the public value of media is complex and rather confusing. This is mainly due to its hybrid intellectual architecture of the public value concept.

Three schools are fighting for academic hegemony: firstly, the beginning of public value research dates to 1995, with Mark H. Moore's seminal book *Creating Public Value: Strategic Management in Government* (1995). Then, Moore presented the public value concept as a normative theory of strategic management in the public sector and saw it as the equivalent of shareholder value in the management of private companies. Social value creation has since become a corporate duty.

Secondly, in contrast to Moore's management perspective, Barry Bozeman's work is concerned with the societal level (Bryson et al., 2015). This is reflected in Bozeman's definition of public values as "those that provide a normative consensus about the rights, benefits, and privileges to which citizens should (and should not) be entitled; the duties of citizens to society, the state and each other; and the principles on which governments and policies should be based" (Bozeman, 2007, p. 17). A central theme in Bozeman's approach is the idea of public value failure, describing situations in which neither the market nor the state provides the necessary outputs and conditions to achieve public values (Bozeman, 2002).

And thirdly, unlike Moore's (1995) and Bozeman's (2007) approaches to public value, Timo Meynhardt (2015; ibid., 2019) uses the term to critically analyze an organizations' contribution to the common good. He believes that current management concepts, such as shareholder value, stakeholder value, customer value, sustainability, or corporate social responsibility, should legitimize themselves with regard to their impact on the common good. In his view, public value emerges for individuals from the experiences made in social structures and relationships.

Meynhardt posits that an organization is valuable to society when it contributes to the common good as perceived by the public (Meynhardt, 2009a, b; 2019). "Public value is situated in relationships between the individual and 'society', founded in individuals, constituted by subjective evaluations against basic needs, activated by and realized in emotional-motivational states, and produced and reproduced in experience-intense practices" (Meynhardt, 2009a, b, p. 212). To put it succinctly: "Public value is what the public values" (Talbot, 2011, p. 28).

Broadly speaking, the public value debate is about the question of which media content conveys values for society, how PSM—usually broadcasting—produce institutionally socially relevant content, how PSM distribute it on diverse platforms and channels, and how it is also accepted and consumed by heterogeneous audiences (Dobusch, 2018).

In principle, it can be determined and measured via four public value dimensions across industries (Faulkner & Kaufman, 2018):

1. Outcome: An outcome would be, for example, a social-economic, ecological, or cultural outcome that is perceived as an improvement of the public sector, such as increased security and good medical care. Quality media achieve a socially valuable outcome through so-called positive externalities in the consumption of, for example, regional news, cultural programs, or the broadcasting of parliamentary debates.
2. Legitimacy and trust, that is, the extent to which an organization and its activities are trusted and seen as legitimate by the public and key stakeholders, which can be achieved, for example, through a transparent and fair process of service provision and distribution.
3. Quality of the service as perceived by customers, managers, etc. as well as the availability and the effort required to consume a service.
4. Efficiency, such as a low level of bureaucracy, a balance of costs and benefits, or even the value that can be generated for resources used.

However, it is crucial that this value contribution to society is also experienced as important by individuals. In economic theory, such acceptance is signaled by the consumer's willingness to pay. Here, we assume that only through individual appreciation in the sense of maximizing the benefits of consumption does social acceptance for the collective good of public service media arise.

The UK's Work Foundation describes this process as follows: "Public value is what the public values, and it is the role of public managers to help determine through the democratic processes of deliberation and public engagement what social outcomes are desirable. It is through such processes that public managers can help to articulate collective citizens' preferences and thereby redress the 'democratic deficit' between public services and citizens" (The Work Foundation, 2006, p. 7).

More recent studies emphasize the need for widening our understanding of public value in media. Mazzucato et al. (2020) developed new metrics that can assess how the BBC delivers against its mission, creates public value, and co-shapes markets. In their report *Creating and Measuring Dynamic Public Value at the BBC*, the authors tackled questions of how to measure the BBC's public value more dynamically and holistically. By widening the picture beyond mere audience reach numbers, it identified three layers of public value in that the BBC creates broader value for both individuals, industry, and society at large. In doing so it has created value for individuals in their experiences as consumers; for society in contributing to a more inclusive, tolerant, and diverse culture; and in industry in taking the kinds of risks necessary for new markets to emerge.

Truly, audience share and some more qualitative metrics such as reach remain important. "Consumption figures help to show the BBC's reach, efficiency, and commercial success—these are key indicators of public value as without successful and widely viewed programming, the BBC would not have the legitimacy and scale to engage the wider public. But by widening the picture beyond numbers, we can see that the BBC creates broader value for individuals, industry and society" (Mazzucato et al., 2020, p. 23; Mazzucato & Semieniuk, 2017; Mazzucato, 2016). According to Mazzucato et al. (2020), there is a need to return to the understanding of the state as a collective value creator, and not limit its role to stabilizing markets. By acting as investor, inventor, innovator, and consumer platform at the same time, the BBC would play an essential role in developing the UK's infrastructure for digital and media innovation.

For public value not to become an empty formula, a central problem must be solved: What counts as public value is not only a problem of definition and agreement upon particular interest groups in society in the sense that PSM automatically create public value as a matter of their remit but, more essentially, predominantly as a problem of measurement and proven evidence in public value media performance.

Evidently, the total benefit that an individual derives from the consumption of TV programs and other services becomes a *verifiable* value in and for society. If this individual media benefit is not generated, no willingness to pay and hence no social value is generated, and thus ultimately no public sphere is created. In the fragmented media society, individual consumer preferences determine the value of a market offering, and ultimately the benefit to the individual consumer. In other words: "The 'value' that an individual attaches to an experience is based on how well the experience satisfies his or her basic needs as assessed against these dimensions. Note that the assessment is a subjective, emotional-motivational, and valanced reaction to an experience of some sort involving the 'public'" (Bryson et al., 2014, p. 450).

However, public value reaches beyond the individual self-interests of media audiences. Public value services are primarily designed to contribute to the common good. Therefore, it predominantly resides in the collectivist interest of society.

This means quite practically that PSM must deliver value not only for individual audiences but also for those who do not individually draw value from consuming their programs and services. Only when PSM are capable to create value that is perceived as valuable and beneficial for *all* members of society (i.e., consumers and non-consumers), will they gain legitimacy and true democratic meaning.

PSM and the Public Value Scorecard (PVSC)

The public value concept theoretically contributes to the debate on organizational legitimacy by providing new insight into how individual and societal well-being are affected by organizational action. As mentioned above, public value cannot merely be delivered, but instead must be perceived and experienced among the publics. Thus, to make valid predictions on their societal value contribution as perceived by their different public(s), as well as on areas of improvement, organizations need valid measurement tools (Meynhardt et al., 2017).

Meynhardt developed a "Public Value Scorecard" (PVSC) framework to help organizations understand and increase their value to society (2009a, b; 2015). The questions raised by this model are: What value are large organizations bringing to society? And, when they are getting it right, how can and should corporations build trust and gain legitimacy within society?

The PVSC framework (see, Fig. 4.1 below) aims at recording an outside-in perspective next to the strategic decision tools of organizations (Meynhardt & Frantz, 2021a, 2021b). It can be used to organize societal feedback from audiences and to reflect one's own strategical approaches with the evaluations and needs within the social environment. Of course, PSM have a strong awareness of their social and democratic responsibility, and, clearly, they strive to understand their customer needs and evaluate their impact among them. However, they do not explicitly engage in dialogue about their social function, unaware of their public value, and thus often do not realize the core of their purpose.

The PVSC is inspired by Kaplan and Norton's Balanced Scorecard (BSC) approaches in public management which shook up the world of

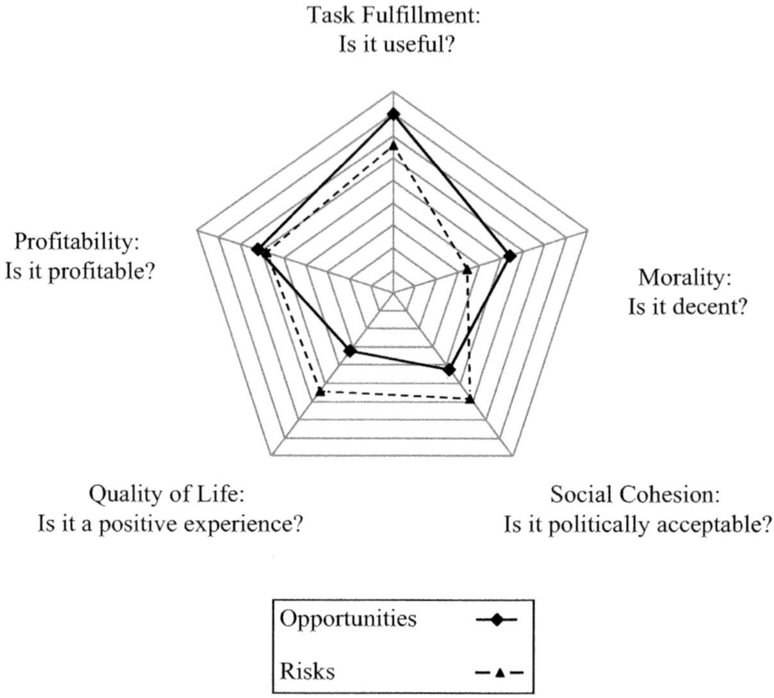

Fig. 4.1 The Public Value Scorecard (PVSC). (Source: Adapted from Meynhardt, 2015 (example))

performance measurement in the 1990s—in both the private and public sectors (Kaplan & Norton, 1992; Moore, 2003). While the BSC provides a synoptic view of the financial, marketing, operations, and human resources perspective and hence look to the supply side forces of a firm's performance, Meynhardt's PVSC draws attention to the demand side and retrieves results of the public value of an organization, service, or project from an individual's subjective judgment of five broad categories: task fulfillment, profitability, morality, social cohesion, and quality of life.

Accordingly, Meynhardt (2015) defines public value as follows:

- Public value is subjective—it, therefore, enquires about people's perceptions instead of gathering "facts."

- Public value, in keeping with needs theory, can be decomposed into several dimensions—different value perspectives are therefore included.
- Public value is non-normative—the scorecard has no value hierarchy (i.e., all five dimensions of the PVSC introduced below contribute equally to the public value score. But since public value ultimately is evaluated by every single recipient, organizations might allocate more weight to certain single public value dimensions).

As introduced by Meynhardt et al. (2014, 2016), the Public Value Scorecard model focuses directly on public value creation along five theory-based basic public value dimensions.

Survey participants answer several questions alongside five public value dimensions (seeking answers to five key questions):

1. Task fulfillment: "Is it useful?"
2. Profitability: "Is it profitable?"
3. Morality: "Is it decent?"—moral-ethical values
4. Social cohesion: "Is it politically acceptable?"
5. Quality of life: "Does it allow for positive experiences?"

As such, the PVSC is explicitly designed to collect evidence from individuals and their perceptions, beliefs, attitudes, values, sentiments, and feelings when judging a specific product or service of value. Hence, by putting emphasis on the micro/individual rather than the meso/organizational and macro/societal level, individuals can be addressed as key actors and central drivers for engagement in visioning a good and just society.

Meynhardt's approach is based on the Cognitive-experiential Self-theory of Epstein (1990), who identified four basic human needs: (1) the need for maximizing pleasure and minimizing pain, (2) the need for self-enhancement, (3) the need for maintaining control and coherence, and (4) the need for relatedness. Accordingly, human beings aim to satisfy their basic needs to ensure personal well-being. Consequently, "an evaluation of any object against basic needs is called a value" (Meynhardt, 2015, p. 321).

Data on the PVSC is typically collected through surveys, specific interview techniques, workshop methods as well as by applying social media analysis (Meynhardt, 2015). Results are schematically represented in a pentagonal profile, directing management attention to perceived opportunities and risks regarding the five dimensions given above.

According to Meynhardt's PVSC, public value is to be solely evaluated subjectively on the level of the individual beneficiary of a public value service. There are different inquiry techniques, all based on the five dimensions, but using various methods to collect data and to provide specific findings for various demands (Meynhardt, 2015, pp. 157–168).

Applying the *prioritizing* version of the PVSC, focus groups of PSM audiences can be asked to assess and prioritize an initiative or program regarding its current or potential Public Value. Participants evaluate a series of statements (see Table 4.1 below), reflecting on their Public Value relevance.

In total, there are 18 statement sets, 9 of which represent opportunities, and the other 9 point to risks, that are connected to a certain program or initiative. Each statement set contains five items, reflecting each Public Value dimension. Further, the nine statement sets of each perspective (opportunities and risks) are categorized into three subcategories, each concerning (a) the present status (general), (b) the short-term development, and (c) the medium and long-term development.

Respondents are asked to rank each value item within the several sets of statement from 5 (being the most important) to 5 (being the least important) values.

By applying a forced-choice mechanism, this method allows for analyzing each public value dimension independently within different situations and strategic perspectives. The categorization helps to identify possible sustainability gaps and provides a dynamic perspective of change over time.

Taken together, a specific public value profile is plotted into the PVSC (Fig. 4.1): the higher the opportunities compared to the risks, the higher the public value.[1]

Based on this, PSM can be evaluated alongside these five dimensions. Integrating the outside-in perspective gives more voice to the people

[1] Fig. 4.1 shows a real example of a leadership team's application of a specific scorecard version to self-assess the public value of its divestment decision (Meynhardt, 2015). From a business perspective (usefulness and profitability), the opportunities (the solid line) clearly outweighed the risks (the dotted line). However, a conflict emerged between the moral-ethical dimension and the political-social one. Whereas the project was seen as bearing a moral risk, the political dimension appeared to be less risky.

Table 4.1 PVSC value statements (generic)

Opportunities	General	The aims of the initiative convince me because they … are factually and technically coherent do not regard human aspects as merely a means to an end incorporate different interests appropriately are oriented to the satisfaction and well-being of those involved are financially and economically attractive	*Not* carrying out the initiative would above all prevent … a solution with innovative content being tried out an important contribution to more fairness being made the politically favorable situation being utilized the public image of those initiating the initiative being improved a lucrative investment being made	The chances of the initiative being successful in the end are great because … the content is well thought out the matter is not just legal but also perfectly legitimized a wide range of interest is being appropriately considered those involved predominantly recognize the opportunities it gives them there is the prospect of making a profit
	Short-Term	**I believe that the initiative will be successful within a short time because …** the fitness for purpose of the content will be recognized nobody suffers on a personal level it does not trigger any insuperable political controversies it provides fun and pleasure it is being handled appropriately economically	**It is immediately obvious that …** the initiative makes sense the self-worth of those involved will be increased any power conflicts that occur will not impede the initiative those involved associate good and enjoyable experiences with it the initiative pays off financially	**It will quickly become apparent that …** the objectives are achievable those in charge handle gray areas fairly conflicts that arise are dealt with constructively the welfare of all is taken into consideration appropriately funding is being used sensibly
	Long-Term	**I am convinced that the initiative will also gain recognition in the medium- to long-term, because …** the cost-benefit ratio is right the matter is fair and just there is a balance of interests it helps meet important needs those involved will benefit materially from it	**Over time it will be recognized that …** the content is worth the expenditure the dignity of the individual is strengthened there is a positive effect on relationships between groups the satisfaction of those involved increases the financial resources are being used sensibly	**In retrospect, the initiative will be acknowledged in that …** the quality of the approach is right the leap of faith is justified the cohesion of different groups is being influenced positively it provides fun and pleasure it is worthwhile from an economic point of view

(*continued*)

Table 4.1 (continued)

Risks	General	**In my view, the greatest risks to the Initiative are that …** there is too much emphasis on the current level of knowledge reservations on moral grounds are not dealt honestly not enough attention is paid to the political effects there is no agreement among those involved the costs are being underestimated	**When difficulties loom, the initiative will be reproached most for …** not solving any really relevant problems having excessive moral expectations provoking tension between people in an irresponsible way tacitly approving disproportionate individual hardship not working efficiently economically	**I believe that in the end, the initiative is most likely to fail because …** it is not possible to make the ideas comprehensible people will have suspicions about the good intentions it does not achieve social balance too few people really have fun with it financial or cost objectives are not being achieved
	Short-Term	**With this initiative, there is a risk in the short term that …** initiatives in this field that are at least as important will be dropped our own credibility will suffer relationships among those involved will be adversely affected too few people will be positively motivated there will be a shortage of funding elsewhere	**The initiative is particularly vulnerable in the current situation because …** the technically superior quality of the approach is not being adequately acknowledged there are doubts whether it would also be equitable under pressure existing relationship structures are being queried in the beginning it will involve losses for different parties in the first place the actual financial effects are still unclear	**A failure would above all immediately …** exacerbate material problems do irreparable moral damage put a strain on existing cooperative relationships adversely affect the well-being of those involved cause financial losses
	Long-Term	**As things stand today it seems to me that it is very uncertain in die medium to long term whether…** the expected long-term benefits will occur the moral and ethical claim will be realized it will ever be accepted in the public power and relationship structure it will gain positive feedback from third parties the potential financial yield will be exploited	**In the longer term, it appears particularly uncertain whether …** the solution is sound and viable enough all will keep to their word those involved will deal with each other in a professional and cooperative way the results will be perceived as rewarding the necessary funding can be found	**In the medium- to long-term, one might pay the price in that …** the path for other solutions is being obstructed once and for all new injustices arise prejudice between groups increase too many people are dissatisfied the economic results are not being properly appreciated

Table is taken from Meynhardt (2015, pp. 161–163)

within the decision-making and programming and leads to a more integrated and sustainable discourse with and within the society.

PSM and the Emergent Issue of Sustainability

In the last 30 years, sustainability has moved beyond its buzzword status. In 2015, all United Nations Member States adopted the 2030 Agenda for Sustainable Development, setting a "shared blueprint for peace and prosperity for people and the planet, now and into the future." The agenda recognizes "that ending poverty and other deprivations must go hand-in-hand with strategies that improve health and education, reduce inequality, and spur economic growth—all while tackling climate change and working to preserve our oceans and forests" (THE 17 GOALS | Sustainable Development (un.org)).

In management theory, notions like corporate social responsibility (Garriga & Mele, 2004) or the Triple Bottom Line (Norman & MacDonald, 2004) have gained currency, helping to illuminate sustainability issues and drive social and environmental reporting and performance in organizations and their interactions with financial outcomes.

However, research has still to provide a greater understanding of how media organizations respond to the imperative of sustainability (Lubin & Esty, 2010) and how economic, social, and environmental performances interact.

Importantly, media management scholars also have a significant—but yet unfulfilled—role in asking questions and helping to make collective decisions related to what media systems, subsystems, and characteristics of them we should be interested in sustaining (Costanza & Patten, 1995).

Finally, the notion of sustainability, in the context of digitally transformed consumer behavior and financially struggling organizations, has also entered scholarly discussions on media. Societal, cultural, environmental, legal, technological, market, and other macro-level interdependencies influence the economic, social, and environmental sustainability of the dominant means of mass communication (broadcasting, publishing, and the Internet).

At the organizational level, the economic sustainability of media players—that is, their capacity to remain in the market for a long time—may depend on efforts and activities as diverse as innovation and technology, collaboration, knowledge management, processes, purchase, and sustainability reporting and communication (Baumgartner & Ebner, 2010).

Similarly, media organizations' social sustainability—anchored on their positive influence on the present and future relationships and stakeholders, such as their value chains or their local communities (Figge et al., 2002)—will hang on critical organizational strategies in human capital development, corporate governance, internal motivation and incentives, ethical behavior, or corporate citizenship. And finally, media organizations' use of resources, emissions, or waste also carries a significant impact on ecological sustainability not always addressed.

Several large-scale and collaborative initiatives are underway to try to address some of these issues. In September 2018, the United Nations launched the SDG Media Compact, an initiative marking a new drive to advance awareness of the Sustainable Development Goals (SDGs). The SDG Media Compact began with 31 founding media and entertainment companies and has grown into a powerful alliance of over 200 members around the world, spanning 160 countries on 5 continents, with a combined audience of about 2 billion people worldwide. The SDG Media Compact seeks to inspire news and entertainment organizations to leverage their resources and talent to amplify and accelerate progress toward achieving the Goals (SDG Media Compact (un.org)).

Scholars have started to provide insights and overviews on how sustainability has been applied and explored in the world of media firms (Berglez et al., 2017). Unfortunately, however, sustainability is still a nascent communication phenomenon. It started as an economic description of the use of resources with avoiding their depletion to maintain an ecological balance (World Commission on Environment and Development, 1987, p. 51); however, the concept of sustainability changed at the end of the 1990s into a future vision of growth, a vision of the future *within* the existing system of capitalism. With a massive wave of corporate communication, sustainability gained fame and, above all, increased its public "glamour"; it even developed into a master frame (Weder et al., 2021), used (and abused) in many contexts of meaning.

The Role of PSM as Advocates of Sustainability

Certainly, media in general and PSM, in particular, are a crucial tool for raising awareness of the SDGs, as intended by the United Nations with the SDG Media Compact Initiative. They, therefore, have an important role to play in achieving the SDGs. However, limiting the media's function to that of an awareness driver would be too narrow a scope. The social significance of media and of PSM, in particular, goes far beyond a promoter function for certain agendas. Their social significance lies deeper.

PSM, which are independent in character and committed to the general interest, have a constitutional function for society. They have the purpose of facilitating constructive social discourse and thereby enabling the social opinion-forming process. In this context, they not only have the task of drawing attention to and informing about socially relevant phenomena and developments such as the SDGs but also of constructively promoting an in-depth discussion of them, reflecting on normative settings, and also pointing out conflicts of goals and values, dilemmas, and challenges (Fetzer, 2018), as well as critically observing their implementation and the activities around them.

First and foremost, PSM have an obligation to society and the common good. They thus take on a function for all socially relevant issues. As a response to global and societal challenges, the SDGs are highly relevant to the common good and accordingly also relevant for PSM. However, in terms of public interest, the role and function of PSM in this regard should not be normatively guided. The PVSC framework presented here can support PSM in determining and shaping their role regarding the achievement of the SDGs from the perspective of society. This procedural approach can identify functions that support the SDGs and their achievement and are socially sustainable: for example, through independent and informed journalism, strong regional relevance, holistic and diverse considerations, or factual enlightenment and education. Furthermore, the sustainability function of PSM can thus also be complemented by other facets that have not yet been captured in the SDGs, such as cultural aspects of sustainability.

PSM can only be a strong advocate for the SDGs if they are well accepted by society and they act in line with their societal function. In this way, PSM are indispensable for the sustainable development and implementation of the SDGs and for society itself.

Conclusion

This study has sought to interrogate the value of PSM in contributing to achieving the Sustainable Development Goals (SDGs).

We reviewed the debate of public value as it relates to PSM and independent journalism and explored the PVSC model as a possible approach to enhance existing performance measurement practices of PSM in the light of the sustainability imperative.

Sustainability comes as the next big challenge of transformational change for the media industry. It refers to quality news media's capacity to operate effectively under sound political, legal, and economic conditions. In a sustainable market environment, it is alleged, journalists operate without interference or fear of violence, and media organizations enjoy stable legal and business conditions that pay decent salaries, discourage media corruption, and promote sector-wide integrity. Ownership structures in the media sector reflect a diversity of views, and citizens trust that the media represent the full range of society's interests, including the information needs of minorities or repressed groups (Forum on Information & Democracy, 2021).

Given the findings of this discussion, we can reasonably conclude the following:

Firstly, we reaffirm the importance of the public value doctrine to support news media in the public interest. Evidently, PSM play a particularly crucial role in supporting public dialogue, enhancing knowledge of ways to support sustainable development, and holding governments accountable. Certainly, healthy news media and independent journalism are more important than ever.

The public value concept theoretically contributes to the debate on organizational legitimacy by providing new insight into how individual and societal well-being are affected by organizational action. However, we stress the notion that public value creation is to be understood as audience-centric and engagement-driven.

Public value services must first be consumed by the publics before being considered to be legitimate. Thus, to make valid predictions on their societal value contribution as perceived by their different public(s), as well as on areas of improvement, news media organizations such as PSM need qualified measurement tools (Meynhardt et al., 2017).

However, we posit that legacy PSM need to become both stronger and more acclaimed, yet more accountable to wider issues of societal impacts. In our view, the public value doctrine for PSM needs to open toward new topical challenges (notably, the sustainable media and communications future alias "sustainability imperative"). This means that PSM must adapt its principles and practicalities to meet SDGs in a mediatized world (Karmasin, 2020; Westlund & Murschetz, 2019).

Mediatization shapes public discourses and thus influences the way in which the Agenda 2030 is reflected, criticized, and implemented. Communication plays an important and sometimes decisive role in the awareness and individual acceptance and the political and economic legitimation of the SDGs.

As it seems, the future of PSM and independent journalism is as much an economic issue as it is a societal one. In fact, the individualization of civic cultures has emerged in tandem with the growth of mediatized communication processes whereby individuals use new technologies, with a tendency toward personalization in the public domain (Alvarez & Dahlgren, 2016; Bennett & Segerberg, 2013; Murschetz, 2018).

Secondly, as a corollary, PSM value can no longer be measured solely based on traditional output performance metrics such as audience share and reach.

Instead, new frameworks to measure audience engagement in a sustainable media future are to be explored. We suggest that PSM benefit from improving the efficacy of their public value remit by exploring the Public Value Scorecard (PVSC) model which measures public value from an audience and societal perspective.

Unsurprisingly, the PVSC's central theme is one of accountability. It aligns with the performance measurement movement within public services which has been in part justified as an increase in customer accountability and participation (Talbot, 2007).

From this perspective, public media value can no longer be measured solely based on traditional modes of measurement such as ratings, charter reviews, evaluations, and metrics.

Instead, when addressing the issue of PSM, performance is more effectively measured by quality-based measures that activate audiences to judge news and information individually (Sehl, 2020). Audience satisfaction and approval ratings, "value for money" measures (as this is, for example, done in the UK by the BBC Trust), or any other new forms of audience engagement measures become equally important (e.g., deep listening, sentiment tracking, collective storytelling models).

In all, the PVSC approach is both integrative and transformative by design. Integrative, as it stresses the centrality of audience engagement to measuring the impact of PSM contributing to the common good. Transformative, as it enables managers to determine whether public value is being created for audience demands, and whether demands for accountability from audiences as citizens are properly met.

Thirdly, there is no doubt about a new quest for a broader notion of PSM performance in an ever more complex world; however, how best to measure value and performance of PSM is less obvious.

Unfortunately, however, scholarly research on performance measurement of PSM regarding underlying theories, core ideas, process, insight or value created, and risks and limitations remain scarce (Anding & Hess, 2001; Kunz et al., 2016; Napoli, 2014; Picard, 2003; Reising, 2013).

Arguably, however, sustainability may challenge PSM principles and core values in rather unpredicted ways. This is because their impact on the environment as well as their "social footprint," including their relationship to employees and external stakeholders and audiences needs to be taken into account more substantially. The social impact (SI) on the society and the key audiences or publics as well as the need to get their license to operate (SLO) (Hurst & Ihlen, 2018) is discussed in various fields of CSR communication research (e.g., Rasche et al., 2017). However, PSM have not (yet) been challenged to consistently introduce responsible business models and respond to sustainability principles.

This paper also only states conceptual considerations to approach the role of PSM in achieving and promoting SDGs. Further research needs to include improving the validity of analysis by generating more insightful and testable propositions to be examined against empirical evidence of the effects of sustainability on PSM performance. This would imply establishing a structural model which postulates effects between the technological, communicative, economic, socio-cultural, and perceptual determinants of sustainable communication on PSM decision-making, audience integration strategies, and the perceived impacts on performance measured against Key Performance Indicators (KPIs) (Barbuio, 2018).

Due to the "public value" that the product or "good" (potentially) carries, there is a second dimension of responsibility that needs to be considered. A so-called communicative responsibility, as Karmasin and Weder describe it, means the responsibility for *what* and *how* a medium communicates. To further understand communicative responsibility next to economic, social, and environmental responsibility of media, the concept of *public service* needs to be bridged with the existing CSR and media management literature. Furthermore, sustainability as an overarching normative framework and guiding principle for responsible behavior and action helps to bring these concepts together and to develop a framework for *what makes media valuable to society*.

As a guideline for a sustainable future, the idea of sustainable resource use and regeneration has developed into a normative framework for individual behavior, but by the same time has been institutionalized as the 17 Sustainable Development Goals by the United Nations (UN, 2021). This "sunshine perspective" on the future, this story of progress, technological innovation, and a renewable energy economy have been communicated by political institutions and business, and organizations of all kinds, shape, and size (Weder et al., 2021). Next to this, the "rainy side" of sustainability, the principle of abundance, individual sacrifices, and environmental degradation have developed as an answer to the "old story" of climate change, as an alternative *to* capitalism, instead of an alternative *within* capitalism. This new story of revolution, cultural change, and innovation needs different ways and channels of communication.

References

Alvarez, C., & Dahlgren, P. (2016). Populism, extremism and media: Mapping an uncertain terrain. *European Journal of Communication, 31*(1), 46–57.

Anding, M., & Hess, T. (2001). Employing the Balanced Scorecard for the online media business. A conceptual framework. *IFIP International Federation for Information Processing, 74*, 354–369.

Barbuio, F. (2018). Performance measurement: A practical guide to KPIs and benchmarking in public broadcasters. Performance measurement a practical guide.pdf (publicmediaalliance.org).

Baumgartner, R. J., & Ebner, D. (2010). Corporate sustainability strategies: Sustainability profiles and maturity levels. *Sustainable development, 18*(2), 76–89.

Benington, J., & Moore, M. H. (2009). *Public value: The theory and practice*. Palgrave.

Benington, J., & Moore, M. H. (2011). Changing value in complex and changing times. In J. Benington & M. H. Moore (Eds.), *Public value: Theory and practice* (pp. 1–30). Palgrave Macmillan.

Bennett, W. L., & Segerberg, A. (2013). *The logic of connective action: Digital media and the personalization of contentious politics*. Cambridge University Press.

Berglez, P., Olausson, U., & Ots, M. (2017). What is sustainable journalism? An Introduction. In P. Berglez, U. Olausson, & M. Ots (Eds.), *What is sustainable journalism? Integrating the environmental, social, and economic challenges of journalism* (pp. xi–xxvi). Peter Lang.

Bozeman, B. (2002). Public-value failure: When efficient markets may not do. *Public Administration Review, 62*(2), 145–161.

Bozeman, B. (2007). *Public values and public interest: Counterbalancing economic individualism*. Georgetown University Press.

Bryson, J. M., Crosby, B. C., & Bloomberg, L. (2014). Public value governance: Moving beyond traditional public administration and the new public management. *Public Administration Review, 74*(4), 445–456.

Bryson, J. M., Crosby, B. C., & Bloomberg, L. (2015). Discerning and assessing public value: Major issues and new directions. In J. M. Bryson, B. C. Crosby, & L. Bloomberg (Eds.), *Public value and public administration* (pp. 1–21). Georgetown University Press.

Centre for Media Pluralism and Media Freedom (CMPF). (2021). Media economy in the pandemic: A European Perspective Technical Report April 2021/01 (by R. Carlini and K. Bleyer-Simon). Media economy in the pandemic: A European perspective (eui.eu).

Costanza, R., & Patten, B. C. (1995). Defining and predicting sustainability. *Ecological Economics, 15*(3), 193–196.

Dobusch, L. (2018). Democratic media public spaces in the age of digital platforms. In K. Mitschka & K. Unterberger (Eds.), *Public open space. On the future of public media* (pp. 308–313). Facultas.

Donders, K. (2021). *Public service media in Europe. Law, theory and practice.* Routledge.

Donders, K., Raats, T., & Tintel, S. (2020). (Re)defining public service media from an economic perspective: Damned if they do, damned if they don't. In M. B. Rimscha & S. Kienzler (Eds.), *Management and economics of communication* (pp. 203–223). https://doi.org/10.1515/9783110589542

Epstein, S. (1990). Cognitive-experiential self-theory of personality. In T. Millon & M. J. Lerner (Eds.), *Handbook of psychology: Personality and social psychology* (Vol. 5, pp. 159–184). John Wiley & Sons Inc.

European Broadcasting Union. (2012). *Empowering society. A declaration on the core values of public service media*. European Broadcasting Union.

European Broadcasting Union. (2020). The value of PSM. EBU—The value of public service media: Executive guide.

Faulkner, N., & Kaufman, S. (2018). Avoiding theoretical stagnation: A systematic review and framework for measuring public value. *Australian Journal of Public Administration, 77*(1), 69–86.

Figge, F., Hahn, T., Schaltegger, S., & Wagner, M. (2002). The sustainability balanced scorecard—Linking sustainability management to business strategy. *Business Strategy and the Environment, 11*(5), 269–284.

Forum on Information & Democracy. (2021). A new deal for journalism. https://informationdemocracy.org/working-groups/sustainability-of-journalism/

Fuchs, C., & Unterberger, K. (2021). *The public service media and public service internet manifesto* (pp. 113–127). University of Westminster Press.

Fuchs, C., & Unterberger, K. (2021). *The public service media and public service internet manifesto.* University of Westminster Press.

Fukumoto, E., & Bozeman, B. (2019). Public values theory: What is missing? *American Review of Public Administration, 49*(6), 635–648. https://doi.org/10.1177/0275074018814244

Garriga, E., & Mele, D. (2004). Corporate social responsibility theories: Mapping the territory. *Journal of Business Ethics, 53*, 51–71.

Gransow, C. (2020). A question of value or further restriction? Public value as a core concept. In P. Savage, M. Medina, & G. F. Lowe (Eds.), *Universalism in public service media* (pp. 113–131). Nordicom, University of Gothenburg.

Horowitz, M., Cushion, S., Dragomir, M., Gutiérrez Manjón, S., & Pantti, M. (2021). A framework for assessing the role of public service media organizations in countering disinformation. *Digital Journalism*. https://doi.org/10.1080/21670811.2021.1987948

Hurst, B., & Ihlen, Ø. (2018). Corporate social responsibility and engagement. In K. A. Johnston & M. Taylor (Eds.), *Handbook of communication engagement* (pp. 133–152). Wiley-Blackwell.

Kaplan, R. S., & Norton, D. P. (1992). The balanced scorecard—Measures that drive performance. *Harvard Business Review, 70*(1), 71–79.

Karmasin, M. (2020). The SDGs in a mediatized world. In global sustainable development goals in a mediatized world (Akademie in Dialog Nr. 18) (pp. 11–17). Austrian Academy of Science.

Karmasin, M., & Bichler, K. (2017). Corporate social responsibility in the media industry: Setting the benchmark or falling behind? In K.-D. Altmeppen, C. A. Hollifield, & J. van Loon (Eds.), *Value-oriented media management: Decision making between profit and responsibility* (pp. 135–147). Springer.

Kelly, G., Muers, S., & Mulgan, G. (2002). *Creating public value: An analytical framework for public service reform*. Cabinet Office.

Kim, S. J. (2018). Audience measurement and analysis. In A. B. Albarran, B. I. Mierzejewska, & J. Jung (Eds.), *The handbook of media management and economics* (2nd ed., pp. 379–393). Routledge.

Kunz, R., Siebert, J., & Mütterlein, J. (2016). Structuring objectives of media companies: A case study based on value-focused thinking and the balanced scorecard. *Journal of Media Business Studies, 13*(4), 257–275.

Lee, P., & Vargas, L. (2020). *Expanding shrinking communication spaces*. Centre for Communication Rights.

Lowe, G. F., Van den Bulck, H., & Donders, K. (2018). *Public service media in the networked society*. Nordicom.

Lubin, D. A., & Esty, D. C. (2010). The sustainability imperative. *Harvard Business Review*. The Sustainability Imperative (hbr.org).

Martin, F., & Lowe, G. F. (2014). The value and values of public service media. In G. F. Lowe & F. Martin (Eds.), *The value of public service media. Ripe@2013* (pp. 19–40). Nordicom.

Mazzucato, M. (2016). From market fixing to market-creating: A new framework for innovation policy. *Industry and Innovation, 23*(2), 140–156.

Mazzucato, M., Conway, R., Mazzoli, E., Knoll, E, & Albala, S. (2020). Creating and measuring dynamic public value at the BBC. UCL Institute for Innovation and Public Purpose, Policy Report (IIPP WP 2020–23).

McQuail, D. (2010). *McQuail's Mass Communication Theory* (6th ed.). Sage.

Meynhardt, T. (2009a). Public value inside: What is public value creation? *International Journal of Public Administration, 32*(3–4), 192–219.

Meynhardt, T. (2009b). Public value: Organisations make society. OrganisationsEntwicklung. *Journal for Corporate Development and Change Management, 4*, 4–7.

Meynhardt, T. (2015). Public value—Turning a conceptual framework into a scorecard. In J. M. Bryson, B. C. Crosby, & L. Bloomberg (Eds.), *Public value and public administration* (pp. 147–169). Georgetown University Press.

Meynhardt, T. (2019). Public value: Value creation in the eyes of society. In A. Lindgreen, N. Koenig-Lewis, M. Kitchener, J. D. Brewer, M. H. Moore, & T. Meynhardt (Eds.), *Public value: Deepening, enriching, and broadening the theory and practice* (pp. 3–23). Routledge.

Meynhardt, T., & Bartholomes, S. (2011). (De)Composing public value: In search of basic dimensions and common ground. *International Public Management Journal, 14*(3), 284–308.

Meynhardt, T., Brieger, S. A., Strathoff, P., Anderer, S., Bäro, A., Hermann, C., Kollat, P., Neumann, J., Bartholomes, S., & Gomez, P. (2016). Public value performance: What does it mean to create value in the public sector? In R. Andeßner, D. Greiling, & R. Vogel (Eds.), *Public sector management in a globalized world* (pp. 135–180). Springer Gabler.

Meynhardt, T., & Frantz, E. (2019). Medialer public value als Beitrag zum Gemeinwohl. Media Perspektiven, 10/2019, 444–451.

Meynhardt, T., & Frantz, E. (2021a). Public value. Gemeinwohl als Zielgröße im Medienmanagement. tv-diskurs, 08/2021, 24–28.

Meynhardt, T., & Frantz, E. (2021b). Purpose controlling: Public value in die balanced scorecard integrieren—Wie das Controlling näher an die Gesellschaft rückt. Controlling—Zeitschrift für erfolgsorientierte Unternehmens steuerung, 78–81.

Meynhardt, T., & Fröhlich, A. (2019). More value awareness for more (public) value: Recognizing how and for whom value is truly created. In A. Lindgreen, N. Koenig-Lewis, M. Kitchener, J. Brewer, M. Moore, & T. Meynhardt (Eds.), *Public value—Deepening, enriching, and broadening the theory and practice* (pp. 23–39). Routledge.

Meynhardt, T., Gomez, P., & Berndt, T. (2017). How non-financial reporting can make use of Public Value: Getting Serious About Society. *The Reporting Times*, 10.

Meynhardt, T., Gomez, P., & Schweizer, M. (2014). The public value scorecard: What makes an organization valuable to society?. https://www.alexandria.unisg.ch/229529/1/EY-Performance-Organization-valuable-to-society1.pdf

Meynhardt, T., & Jasinenko, A. (2020). Measuring public value: Scale development and construct validation. *International Public Management Journal*. https://doi.org/10.1080/10967494.2020.1829763

Moore, M. H. (1995). *Creating public value: Strategic management in government*. Harvard University Press.

Moore, M. H. (2003). The PVSC: A rejoinder and an alternative to 'Strategic performance measurement and management in non-profit organizations' by R. Kaplan. Hauser Center for Non-profit Organizations. Working paper #18.

Moore, M. H. (2013). *Recognizing public value*. Harvard University Press. Recognizing Public Value | Harvard Kennedy School.

Mulgan, G. (2011). Effective supply and demand and the measurement of public and social value. In J. Benington & M. H. Moore (Eds.), *Public value theory and practice* (pp. 212–223). Palgrave Macmillan.

Mulgan, G., Breckon, J., Tarrega, M., Bakhshi, H., Davies, J., Khan, H., & Finnis, A. (2019). *Public value. How can it be measured, managed and grown?* NESTA.

Murdock, G. (2021). Public service media for critical times: Connectivity, climate, and corona. In C. Fuchs & K. Unterberger (Eds.), *The public service media and public service internet manifesto* (pp. 69–111). University of Westminster Press.

Murschetz, P. C. (2018). Political engagement of individuals in the digital age. In J. Servaes (Ed.), *Handbook of communication for development and social change*. Springer. https://doi.org/10.1007/978-981-10-7035-8_85-1

Murschetz, P. C. (2020). State aid for independent news journalism in the public interest? A critical debate of government funding models and principles, the market failure paradigm, and policy efficacy. *Digital Journalism, 8*(6), 720–739.

Nabatchi, T. (2018). Public values frames in administration and governance. *Perspectives on Public Management and Governance, 1*, 59–72.

Napoli, P. M. (2012). Audience evolution and the future of audience research. *International Journal on Media Management, 14*(2), 79–97.

Napoli, P. M. (2014). Measuring media impact. An overview of the field. measuringmedia.pdf (learcenter.org).

Newman, N. (2021). Journalism, media, and technology trends and predictions 2021. Journalism, media, and technology trends and predictions 2021 | Reuters Institute for the Study of Journalism (ox.ac.uk)

Norman, W., & MacDonald, C. (2004). Getting to the bottom of 'Triple Bottom Line'. *Business Ethics Quarterly, 14*, 243–262.

Rasche, A., Morsing, M., & Moon, J. (2017). *Corporate social responsibility: Strategy, communication, governance*. Cambridge University Press.

Reising, W. (2013). Performance management im öffentlich-rechtlichen Rundfunk. In M. Gmür, R. Schauer, & L. Theuvsen (Eds.), *Performance management in nonprofit-organisationen: Theoretische grundlagen, empirische Ergebnisse und Anwendungsbeispiele* (pp. 136–145). Haupt.

Rutgers, M. R. (2015). As good as it gets? On the meaning of public value in the study of policy and management. *The American Review of Public Administration, 45*, 29–45.

Saurwein, F., Eberwein, T., & Karmasin, M. (2019). Public service media in Europe: Exploring the relationship between funding and audience performance. *Javnost—The Public, 26*(3), 291–308. https://doi.org/10.1080/13183222.2019.160281

Sehl, A. (2020). Public service media in a digital media environment: Performance from an audience perspective. *Media and Communication, 8*(3), 359–372.

Serong, J. (2017). The public broadcasters and public value. On the untapped potential of the concept of public value. *Communicatio Socialis, 52*(2), 20–35.

Talbot, C. (2007). Performance management. In E. Ferlie, L. E. Lynn Jr., & C. Pollitt (Eds.), *The Oxford handbook of public management*. Oxford University Press.

Talbot, C. (2011). Paradoxes and prospects of 'public value'. *Public Money & Management, 31*(1), 27–34.

The Work Foundation. (2006). Deliberative democracy and the role of public managers. Final report of The Work Foundation's public value consortium (by L. Horner, R. Lehki, & R. Blaug).

United Nations. (2020). Take action for the sustainable development goals. https://www.un.org/sustainabledevelopment/sustainable-development-goals/

United Nations. (2020). SDG media compact. https://www.un.org/sustainabledevelopment/sdg-media-compact-about/

Van den Bulck, H. (2015). Public service media accountability in recent decades: A progressive shift from state to market. In K. A. Ibarra, E. Nowak, & R. Kuhn (Eds.), *Public service media in Europe. A comparative approach* (pp. 73–89). Routledge.

Van Dijck, J., Poell, T., & de Waal, M. (2018). *The platform society. Public values in a connective world*. Oxford University Press.

Weder, F., Karmasin, M., Krainer, L., & Voci, D. (2021). Sustainability communication as critical perspective in media and communication studies—An introduction. In F. Weder, L. Krainer, & M. Karmasin (Eds.), *The sustainability communication reader*. Springer VS. https://doi.org/10.1007/978-3-658-31883-3_1

WEF—World Economic Forum. (2020). *Understanding value in media: Perspectives from consumers and industry*. World Economic Forum Publication.

Westlund, O., & Murschetz, P. C. (2019). Reviewing the Nexus of participatory journalism and mediatized engagement. *JOCIS—Journal of Creative Industries and Cultural Studies, 4*, 54–73.

World Commission on Environment and Development. (1987). https://sustainabledevelopment.un.org/content/documents/5987our-common-future.pdf

CHAPTER 5

Sovereign Communication: Realising First Nations' Media and Information Literacy and Sustainability in Australia

Holly Randell-Moon

Abstract Consideration of First Nations' sustainability highlights the necessity for an SDG-18 Communication for All. Communication networks and the transmission of knowledge and information among First Nations have been central to their cultural and language survival. In Australia, First Nations are higher than average consumers of mobile technologies and social media and have been active in the creation of media networks. The latter play an important role in circulating First Nations' voices in the Australian media landscape as it has been well established that Australian news reporting has been harmful to First Nations. The production of stereotypical and racialising news media on First Nations has been coincident with settler colonisation in countries such as Australia. Misinformation about First Nations continues through deficit discourse

H. Randell-Moon (✉)
School of Indigenous Australian Studies, Charles Sturt University, Dubbo, NSW, Australia
e-mail: hrandell-moon@csu.edu.au

J. Servaes, M. J. Yusha'u (eds.), *SDG18 Communicaton for All, Volume 2*, Sustainable Development Goals Series,
https://doi.org/10.1007/978-3-031-19459-7_5

and the framing of First Nations through statistics as deprived in comparison to non-Indigenous socio-economic standards. The sustainability of First Nations is inextricably connected to the accessibility, contestation and creation of communication platforms that centre First Nations' information, perspectives and goals. An SDG-18 Communication for All would not only support the important role of First Nations to the global communications environment, it would create a policy framework and information literacy imperative to ensure First Nations' sovereign communication.

Keywords SDG-18 communication for all • First Nations • Indigenous • Communication • Development • Sustainability • Sovereignty • Self-determination

Introduction

Consideration of First Nations' sustainability highlights the necessity for an SDG-18 Communication for All. Communication networks and the transmission of knowledge and information among First Nations have been central to their cultural and language survival. In Australia, First Nations are higher than average consumers of mobile technologies and social media and have been active in the creation of media networks. The latter play an important role in circulating First Nations' voices in the Australian media landscape as it has been well established that Australian news reporting has been harmful to First Nations (see McCallum et al., 2012; Randell-Moon, 2017; Thomas et al., 2020). The production of stereotypical and racialising news media on First Nations has been coincident with settler colonisation in countries such as Australia (see Warren, 2020). Misinformation about First Nations continues through deficit discourse and the framing of First Nations through statistics as deprived in comparison to non-Indigenous socio-economic standards. First Nations' activism and media and information literacy has attempted to address these problems through the adoption of respectful cultural protocols when reporting on First Nations and professional guidelines regarding unnecessary emphasis on race and ethnicity. There is further work on increasing First Nations' sovereignty in media and information landscapes through Indigenous data sovereignty and routinising First Nations' experts and inputs into media and communications policy regulation. The sustainability of First Nations is inextricably connected to the accessibility, contestation and creation of communication platforms that centre First Nations' information, perspectives and goals. This chapter contends that an SDG-18 Communication for All would not only support the important role of First Nations to the global communications environment, it would create a policy framework and information literacy imperative to ensure First Nations' sovereign communication.

Focusing specifically on media and communication technologies in an Australian context, this chapter outlines why an SDG-18 Communication for All would be particularly important to First Nations' sustainability in policy, regulatory and representational terms and would help to illustrate First Nations' self-determination and development goals. The first section contextualises First Nations' communication development goals within the absence of a specifically named SDG for Indigenous peoples and why communication development for First Nations is important when nation-states, responsible for settler colonisation, are the policy interlocutor for First Nations' developments. The second section discusses the Australian news and communications media landscape which has continuously failed to accurately represent and support First Nations' development through the production of racial stereotyping and deficit discourse. The third section considers how dominant accounts of media and information literacy exclude the history of racial science and racial stereotyping from misinformation and disinformation policy and education. The final section considers the production of First Nations' media in Australia and focusing on the COVID-19 pandemic, why sovereign communication is necessary for First Nations' sustainability. Each of these sections demonstrates why an SDG-18 Communication for All would help to promote First Nations' sovereign communication and situate First Nations' self-determination and development goals within the global media and information environment.

Terminology for First Nations is a contextual, contested and evolving discursive landscape as institutions and professions work to incorporate respectful and authentic references to First Nations in Australia and elsewhere. As many of these institutions and professions were founded on racist and racialising assumptions towards Indigenous peoples, attending to language and its capacity to inform and construct communities and subjects is important (McGloin & Carlson, 2013). This chapter uses the term First Nations to refer to Aboriginal and Torres Strait Islander Nations and communities in Australia. This is consistent with the recommendations and self-identifications of these Nations and communities. For global references, I use the term Indigenous peoples. The policies and research discussed sometimes use different terminology and this is kept intact to preserve the integrity of the sources. I examine historically racist terminology and discourse and include this material to explicate the role of language and communication in harming First Nations' aspirations for sovereignty and self-determination. I am a non-Indigenous cis-gendered woman with settler convict ancestry, writing on unceded Wiradyuri Country. I locate myself within communication paradigms that have privileged my family and community. It is these communication paradigms that require dismantling for the sustainability of First Nations' communication and development. The latter can be supported by an SDG-18 Communication for All that recognises and attempts to ameliorate asymmetries of power in the current global communications landscape.

First Nations and the SDGs

The SDGs provide an international framework connecting the mitigation of climate change with the alleviation of socio-economic disadvantage. Though social identities such as gender (SDG-5) are distinguished as requiring particular attention, First Nations and Indigenous peoples are not specifically recognised in the goals despite the United Nations acknowledging that 'reducing inequalities is of particular relevance to indigenous peoples, who are almost universally in situations of disadvantage vis-à-vis other segments of the population' (United Nations, Department of Economic and Social Affairs, Indigenous Peoples, n.d.). Indigenous peoples are mentioned in the target goals for SDG-2 Zero Hunger and SDG-4 Quality Education (United Nations, Department of Economic and Social Affairs, Indigenous Peoples, n.d.). The review of the goals also explicitly includes Indigenous peoples' participation (United Nations, Department of Economic and Social Affairs, Indigenous Peoples, n.d.) and the Indigenous Peoples Major Group is one of the nine Major Groups in the sustainable framework (Indigenous Peoples Major Group, n.d.). Nevertheless, the lack of specifically named goals for First Nations is concerning. First Nations' sustainability is threatened by language extinction (United Nations Permanent Forum on Indigenous Issues, n.d.) and epistemicide (the loss of cultural knowledge, laws and science) (Watson, 2018), which are exacerbated by the effects of climate change. First Nations bear a disproportionate burden of the impact of man-induced climate change despite contributing comparatively little to its development and receive comparatively little financial compensation for the environmental protection their land and water management economies provide to global climate change mitigation (Kaimowitz, 2021).

Within dominant development paradigms, First Nations are often constructed as requiring assistance rather than being positioned as contributors to growth paradigms (see tebrakunna country, Lee & Eversole, 2019). This can be illustrated in the specific references to First Nations in the goals SDG-2 Zero Hunger (United Nations, n.d.-b) and SDG-4 Quality Education (United Nations, n.d.-c) where Indigenous peoples require liberation from poverty and educational disadvantage. With respect to the latter, this disadvantage is largely addressed through the recuperation of Indigenous peoples into educational norms (i.e. the amelioration of disadvantage through access to non-Indigenous education) rather than the promotion of Indigenous forms of literacy and knowledge. The Indigenous Peoples Major Group spoke about the importance of self-determination in realising the SDGs for First Nations (see DeLuca, 2017). Self-determination is the foundation for the United Declaration on the Rights of Indigenous Peoples (see Cowan, 2013). This declaration affirms 'the fundamental importance of the right to self-determination of all peoples, by virtue of which they freely determine their political status and freely pursue their economic, social and cultural development' (United Nations, n.d.-d, pp. 5–6). The Indigenous Peoples Major Group expressed concern that SDG-1 No Poverty specifies 'ownership and control over land and other forms of property' (United Nations, n.d.-a) in ways that imply individual property rights and does 'not fully reflect the special situations of Indigenous Peoples and could be detrimental for traditional economies that are based on subsistence and harmonious relationship with natural environment' (DeLuca, 2017). Further, land encompasses more than economic sustenance for Indigenous peoples and includes the maintenance of cultural knowledges, languages and identities (DeLuca, 2017). Goals related to clean energy (SDG-7) and water (SDG-6) may also rationalise the appropriation of Indigenous lands under policy exigencies to combat climate change (DeLuca, 2017).

First Nations' knowledges, expertise and land assets are able to realise a number of the existing SDGs. As noted by the Major Group for Indigenous Peoples, while Indigenous peoples represent less than 5% of the global population (United Nations Permanent Forum on Indigenous Issues, 2010), 'The lands that we are protecting conserve 80 percent of the world's biodiversity' (DeLuca, 2017). In an Australian context, the

Indigenous Estate, land managed by First Nations, constitutes approximately 20% of the Australian land mass and has high biodiversity and environmental value (Altman et al., 2007). The sustainable management of Indigenous-controlled land assets reflects the broader need for climate change action to be co-extensive with Indigenous self-determination and Indigenous sovereignty (see Porter et al., 2020).

The positioning of First Nations as needing assistance in development paradigms obscures how the development of nation-states has often occurred through the destruction and violence perpetrated against Indigenous peoples. Tanganekald, Meintangk and Boandik First Nations' Peoples scholar Irene Watson connects the violence of land dispossession and environmental destruction which occurred through settler colonisation to contemporary Indigenous socio-economic realities. For Watson, 'the violence we are currently observing in Aboriginal communities can be sourced in the invasion and colonisation of Australia' (2007, p. 97; see also Atkinson, 2002; MacDonald, 2010). Colonisation enabled the 'rampart and ravenous development of our natural world' (Watson, 2007, p. 100, 2009, p. 6) and has facilitated 'a lifestyle that has murdered ours as it eats into the future of us all' (2002, para. 9). She notes that over the past 200 years, Australia has experienced 'the highest rate of mammalian extinction in the world' (Watson, 2018, p. 129). Colonial and later governing bodies enacted intense forms of surveillance, management and violence on Indigenous families (Watson, 2007), disrupting or ignoring matriarchal and matrilineal forms of authority (2007) and contributing to First Nations' gender inequalities and poverty.

Watson also notes that Indigenous peoples are not recognised as sovereign subjects of international law and can only receive recognition through human rights frameworks via the interlocutor of a nation-state (2018, pp. 122–123). As noted above, the United Nations Declaration on the Rights of Indigenous Peoples centres self-determination to First Nations' development paradigms. However, Article 46 stipulates that the declaration should not be 'construed as authorizing or encouraging any action which would dismember or impair, totally or in part, the territorial integrity or political unity of sovereign and independent States' (United Nations, n.d.-c, pp. 28–29). For this reason, Shawnee/Lenape scholar Steven T. Newcomb argues that the declaration is underpinned by development paradigms that render Indigenous peoples' rights conspicuous because they are 'dominated peoples' (2011).

Indigenous sovereignty encompasses the political, governance and developmental aspects of self-determination but also centres custodial relationships to the environment to the sovereign status of First Nations. As Watson explains,

> Aboriginal relationships and obligations to our territories are informed by Aboriginal laws, cultures and knowledge systems. For many First Nations, relationships to land are integral to kinship systems. … The natural world is referred to as 'mother', and features of the land are often known as places of the grandfather or grandmother. Arising from relationships to land are obligations to care for country as one would care for oneself. This is a relational connection to land which is a core difference between Aboriginal relations to land and those of colonial legal systems that treat land as property and a mere commodity. (2018, p. 119) (see also Graham, 2008)

As Watson writes, First Nations' sovereignty cannot be extinguished. 'Aboriginal law cannot be assimilated or extinguished, for there is no principle within Aboriginal jurisprudence which enables extinguishment. The logic that our law could be extinguished would assume that as Aboriginal Peoples we have consented to our own genocide and/or juridicide, an idea which goes against reason, morality and law' (2018, p. 122). First Nations continue therefore to exercise sovereignty in Australia and elsewhere and acquit their custodial responsibilities despite the obstacles of the nation-state and other development instruments that do not recognise this sovereignty as co-extensive with First Nations' development. The communication of these sovereign responsibilities and assertion of self-determination through communication technologies is a crucial element of First Nations' development.

The right to communicate is and has been historically central to assertions of Indigenous sovereignty. This can be evidenced in one of the first Indigenous petitions to the Crown, signed by Walter George Arthur of the Ben Lomond community, protesting the treatment of non-Indigenous colonial authorities in Flinders Island, Tasmania (Stevens, 2017). Later, the 1963 Yirrkala bark petitions from the Yolngu people asserted their sovereignty and rights to governance of their lands (Milirrpum et al., 1963). Yorta Yorta leader William Cooper petitioned the Crown in the 1930s regarding the treatment of Indigenous peoples, which was reported in on newspapers at the time (Markus, 1983). The Larrakia people from central Australia, in the Northern Territory, presented a petition to the

Crown in 1972 outlining how their Country had been taken without a treaty (Thomas, 2020). The seminal 1938 Day of Mourning protest held within and outside of Australian Hall, on Elizabeth Street, central Sydney, also utilised communication technologies to advance First Nations' self-determination. The protest was organised by the Aborigines Progressive Association and coincided with the non-Indigenous public holiday Australia Day, which at the time celebrated 'the 150th Anniversary of the whitemen's seizure of our country' and 'callous treatment of our people' (Patten & Ferguson, n.d.). The Association issued a pamphlet outlining the discriminatory treatment of First Nations by a range of public institutions such as the mainstream media and government. The protest remains a landmark of Indigenous resistance and was reported on by the non-Indigenous news media (see Standfield et al., 2014; McGregor, 2011).

Despite being significant consumers of new media and information technologies (see Townsend et al., 2016; Shaw et al., 2014; Rice et al., 2016), First Nations are not positioned within telecommunications infrastructure developments as growth stakeholders or sovereign peoples whose Country telecommunications takes place on. First Nations are not mentioned in the *Telecommunications Act 1997* (Cth) or the Act legislating the NBN, the *National Broadband Network Companies Act 2011* (Cth). The *Native Title Act 1993* (Cth), which legislates First Nations' rights to land, has provisions for the construction of infrastructure including 'a cable, antenna, tower or other communication facility' (253, *infrastructural facility* [h]). As with the comments above regarding the acquisition of Indigenous lands for clean energy projects, this can also occur with respect to a range of infrastructure (see Fisher, 2000). The Native Title Amendment (Infrastructure and Public Facilities) Bill 2020 updated these provisions without necessarily providing for greater self-determination for Indigenous peoples (Commonwealth of Australia, 2019–2020). Generally First Nations' land assets are only viewed as infrastructurally significant for communications development when they are needed for the broader non-Indigenous community or other business interests.

The general exclusion of technologies from policy and legal domains related to Indigenous cultures, such as land rights, is not incidental. Despite having the right to self-determine how cultures are developed and maintained in international law (Article 5, United Nations, n.d.-c), Australian law has found that the incorporation of technologies such as motor boats and metal tools is inconsistent with pre-invasion of First

Nations' cultures and sufficient to demonstrate that First Nations' cultures and rights to land therefore no longer exist (Moreton-Robinson, 2004, para. 16). Yugambeh writer Maddee Clark argues these constructions of First Nations in opposition to technology reinforce

> [o]ne of the central fantasies of colonisation in Australia ... that Aboriginal people have no future. Much of telling Indigenous history to non-Indigenous people is unseating the idea that we are dead or that we belong only to the past. It is always much more digestible to non-Indigenous minds that Aboriginal people are dead, tragically/no longer have culture/are dying out/don't really live in the south eastern states; than it is to accept images of resistance, life, and adaptation. (2016)

There are numerous examples of First Nations' technological and communications innovation such as the invention of television (see Michaels, 1986) and telecommunications networks (see Casey et al., 1999), which were often initiated due to poor or no service for rural communities. First Nations' communities tend to remain in rural areas in contrast to non-Indigenous population decline. First Nations' communities are also disproportionately affected by telecommunications debt in order to participate in networked forms of communication (Cartwright & McAuliffe, 2020). An SDG-18 Communication for All would help to realise not only how essential telecommunications are for Indigenous peoples' development goals but also how important First Nations stakeholders are to growth-focused communications policies and development. This SDG would not just recognise First Nations as recipients of communications services but as self-determining communities with developmental goals tied to communications infrastructures and futures. The following section discusses the media and communications landscape in Australia in order to illustrate the importance of First Nations' self-determined communication.

First Nations and Australian Media

It has been well established that Australian news reporting has been harmful to First Nations (see McCallum et al., 2012; Randell-Moon, 2017; Thomas et al., 2020). The production of stereotypical and racialising news media on First Nations has been coincident with settler colonisation in countries such as Australia (see Warren, 2020). Early news media in

Australia were crucial in justifying settler colonial violence and racialising ideas about First Nations; though this media also provided a platform at times for critiques of this violence and the colonial treatment of First Nations. Nevertheless news salience regarding First Nations as colonial and then political 'problems' requiring intervention has been a consistent feature of the development and sustaining of news media economies in Australia.

The contemporary media landscape in Australia consists of public and private television and radio broadcasting as well as subscription television cable and media streaming services. The two public television broadcast channels have provisions that enable the inclusion of First Nations' content. The Special Broadcasting Service (SBS) has a Charter which specifics its content must meet 'communications needs of Australia's multicultural society, including ethnic, Aboriginal and Torres Strait Islander communities' (Section 6: 2[a]; *Special Broadcast Service Act 1991* [Cth]). The Australian Broadcasting Corporation (ABC), which also broadcasts public radio, does not specifically mention First Nations in its Charter (Section 6; *Australian Broadcasting Corporation Act 1983* [Cth]) but its television and radio services do contain First Nations' media content. New media developments such as online platforms and social media have enabled First Nations to develop and disseminate media content in a comparatively cost-reduced production environment. With respect to commercial broadcasters and media companies, Australian media is one of the most concentrated globally with many media companies largely owned by two or three companies (see Dwyer et al., 2021). This media concentration has implications for diversifying media and the benefits this diversification would have for First Nations.

Australian media and news media in particular have been found to perpetuate racialising and deficit discourse with respect to First Nations. 'Racialisation refers to the construction of persons and communities as "raced" or "ethnic"' (Randell-Moon, 2019a, p. 9). Racialisation is broader than racial stereotyping because it perpetuates and makes race salient to understandings of communities. Racial stereotypes 'refer to a reductive set of common sense ideas and characteristics that are repeatedly attributed to and generalized about a particular social grouping' (Randell-Moon, 2019b, p. 1). Ruth McCausland writes, 'There is a substantial body of research that demonstrates that the media over-reports or disproportionately focuses on the alleged criminal activity of Indigenous and other non-white Australians' (2004, p. 86). This demonstrates processes of racialisation where First Nations' communities are 'raced' and associations between criminality and First Nations as a whole are reproduced in the media. McCausland also notes how mainstream news media frequently portrays issues without contextualising information on the history of settler colonisation. For instance, news reports on the Port Arthur shooting massacre in 1996 described the event as surpassing 'any other documented in Australia's history' and that it was 'one of the worst mass shootings of all time' (p. 89; see also Banerjee & Osuri, 2000). These descriptions ignore mass shootings of First Nations and in particular the 'Black Line', a series of military and civilian campaigns in Tasmania intended to kill all First Nations residing on the island (see Ryan, 2013).

In my own research, I have shown how racialising discourse and the denial of First Nations' peoples as sovereign occur in the reporting of media events (see Randell-Moon, 2006, 2017, 2019b). Fiona Nicoll has argued that mainstream news media perpetuates colonial 'ways of seeing' (2008, p. 58) by framing 'Indigenous people as domestic rather than sovereign subjects' (2008, p. 64). This negation of Indigenous peoples as sovereign subjects is reinforced by media tropes of Aboriginal dysfunction and child abuse as a 'spectacle' for non-Indigenous consumption (2008, p. 67). 'Such framing disavows the role of colonisation in producing the very social problems constructed as endemic in Indigenous communities by the media' (Randell-Moon, 2017, p. 12). Amanda Porter has found that Australian news media reporting on the Black Lives Matter anti-racist movement in the United States differs from similar protests in Australia (2015). Where reporting on Black Lives Matter in the United States includes contextual information regarding the history of slavery and institutional racism, in an Australian context, the history of settler colonisation and institutional racism is not included. Porter argues that without this contextual information, news media reporting on First Nations' protests align with Stanley Cohen's notion of 'moral panics' (1980) where fear is encouraged in relation to social out-groups.

> The Australian media's propensity for moral panic and sensationalist cliché in its reports on Indigenous resistance towards police brutality is apparent. Given that, in contemporary Australia, six out of 10 Australians have had little or no contact with Indigenous Australians ... moral panic does little to help dispel stereotypes and misinformation about Indigenous affairs. (2015, p. 300) (see also Kerr & Cox, 2016)

Research has demonstrated that exposure to stereotypes depresses educational and professional performance. 'Media play a crucial role in the establishment of a social identity in terms how individuals align and identify themselves with particular social groupings and help create social representations. It is this form of social identification that exposes individuals to stereotype threat. In identifying with a social group, there is a risk of identifying and being identified with the stereotypes of that group. Importantly, the media are a key source of information about social groups for individuals who do not belong to that group or know them in person' (Randell-Moon, 2019b, p. 3). As found in other settler colonial contexts such as the United States (Leavitt et al., 2015), few non-Indigenous peoples personally know individuals who are First Nations, making the media their primary source of information about this group. Aboriginal scholar Marcia Langton theorises this relationship as the construction of 'Aboriginality'—a set of stereotypes and knowledges drawn from the media. 'Aboriginality' is 'produced by Anglo-Australians, not in dialogue with Aboriginal people, but from other representations such as the "stone age savage", the "dying race"' (1993, p. 34).

First Nations have challenged stereotypical and racially discriminatory media representations. In 2009, a news media commentator was found to have breached the *Racial Discrimination Act 1975* (Cth) in two articles written for the *Herald Sun* and *The Weekly Times* which 'implied light-skinned people who identified as Aboriginal did so for personal gain' (ABC/AAP, 2011). In 2018, the Yirrkala Aboriginal community sued Channel Seven, a commercial television broadcaster, for using 'images of adults from Yirrkala in the backdrop to a controversial Sunrise segment calling for Aboriginal children to be adopted by white families' (Wahlquist, 2019). The segment featured an all-white panel discussing Aboriginal child removals and did not include contextual information on the history and trauma associated with colonial and later governmental removals of First Nations' children (Human Rights & Equal Opportunity Commission, 1997). These children are known as the Stolen Generations and these practices are considered a form of cultural genocide (see Beresford & Omaji, 2000). The Yirrkala community had no relationship to the issues being discussed in the *Sunrise* segment. The fact that footage of any Aboriginal community was considered suitable to run during this segment and that offensive articles which breach the *Racial Discrimination Act* are printed in newspapers indicates how powerful conceptions of Aboriginality are in the production of Australia media content. These examples indicate that existing legal mechanisms can resolve problematic media representations when pursued by First Nations. An SDG-18 Communication for All has the potential to provide a more robust framework for rights to communication that are free from discrimination and informed by communication development paradigms which explicate the connections between communication and self-determination.

There is considerable research on the role of deficit discourse in media portrayals of First Nations. Deficit discourse more broadly encompasses racialising and stereotypical treatments of First Nations. The presentation of First Nations as 'deficit' and as negatively positioned in relation to non-Indigenous peoples is considered a contemporary evolution of colonial discourse which used racial science to supposedly evidence Indigenous peoples' inferiority (Walter, 2016). Deficit discourse works to undermine First Nations' development goals by justifying instead non-Indigenous determined forms of development and intervention into First Nations' communities. In their report, 'Deficit Discourse and Indigenous Health: How Narrative Framings of Aboriginal and Torres Strait Islander People Are Reproduced in Policy', William Fogarty et al. show how

> [d]eficit discourse operates across a range of intersecting fields including education and health; it circulates in policy, media, everyday conversations and beyond. Media and political discourses often operate in tandem, reproducing negative discourses about Aboriginal and Torres Strait Islander people. McCallum and Waller (2012), for example, found that between 1988 and 2008, Australia's news media paid little attention to Aboriginal and Torres Strait Islander policy issues generally, unless they were controversial. (Fogarty et al., 2018, p. viii)

This research was corroborated in another study by Melissa J. Stoneham, Jodie Goodman and Mike Daube which

> examined the media portrayal of Indigenous Australian public health issues in selected media over a twelve month period and found that, overwhelmingly, the articles were negative in their portrayal of Indigenous health. A total of 74 percent of the coverage of Australian Indigenous related articles were negative, 15 percent were positive, and 11 percent were neutral. The most common negative subject descriptors related to alcohol, child abuse, petrol sniffing, violence, suicide, deaths in custody, and crime. (Stoneham et al., 2014; see also Fforde et al., 2013)

Media can play an important role in publicising inquiries and some issues of importance for First Nations. For instance, the authors of the 'Bringing Them Home' report (Human Rights & Equal Opportunity Commission, 1997), which detailed systemic child removals, were able to liaise with media to promote the testimony and personal stories from the report (McCausland, 2004, pp. 94–95). However research continues to demonstrate how the mainstream news media reports on First Nations' communities in ways that harm First Nations' aspirations, policies and development goals. In a study examining 45 years of media reporting on Indigenous policy, Amy Thomas, Andrew Jakubowicz and Heidi Norman found 'that the selected media have generally failed to represent Aboriginal agency, and account for the complexity of the Aboriginal polity … by ignoring the standpoints of the Aboriginal polity and thereby presenting Aboriginal social issues as a failure, on the part of Aboriginal peoples, to adapt to non-Aboriginal norms and behaviours, the media have repeatedly failed' (Thomas et al. 2020, p. 8; see also McCallum & Waller, 2017). Given the current media landscape in Australia, it is not clear if sufficient progress has been made with respect to including appropriate contextual information, avoiding stereotypical treatment and prioritising First Nations' determined policy agendas and developmental goals. An SDG-18 Communication for All could more clearly demonstrate the relationship between communication and self-determination for First Nations as the foundation for culturally respectful media content and representation.

First Nations' Media and Information Literacy

Understanding how the current Australian media landscape constrains First Nations' communication and representation requires media and information literacy. UNESCO defines media and information literacy as 'a set of competencies that help people to maximize advantages and minimize harms. Media and information literacy covers competencies that enable people to critically and effectively engage with: communications content; the institutions that facilitate this content; and the use of digital technologies' (Grizzle et al., 2021, p. v). The attention not just to content but the technologies and institutions used to 'facilitate this content' means going 'beyond formal education systems to develop new tools to reach all people, of all ages, through a life-long learning approach that responds to the constantly changing information environment' (p. iv). Media and information literacy requires the inclusion of diverse community groups in all forms of media production and dissemination, including Indigenous peoples (which is spelled in the lower case 'i' in this report), to ensure 'equal access to information and knowledge' (p. 15).

UNESCO's 'Think Critically, Click Wisely!' report includes a section on 'Representation in Media and Information' (p. 77) that explains how media and information represent minority groups, including First Nations, to influence consumers' views of these groups. The report notes the problems with mainstream media and the representation minority groups including Indigenous peoples (p. 177). As I have written elsewhere, 'Media literacy of the identities and communities circulated through the media and which form the basis of knowledge about social groups, for self-identification and group categorization of others, is an important first step for comprehending stereotype formation' (Randell-Moon, 2019b, p. 3). However, '[t]he ability to mitigate stereotype threat through media literacy depends on the media environment and the information about an individual's social group they have access to' (p. 4). As discussed in the previous section, if audiences only know Indigenous peoples through the media in deficit terms, media and information literacy is critical to understanding and countering this knowledge.

Media and information literacy is also increasingly viewed as important for combating misinformation and disinformation. UNESCO's *Journalism, 'Fake News' & Disinformation: Handbook for Journalism Education and Training* defines the disinformation as 'deliberate (often orchestrated) attempts to confuse or manipulate people through delivering dishonest information to them'. Misinformation 'is generally used to refer to misleading information created or disseminated without manipulative or malicious intent' (Ireton & Posetti, 2018, p. 7). Although First Nations are not mentioned in this report, their experiences of settler colonial and governmental authorities involve misinformation and disinformation that is further exacerbated by the lack of historically contextual information regarding First Nations' policies and issues as discussed earlier. The International Center for Journalists' *A Short Guide to the History of 'Fake News' and Disinformation* provides a genealogy of disinformation linked to war and military propaganda (Posetti & Matthews, n.d.). The 'Australian Perspectives on Misinformation' report (O'Neil & Jensen, 2020) also discusses disinformation in the context of war. None of these genealogies and explanations of misinformation and disinformation include the invention of racial science or settler colonisation and invasion as wars that promoted false and damaging knowledge and information of

Indigenous peoples. An understanding of the history of racism and its role in misinformation and disinformation is necessary in order to comprehend the racial stereotyping experienced by First Nations (and other minority groups) in relation to media and information environments.

Disinformation in particular is a problem that First Nations have been dealing with for hundreds of years. As noted above, the development of news media in the colonies promoted disinformation about First Nations during frontier violence and this violence was justified through racial science (see Anderson, 2005). Racial science was so pervasive globally that it had to be debunked by the United Nations in the middle of the twentieth century (Tucker, n.d.). Racial science and eugenics informed government policy in Australia (Anderson & Perrin, 2008) and continued to do so after the UN conferences (see Beresford & Omaji, 2000). The persistence of racial science continues to influence media and information economies. Angela Saini's book, *Superior: The Return of Race Science* (2019), notes the expansion of racism and racial science in political parties in Europe, the United Kingdom and North America. Troublingly, critical race theory, which provides an understanding of the construction of race and its historical and contemporary impact on society, is being subject to political calls for removal from education curriculum (Anderson & Gatwiri, 2021). If racial literacies are not viewed as important to policy and education frameworks, then misinformation and disinformation on First Nations and other racialised groups are likely to continue.

Because of the historical legacies of colonisation and racist governmental approaches to First Nations, new and emerging information and communications technologies may also reproduce stereotypical practices and frameworks that negate Indigenous self-determination. Noongar scholar Tristan Kennedy's research on social media has found that First Nations' consumers experience persistent negativity. In the study, 97% of respondents reported that they 'encountered negative content at least every week', 62% on a daily basis, 78% 'had witnessed hate speech at least weekly over a six-month period' and 48% 'had reported content more than five times' (2021) (see also Carlson & Kennedy, 2021). Further research has found that negative comments and online trolling impact First Nations' engagement with online media and social media (Brown et al., 2021). Racial discrimination legislation and policy may need to be updated to reflect contemporary forms of cyber racism and hate speech (Jakubowicz, 2017) and First Nations consumers of mobile and new media technology face unique cyber safety experiences (Rennie & Yunkaporta, 2016).

Katherine M. Bell with Andrea Cervantez argue that traditional notions of media objectivity obscure practices of racialisation and racism by separating 'racist speech and actions from mainstream values, placing it as a fringe anomaly' (2021, p. 1143). As with the presentation of misinformation and disinformation's history above, racial science and racism are presented as separate to the development of media and information economies as though racial science and racism are separate from the development of nation-states such as Australia.

First Nations' activism and media and information literacy has attempted to address these problems through the adoption of respectful cultural protocols when reporting on First Nations and professional guidelines regarding unnecessary emphasis on race and ethnicity. For instance, the Media, Entertainment & Arts Alliance (MEAA) Journalist Code of Ethics, section 2 states: 'Do not place unnecessary emphasis on personal characteristics, including race, ethnicity' (Media, Entertainment & Arts Alliance, 2021). Media Diversity Australia, 'in partnership with National Congress of Australia's First Peoples and with the support of the Australian Broadcasting Corporation', have developed a substantive and accessible guide for news reporting on First Nations (2018). This guide includes advice on terminology, kinship, scared knowledge and sites, selecting appropriate spokespersons and cultural protocols relating to deceased Indigenous persons.

Advocacy to increase First Nations' experts and sources on matters relating not just to First Nations, but also non-Indigenous events, policy and public debate, draw attention to power and access in relation to communication platforms. In their submission to the recent parliamentary inquiry on Media Diversity in Australia, First Nations Media Australia reported, 'While there have been some improvements in reporting protocols over the past decade, there is still long road ahead to reach balanced and fair reporting on matters relating to First Nations communities. We are regularly provided with examples of entirely non-Indigenous panels on news, magazine and current affairs programs, discussing matters which affect First Nations communities' (2020, p. 11). This is supported by research from Michael Meadows where Indigenous sources are usually quoted last in news stories (2001). First Nations have a range of expertise on policy matters as well as institutional racism and structural inequalities. The First Nations Media Australia submission noted for instance that two commercial broadcast channels reported on Black Lives Matter protests without input from peoples of colour (2020, p. 11). Earlier, it was discussed how a commercial broadcaster featured an all non-Indigenous panel debating Aboriginal child removals.

It is important that the development of information and communication technologies addresses Indigenous data sovereignty and self-determination. Notions of open-access data and digital commons are 'another colonial mash up where their cultural materials and knowledge remain separated from the social-property systems in which they were and continue to be produced' (Christen, 2007, p. 7). Because digital and communications infrastructure and policy have largely been established by non-Indigenous peoples, 'the hegemonic assumptions of the global good of new media technologies have to be accepted by Indigenous people in order to "progress" or have their voices heard' (Rekhari, 2009, p. 177). Discourses surrounding 'digital natives' problematically reproduce colonial ideas of information and communication landscapes as 'open' and 'available' for 'conquest' (Byrd, 2014). As the 2003 'Indigenous Position Paper for the World Summit on the Information Society' states:

> Our collective knowledge is not merely a commodity to be traded like any other in the market place. We strongly object to the notion that it constitutes a raw material or commercial resource for the knowledge-based economy of the Information Society … [we] strongly reject the application of the public domain concept to any aspect related to our cultures and identities … [we] reject the application of IPR (intellectual property rights) regimes to assert patents, copyrights, or trademark monopolies for products, data, or processes derived or originating from our traditional knowledge or our cultural expressions. (in Christen, 2005, p. 328)

Research into the search engines and architecture of online systems also demonstrates pervasive stereotyping. Searching the World Wide Web for information involves a social interaction with knowledge where questions 'result in clear stereotypes' (Baker & Potts, 2013, p. 192) through 'the predictive capabilities that exist in many of the search engine interfaces' (Elers, 2014, p. 216). This is known as algorithmic racism (see Noble, 2018) where the iterative construction of online knowledge 'taught stereotypes to search engines and even trained them to hastily present these as results of "top relevance"' (Baker & Potts, 2013, p. 201). For this reason, internet infrastructure and knowledge systems are premised on a 'mutated colonial logic' (Christen, 2005, p. 334) where the World Wide Web as a knowledge repository relies on Enlightenment conceptions of knowledge acquisition as a universal good and reinforces rather than explains social hierarchies.

First Nations' governance and cultural responsibilities with respect to data planning and sharing are growing. Indigenous data sovereignty is a key concern of First Nations' governance (see Kukutai & Taylor, 2016). Indigenous data sovereignty refers to self-determination in how data is collected and used by and for First Nations. As the editors of *Indigenous Data Sovereignty* note, Indigenous data sovereignty

> considers the implications of UNDRIP [United Nations Declaration on the Rights of Indigenous Peoples] for the collection, ownership and application of statistics pertaining to indigenous peoples and what these might mean for indigenous peoples' sovereignty over data about them, their territories and ways of life. (Kukutai & Taylor, 2016, p. 2)

In order to benefit from these infrastructural investments, digital access to and management of data is crucial for development. The first two recommendations from OECD (Organisation for Economic Co-operation and Development) Rural Policy Reviews report, 'Linking Indigenous Communities with Regional Development', are

1. Improving Indigenous statistics and data governance.
2. Creating an enabling environment for Indigenous entrepreneurship and small business development at the regional and local levels. (2019, p. 6)

Maggie Walter, from the pairrebenne and Tasmanian Aboriginal Briggs family, argues for an expansive definition of data and sovereignty where digital rights for First Nations cover the entire ecosystem of data, including data collection, management, access, interpretation, dissemination and reuse of data (2020). Walter argues that contemporary deficit discourse has antecedents in earlier colonial and Protection era reports, which constructed First Nations as developmentally lacking and in need of intervention (2020). As with stereotypical media representations, where non-Indigenous peoples only 'know' First Nations through the media they consume, only knowing First Nations through the 'statistical Indigene' also reproduces stereotypical knowledge and ill-conceived policy (Walter, 2016, p. 81). The Australian Government's *Best Practice Guide to Applying Data Sharing Principles* (Australian Government,

Department of the Prime Minister and Cabinet, 2019) does not refer to First Nations or their unique experiences and need for data governance. As discussed above, common ideas regarding open data and interoperability across data systems may be harmful for First Nations by breaching intellectual property rights and making it easier to reproduce deficit discourse about First Nations (Walter, 2020). Designing systems to make data mining more efficacious is also a problem for protecting First Nations' intellectual property (Walter, 2020). The lack of disaggregated data for Indigenous peoples in the SDGs is a potential problem for addressing the specific development and governance needs of First Nations (United Nations, Department of Economic and Social Affairs, Indigenous Peoples, n.d.). First Nations already have complex systems for managing information and data. These include the Global Indigenous Data Alliance (n.d.), British Columbia's First Nations Data Governance Initiative (n.d.) and Maiam nayri Wingara (n.d.). The sustainability of Indigenous data sovereignty is inextricably connected to First Nations' nation-building and self-determination.

International frameworks for media and information literacy recognise the importance of combating not just misinformation and disinformation but increasing consumers' understandings of the digital architecture and media landscape in which knowledge and information circulates. First Nations and the contextual history of racial science and settler colonisation are not well represented in contemporary media and information literacy research and policies. Further, common notions of digital rights as encompassing open data access and interoperability may hinder First Nations' intellectual property rights and reproduce informational and data stereotypes. Indigenous data sovereignty aligns with the SDG-18 Communication for All which recognises the relationship between communication and sustainable development.

Sovereign Communication

As explained earlier, UNESCO's 'Think Critically, Click Wisely!' report notes the value of community media and media founded by minority groups for promoting media and information literacy (2021, p. 205). While there is some space in public broadcast media for First Nations' content as discussed earlier, an SDG-18 would bolster legislative, sector and policy frameworks to ensure First Nations' media is produced, promoted and accessible. More broadly, an SDG-18 would promote media literacy and diversity as inclusive of First Nations and could be used to support an increase in First Nations' experts and sources in all media and for First Nations to have input into media regulation and online media and information communications' content and data governance.

According to the peak body of First Nations Media Australia, 'There are roughly 60 First Nations media organisations operating in over 235 communities across Australia, producing media content in more than 25 languages' (2020–2021). There are two national newspapers, *Koori Mail* and the *National Indigenous Times.* The Central Australian Aboriginal Media Association (CAAMA) was founded in 1980 and involves radio and television. The Warlpiri Media Association, operating as PAW Media and Communications, was also developed in the 1980s to focus on radio and television. The Australian Indigenous Communications Association represents all First Nations' media. National Indigenous Television was launched in 2007 and is broadcast free on SBS as well as other pay subscription channels. IndigiTube launched in 2009 promoting radio, podcasts and other audio-visual content. Since 2014, the ABC offers some Indigenous language services such as Warlpiri, Yolngu Matha and Kriol (ABC, 2021). IndigenousX is a multi-platform media and training service with a column in *The Guardian* and the Wakul app, which aggregates Indigenous news media content and operates a twitter presence for social networking news (Nolan et al., 2020).

Social Ventures Australia completed a cost analysis of Indigenous broadcasting for the Department of Prime Minister and Cabinet.

> There are over 120 Australian Government funded Indigenous Broadcasting Services (IBSs) operating in Australia, with further unfunded IBS transmission sites. They vary in size from very small remote services to large community radio broadcasting services, and together, they reach an estimated audience of at least 100,000 Indigenous listeners who listen regularly. The most substantial investment in Indigenous broadcasting is provided by the Culture and Capability Programme under the Indigenous Advancement Strategy (IAS) which is administered by the Department of the Prime and Minister and Cabinet (PM&C). (2017, p. 4)

In addition to foundational outcomes such as strengthening community and increasing community aspirations (p. 4), the report found that Indigenous broadcasting had a \$2.87 return on investment (p. 5).

Commercial and privately established First Nations' media have also proliferated to deliver Indigenous-determined media content to consumers. This media also requires protection and support in recognition of the particular status of First Nations as subject to historical and contemporary media harms as well the developmental goals of First Nations. On February 18, 2021, Facebook blocked news to Australian consumers of the platform for several days due to Australian legislation that would enable news organisations to be paid for news content on the platform (what became the News Media Bargaining Code, specifically the *News Media and Digital Platforms Mandatory Bargaining Code, Treasury Laws Amendment [News Media and Digital Platforms Mandatory Bargaining Code] Act 2021* [Cth]). First Nations were not considered in the Australian Competition and Consumer Commission's *Digital Platforms Inquiry* (2019), which formed the basis of the legislation. Nyangbal, Arakwal and Dunghutti journalist Naomi Moran, manager of *Koori Mail*, has stated that the Australian Parliament were warned by First Nations Media Australia about the potential dangers to First Nations' social media companies and organisations if companies such as Facebook contested the regulation during negotiations (First Nations Media Australia and Community Broadcasting Association of Australia [CBAA], 2020). After the ban, Moran commented:

> The reason First Nations media exists is due to the complete and ignorant failure of mainstream media to represent our interests and perspectives. That's why Facebook's abrupt shutdown of many of our pages, in a sweeping measure to punish the Australian government for its somewhat clumsy attempt to support Australian journalists, is a particularly bitter pill to swallow. The First Nations Media Australia site has since been reinstated as we are a peak body, not a publisher. However, members such as Ngaarda Media in Roebourne, 3KND in Melbourne and Bumma Bippera in Cairns are just a few examples of essential services still waiting to have their page restrictions resolved. (2021)

As discussed earlier with respect to telecommunications infrastructure, First Nations are not considered stakeholders in dominant media policy and regulation domains. This is despite First Nations being higher than average consumers of mobile and online technologies. Aboriginal scholar Bronwyn Carlson, along with others, has conducted extensive research into the value of social media and online communication for First Nations' news, culture and identity (Frazer & Carlson, 2017; Carlson & Frazer,

2018; Carlson, 2021; Carslon & Berglund, 2021). Communications technologies have also been mobilised to address First Nations' development issues such as health. For instance, the hashtag #IHMayDay, initiated by Murri health academic Lynore Geia, was used to promote daylong social media conversation about Indigenous health (Sweet et al., 2015).

The importance of First Nations' media and connectivity is illustrated by the recent COVID-19 pandemic. Australian governments have no pandemic preparedness response for First Nations despite this group being vulnerable due to institutional problems and discrimination in the health system. The earlier H1N1 swine flu pandemic killed Indigenous Australians at six times the rate of the general population (Cousins, 2020), with Indigenous peoples making up 2.5% of the Australian population and an overwhelming 11% of 'cases recorded' (Cousins, 2020). Due to the lack of infrastructural support and health services in rural towns with predominantly Indigenous populations, state institutions adopted what they perceived as the best response in the short amount of time available: declaring entire communities and townships biosecurity zones in need of protection. Protecting the designated areas involved putting roadblocks outside of certain communities (Faa & Stunzner, 2020), which were enforced by police, and travel plans required approval by a Biosecurity Officer (Australian Government, 2020).

Residents of the Yarrabah community in North Queensland protested elements of the lockdown, which were kept in place while restrictions were easing for non-Indigenous populated communities in May (Faa & Stunzner, 2020). In late May, the Queensland Human Rights Commission recommended lifting the restrictions along with more government consultation with communities (Queensland Human Rights Commission, 2020). A number of residents argued that the biosecurity zones were reminiscent of the earlier Protection Acts (Armbruster & Truu, 2020; Faa & Stunzner, 2020), which enforced segregation and police control of Indigenous mobility under the auspices of protection. It should be pointed out that the majority of Indigenous Australians live in urban centres, which was a major flaw of the government's response (see Stanley et al., 2020; Dalzell, 2020).

The Wilcannia community in New South Wales, located on Barkindji Country, was particularly vulnerable during the second wave of the delta variant of the pandemic (as was regional New South Wales in general). Due to housing shortages, social distancing was a problem along with the lack of access to health services. The state government believed the

Commonwealth government was taking responsibility (Jenkins, 2021) and vice versa which left the community to their own initiative to solve a major health problem. As with the Yarrabah community, the importance of access to communication technologies and the means to communicate these issues are illustrated in the following report: 'The Maari Ma Aboriginal health corporation wrote to the Indigenous Australians minister, Ken Wyatt, in March 2020, outlining "grave fears" for the far western New South Wales town if Covid were to spread to the vulnerable population there' (Allam, 2021). Eventually, urgent supplies were sent to Wilcannia after social media activism and news media reporting on the crisis.

Media reporting on the risks for First Nations in regional News South Wales during the second wave also tended to reproduce deficit discourse in ways that pathologise First Nations and lead to the erasure of systemic responsibilities. For instance, terms such as 'overcrowded housing' (Jenkins, 2021) and 'vulnerable indigenous communities' (Taylor & Jackson, 2021, p. 4) (note the lower case 'i' here) ignore structural issues and located the risks of COVID-19 with First Nations themselves. The salience of 'Indigenous' towns was used to present First Nations as rendering these towns susceptible to COVID-19, for instance, 'Regional towns home to large Indigenous populations and without the capacity to deal with a Covid-19 outbreak' (Lam, 2021, p. 5). The lack of contextualising information draws attention away from and simultaneously normalises institutional and government failure to adequately support First Nations. Some reporting aligned the criminalisation and racialisation of First Nations with disease: 'The virus arrived in the town with an unsuspecting carrier who had returned home after a run-in with the law in the nearby regional centre of Dubbo' (Jackson, 2021, p. 5).

Access to media and communications technologies is crucial to countering these harmful narratives. As this tweet from Widjabul Wia-bul organiser Larissa Baldwin notes, 'Aboriginal deaths from COVID-19 were preventable ... 18 months on no recorded deaths until today. Our communities did everything we could to keep our mob safe, we knew the risks. @ScottMorrisonMP [the Australian Prime Minister] & @GladysB [the New South Wales State Premier] any Black Death from Covid19 is on you—you chose not to protect us' (see also Griffiths, 2021). Galari Wiradyuri academic Sue Green's article in *The Conversation* illustrates the contextual and structural issues necessary for understanding the impact of COVID-19 on First Nations: 'The COVID-19 crisis in Wilcannia demonstrates how entrenched neglect, combined with a global pandemic, have created a perfect storm impacting the most marginalised people in society. The treatment of the Barkindji people of Wilcannia is appalling by anyone's standards and should be unacceptable to every Australian' (2021; see also Williamson, 2021). Green points out that the deployment of police and military, because they are easier to mobilise in an emergency and their equipment is easier to sanitise, is not welcoming and inclusive for First Nations, who have traumatic experiences with these organisations. Comments from officials regarding the attendance at a funeral being an illegal social gathering also present First Nations' cultural practices as putting the latter at risk. Finally, Green (2021) notes that First Nations have legitimate reasons to be wary of vaccines and hospitals given the history of medical experimentation and quarantine based on racial hygiene in the early twentieth century (see Sweet et al., 2016).

Media and communication sovereignty aligns with the development of Aboriginal community-controlled health organisations. The latter refers to changes in the delivery of health services to support Indigenous autonomy and determination over health priorities from the latter part of the twentieth century and in response to mainstream healthcare racism affecting Indigenous engagement with health services (see Alford, 2014; Foley, 1991; Bulloch et al., 2019; Phillips, 2003). The response to COVID-19 from the Aboriginal community-controlled health sector included multiple language health information services (Cousins, 2020), early advice, responses to Indigenous communities in urban areas (Stanley et al., 2020) and a relational rather than distanced approach to managing the pandemic. Social media were also important for promoting vaccination such as this video from Wiradyuri Elder Aunty Margaret Walker who advised the practice of social distancing through technology: '[Y]ou can't catch the virus through the phone' (ABC Western Plains, 2021). The 'value of Aboriginal control' (Stanley et al., 2020) is reflected in the statistics where during the first wave in 2020 in Australia, First Nations had one of the lowest infection rates in the world and no deaths were reported (Dalzell, 2020). As of writing, there have unfortunately been ten First Nations' death and infection rates are twice that of non-Indigenous Australians (AAP, 2021); this is still comparatively low compared globally with Indigenous populations.

First Nations have demonstrated cultural resilience, creativity and innovation in continuing their use of technologies to maintain sovereign communication. These practices have occurred in relation to being under-served by mainstream media economies and in relation to health crises. Sovereign communication covers all aspects of the media and information landscape from self-determining content, format, dissemination and data governance. An SDG-18 would promote this holistic understanding of self-determination and development in relation to communication and the important role of First Nations' sustainability in the contemporary media and information environment.

Conclusion

I have provided an outline of the media and communication landscape in Australia as well as the history of racial science and settler colonisation to illustrate how the dominant mode of communication towards First Nations is authority. The production of racial stereotypes and deficit discourse justifies non-Indigenous policy development and intervention into First Nations' communities. First Nations have their own development goals and exercise self-determination in governance, culture and sustainability. Examining news media, media and information literacy, social media, media and data policy, and telecommunications infrastructure against the backdrop of settler colonisation, racial science and deficit discourse, I have sought to illustrate the importance of sovereign communication for First Nations' sustainability. An SDG-18 Communication for All would therefore not only illustrate the importance of First Nations as stakeholders to communication, but the importance of sovereign and self-determined communication to sustainable development goals for First Nations. An SDG-18 Communication for All would promote:

- an understanding of self-determination as a communication right in the context of settler colonial nation-states being the interlocutors for First Nations' policy and development;
- a historical and contemporaneous understanding of the importance of communication in all its forms (medium, infrastructure, governance, policy and regulation) for sustaining First Nations' sovereignties and self-determined development;
- the creation of a policy framework and information literacy imperative to understand the racialising and deficit discourse produced about First Nations;
- the value of First Nations' media content and presence in contemporary media and communications environments;

- the legislative, sector and policy frameworks to ensure First Nations' media are produced, promoted and accessible;
- an understanding of the importance of Indigenous data sovereignty in the contemporary media and communications environment;
- an understanding of the importance of securing First Nations' input into media and communications policy and regulation; and
- the support for First Nations' media as directly connected to sustainable governance, cultures, languages and knowledges.

References

AAP. (2021, October 14). Indigenous people infected with Covid Delta strain at twice the rate of other Australians. *The Guardian*. https://www.theguardian.com/australia-news/2021/oct/14/indigenous-people-infected-with-covid-delta-strain-at-twice-the-rate-of-other-australians

ABC. (2021). News in Indigenous languages. https://www.abc.net.au/news/indigenous-news-service/

ABC Western Plains. (2021, August 18). https://m.facebook.com/story.php?story_fbid=2476390992505190&id=987098678101103

ABC/AAP. (2011, September 29). Bolt breached discrimination act, judge rules. *ABC News*. https://www.abc.net.au/news/2011-09-28/bolt-found-guilty-of-breaching-discrimination-act/3025918?nw=0

Alford, K. (2014, April 2). *Economic value of Aboriginal community controlled health services*. Canberra: National Aboriginal Community Controlled Health Organisation. Retrieved August 1, 2020, from https://apo.org.au/sites/default/files/resource-files/2014-04/apo-nid39333.pdf

Allam, L. (2021, August 30). Wilcannia Covid outbreak: leaked letters show federal government was warned last year of potential catastrophe. *The Guardian*. https://www.theguardian.com/australia-news/2021/aug/30/wilcannia-covid-outbreak-leaked-letter-shows-federal-government-was-warned-last-year-of-potential-catastrophe

Altman, J. C., Buchanan, G., & Larsen, L. (2007). *The environmental significance of the Indigenous estate: Natural resource management as economic development in remote Australia*. CAEPR Discussion Paper No. 286/2007. https://caepr.cass.anu.edu.au/sites/default/files/docs/2007_DP286_0.pdf

Anderson, K., & Perrin, C. (2008). How race became everything: Australia and polygenism. *Ethnic and Racial Studies, 31*(5), 962–990.

Anderson, L., & Gatwiri, K. (2021). The Senate has voted to reject critical race theory from the national curriculum. What is it, and why does it matter? *The Conversation*. https://theconversation.com/the-senate-has-voted-to-reject-critical-race-theory-from-the-national-curriculum-what-is-it-and-why-does-it-matter-163102

Anderson, W. (2005). *The cultivation of whiteness: Science, health and racial destiny in Australia*. Melbourne University Press.
Armbruster, S., & Truu, M. (2020, May 28). Just 50 kilometres from Cairns, this Indigenous community wants its coronavirus travel ban eased. *SBS News*. Retrieved August 1, 2020, from https://www.sbs.com.au/news/just-50-kilometres-from-cairns-this-indigenous-community-wants-its-coronavirus-travel-ban-eased
Atkinson, J. (2002). *Trauma trails, recreating song lines: the transgenerational effects of trauma in Indigenous Australia*. Spinifex Press.
Australian Competition and Consumer Commission. (2019). *Digital platforms inquiry*. Canberra: Commonwealth of Australia. https://www.accc.gov.au/system/files/Digital%20platforms%20inquiry%20-%20final%20report.pdf
Australian Government. (2020, April 29). Factsheet: Remote community entry requirements in place under the *Biosecurity Act 2015*. Retrieved August 1, 2020, from https://www.health.gov.au/sites/default/files/documents/2020/04/remote-community-entry-requirements-in-place-under-the-biosecurity-act-2015_0.pdf
Australian Government, Department of the Prime Minister and Cabinet. (2019, March 15). *Best practice guide to applying data sharing principles*. https://www.pmc.gov.au/sites/default/files/publications/data-sharing-principles-best-practice-guide-15-mar-2019.pdf
Baker, P., & Potts, A. (2013). 'Why do white people have thin lips?' Google and the perpetuation of stereotypes via auto-complete search forms. *Critical Discourse Studies, 10*(2), 187–204.
Banerjee, S. B., & Osuri, G. (2000). Silences of the media: Whiting out Aboriginality in making news and making history. *Media, Culture & Society, 22*(3), 263–284.
Bell, K. M., & Cervantez, A. (2021). News coverage of racism, white supremacy, and hate speech. In S. J. A. Ward (Ed.), *Handbook of global media ethics* (pp. 1143–1161). Springer.
Beresford, Q., & Omaji, P. (2000). *Our state of mind: racial planning and the stolen generations*. Fremantle Arts Centre Press.
British Columbia's First Nations Data Governance Initiative. (n.d.). https://www.bcfndgi.com/
Brown, C., Yap, M., Thomassin, A., Murray, M., & Yu, E. (2021). 'Can I just share my story?' Experiences of technology-facilitated abuse among Aboriginal and Torres Strait Islander women in regional and remote Australia. *Journal of Global Indigeneity, 5*(2). https://www.journalofglobalindigeneity.com/article/29716-can-i-just-share-my-story-experiences-of-technology-facilitated-abuse-among-aboriginal-and-torres-strait-islander-women-in-regional-and-remote-aust

Bulloch, H., Fogarty, W., & Bellchambers, K. (2019). *Aboriginal Health and Wellbeing Services: Putting community-driven, strengths-based approaches into practice.* Carlton South: The Lowitja Institute. Retrieved August 1, 2020, from https://www.lowitja.org.au/content/Image/Aboriginal_Health_and_Wellbeing_services_DD3_FINALwith_links.pdf

Byrd, J. A. (2014). Tribal 2.0: Digital natives, political players, and the power of stories. *Studies in American Indian literatures, 26*(2), 55–64.

Carlson, B. (2021). Indigenous internet users: learning to trust ourselves. *Australian Feminist Studies, 36*(107), 9–25.

Carlson, B., & Berglund, J. (Eds.). (2021). *Indigenous peoples rise up: the global ascendency of social media activism.* Rutgers University Press.

Carlson, B., & Frazer, R. (2018). Yarning circles and social media activism. *MIA: Media International Australia, 169*(1), 43–53.

Carlson, B., & Kennedy, T. (2021). Us mob online: The perils of identifying as Indigenous on social media. *Genealogy, 5*(2). https://www.mdpi.com/2313-5778/5/2/52

Cartwright, C., & McAuliffe, C. (2020). *Telecommunications debt in rural and remote Indigenous Central Australian communities: Loans & phones project phase 3.* MoneyMob Talkabout. https://accan.org.au/MoneyMob%20Telco%20Report.pdf

Casey, J., Ross, R., & Warren, M. (1999, April). *Native networking: Telecommunications and information technology in Indian country.* Washington: Benton Foundation. Retrieved February 11, 2016, from http://eric.ed.gov/?id=ED430769

Christen, K. (2005). Gone digital: Aboriginal remix and the cultural commons. *International Journal of Cultural Property, 12*, 315–345.

Christen, K. (2007, April 28). The politics of search: Archival accountability in Aboriginal Australia. *MIT5: Media in Transition 5 Conference, Technological Translations and Digital Dilemmas Panel.*

Clark, M. (2016, April 6). Coded devices. http://2016.nextwave.org.au/essays/coded-devices/

Cohen, S. (1980). *Folk devils and moral panics: The creation of the mods and rockers.* Martin Robertson.

Commonwealth of Australia. (2019–2020). Native title amendment (infrastructure and public facilities) Bill 2020 Explanatory Memorandum. https://parlinfo.aph.gov.au/parlInfo/download/legislation/ems/r6599_ems_e759764f-730d-4a88-aa7e-e8f299d08c15/upload_pdf/JC000091.pdf;fileType=application%2Fpdf

Cousins, S. (2020, May 19). Indigenous Australians avert an outbreak—for now. *Foreign Policy.* Retrieved August 1, 2020, from https://foreignpolicy.com/2020/05/19/indigenous-australians-avert-coronavirus-outbreak-for-now-aboriginal/

Cowan, A. (2013, March). UNDRIP and the Intervention: Indigenous self-determination, participation, and racial discrimination in the Northern Territory of Australia. *Pacific Rim Law & Policy Journal, 22*(2), 247–310.

Dalzell, S. (2020, July 1). Government's coronavirus response overlooked crucial details about Indigenous population: report. *ABC News*. Retrieved August 1, 2020, from https://www.abc.net.au/news/2020-07-01/government-warned-coronavirus-blind-spot-testing-indigenous/12407544

DeLuca, D. (2017, December). What do the sustainable development goals mean for Indigenous peoples? *Cultural Survival Quarterly Magazine.*. https://www.culturalsurvival.org/publications/cultural-survival-quarterly/what-.do-sustainable-development-goals-mean-indigenous

Dwyer, T., Wilding, D., & Koskie, T. (2021). Australia: Media concentration and deteriorating conditions for investigative journalism. In J. Trappel & T. Tomaz (Eds.), *The media for democracy monitor 2021: How leading news media survive digital transformation* (Vol. 1, pp. 59–94). Nordicom, University of Gothenburg.

Elers, S. (2014). Maori are scum, stupid, lazy: Maori according to Google. *Te Kaharoa, 7*, 16–24.

Faa, M., & Stunzner, I. (2020, May 14). Coronavirus laws discriminate against Indigenous Australians, communities say. *ABC News*. Retrieved August 1, 2020, from https://www.abc.net.au/news/2020-05-14/coronavirus-queensland-indigenous-restrictions-yarrabah/12230492

Fforde, C., Bamblett, L., Lovett, R., Gorringe, S., & Fogarty, B. (2013). Discourse, deficit and identity: Aboriginality, the race paradigm and the language of representation in contemporary Australia. *Media International Australia, 149*, 162–173.

First Nations Media Australia. (2020, December). Media diversity in Australia, Senate standing committees on environment and communications, submission from first nations media Australia. https://firstnationsmedia.org.au/sites/default/files/files/Submissions/Media%20Diversity%20in%20Australia%20submission%202020.pdf

First Nations Media Australia. (2020–2021). Our media matters. https://firstnationsmedia.org.au/our-media

First Nations Media Australia and Community Broadcasting Association of Australia (CBAA). (2020, June). Mandatory news media bargaining code—Concepts Paper Joint response to the ACCC. https://www.accc.gov.au/system/files/First%20Nations%20Media%20Australia%20and%20Community%20Broadcasting%20Association%20of%20Australia_0.pdf

Fisher, D. E. (2000). Indigenous interests and infrastructure development in Queensland. *Journal of Energy & Natural Resources Law, 18*(1), 67–90.

Fogarty, W., Bulloch, H., McDonnell, S., & Davis, M. (2018). *Deficit discourse and Indigenous health: How narrative framings of Aboriginal and Torres Strait*

Islander people are reproduced in policy. The Lowitja Institute & National Centre for Indigenous Studies.

Foley, G. (1991). Redfern Aboriginal medical service: 20 years on. *Aboriginal and Islander Health Worker Journal, 15*(4), 4–8.

Frazer, R., & Carlson, B. (2017). Indigenous memes and the invention of a people. *Social Media & Society, 3*(4), 1–12.

Global Indigenous Data Alliance. (n.d.). https://www.gida-global.org/

Graham, M. (2008). Some thoughts about the philosophical underpinnings of Aboriginal worldviews. *Australian Humanities Review, 45*, 181–194.

Green, S. (2021, September 16). COVID in Wilcannia: a national disgrace we all saw coming. *The Conversation*. https://theconversation.com/covid-in-wilcannia-a-national-disgrace-we-all-saw-coming-167348

Griffiths, K. (2021, August 31). The first Indigenous COVID death reminds us of the outsized risk NSW communities face. *The Conversation*. https://theconversation.com/the-first-indigenous-covid-death-reminds-us-of-the-outsized-risk-nsw-communities-face-166888

Grizzle, A., Wilson, C., Tuazon, R., Cheung, C. K., Lau, J., Fischer, R., Gordon, D., Akyempong, K., Singh, J., Carr, P. R., Stewart, K., Tayie, S., Suraj, O., Jaakkola, M., Thésée, G., & Gulston, C. (2021). *Think critically, click wisely! media and information literacy curriculum for educators & learners*. United Nations Educational, Scientific, and Cultural Organization. https://unesdoc.unesco.org/ark:/48223/pf0000377068/PDF/377068eng.pdf.multi

Human Rights & Equal Opportunity Commission. (1997). *Bringing them home: Report of the national inquiry into the separation of Aboriginal and Torres Strait Islander children from their families*.

Indigenous Peoples Major Group. (n.d.). Indigenous peoples major group position paper on proposed SDG indicators. https://www.forestpeoples.org/sites/fpp/files/publication/2015/10/sdg-indicatorsfinal-web1.pdf

Ireton, C., & Posetti, J. (2018). *Journalism, 'fake news' & disinformation: Handbook for journalism education and training*. United Nations Educational, Scientific, and Cultural Organization. https://unesdoc.unesco.org/ark:/48223/pf0000265552/PDF/265552eng.pdf.multi

Jackson, S. (2021, August 13). Frantic race to vaccinate as Indigenous township exposed. *The Australian*, 5.

Jakubowicz, A. (2017). Alt_Right white lite: Trolling, hate speech and cyber racism on social media. *Cosmopolitan Civil Societies: an Interdisciplinary Journal, 9*(3), 41–60.

Jenkins, K. (2021, September 8). Government attention 'too late' for COVID-hit Wilcannia. *SBS News*. https://www.sbs.com.au/nitv/article/2021/09/08/government-attention-too-late-covid-hit-wilcannia

Kaimowitz, D. (2021, October 25). Indigenous peoples must be central to tackling the climate crisis. *IISD—SDG Knowledge Hub*. https://sdg.iisd.org/commentary/guest-articles/indigenous-peoples-must-be-central-to-tackling-the-climate-crisis/

Kennedy, T. (2021, June 11). 97% of Indigenous people report seeing negative social media content weekly. Here's how platforms can help. *The Conversation.* https://theconversation.com/97-of-indigenous-people-report-seeing-negative-social-media-content-weekly-heres-how-platforms-can-help-162353

Kerr, T. A., & Cox, S. (2016). Media, machines and might: Reproducing western australia's violent state of Aboriginal protection. *Somatechnics, 6*(1), 89–105.

Kukutai, T., & Taylor, J. (2016). Data sovereignty for Indigenous peoples: current practice and future needs. In T. Kukutai & J. Taylor (Eds.), *Indigenous data sovereignty: Toward an AGENDA* (pp. 1–17). ANU E-Press. http://press-files.anu.edu.au/downloads/press/n2140/pdf/ch01.pdf

Lam, J. (2021, August 12). Locals in fear as virus spreads to Indigenous town. *The Australian*, 5.

Langton, M. (1993). *'Well, I heard it on the radio and I saw it on the television': An essay for the Australian Film Commission on the politics and aesthetics of filmmaking by and about Aboriginal people and things.* Australian Film Commission.

Leavitt, P. A., Covarrubias, R., Perez, Y. A., & Fryberg, S. A. (2015). "Frozen in Time": The impact of Native American media representations on identity and self-understanding. *Journal of Social Issues, 71*(1), 39–53.

MacDonald, G. (2010). Colonizing processes, the reach of the state and ontological violence: Historicizing Aboriginal Australian experience. *Anthropologica, 52*(1), 49–66.

Maiam nayri Wingara. (n.d.). https://www.maiamnayriwingara.org/

Markus, A. (1983). William Cooper and the 1937 petition to the King. *Aboriginal History, 7*, 46–60.

McCallum, K., Meadows, M., Waller, L., Dunne Breen, M., & Reid, H. (2012). *The media and Indigenous policy: How news media reporting and mediatized practice impact on Indigenous policy.* University of Canberra.

McCallum, K., & Waller, L. (2017). *The dynamics of news and Indigenous policy in Australia.* Intellect Books.

McCausland, R. (2004). Special treatment: The representation of Aboriginal and Torres Strait Islander people in the media. *Journal of Indigenous Policy, 4*, 84–98.

McGloin, C., & Carlson, B. L. (2013). Indigenous studies and the politics of language. *Journal of University Teaching & Learning Practice, 10*(1) https://ro.uow.edu.au/jutlp/vol10/iss1/3/

McGregor, R. (2011). *Indifferent inclusion: Aboriginal people and the Australian nation.* Aboriginal Studies Press.

Meadows, M. (2001). *Voices in the wilderness: Images of Aboriginal people in the Australian media.* Greenwood Press.

Media Diversity Australia. (2018, July). *Reporting on Aboriginal and Torres Strait Islander peoples and issues: An introductory resource for the media.* https://

diversityarts.org.au/app/uploads/ReportingonAboriginalandTorresStraitIslanderPeoplesandIssues_Handbookv2.pdf

Media, Entertainment & Arts Alliance. (2021). *MEAA journalist code of ethics.* https://www.meaa.org/meaa-media/code-of-ethics/

Michaels, E. (1986). *The Aboriginal invention of television in Central Australia 1982–1986.* Australian Institute of Aboriginal Studies.

Milirrpum, Djalalingba, Daymbalipu, Dhayila, Dundiwuy, Dhunggala, Raiyin, Manunu, Larrakan, Wulanybuma, Wawunggmarra, Nyabilingu. (1963). Transcript of the Yirrkala Bark petitions 1963 (From Wells) To The Honourable The Speaker and Members of the House of Representatives in Parliament Assembled. https://aiatsis.gov.au/sites/default/files/2020-09/transcript-yirrkala-bark-petitions-1963-4.docx

Moran, N. (2021, February 23). First Nations media has been caught in the crossfire of Facebook's battle with Australian news. *The Guardian.* https://www.theguardian.com/commentisfree/2021/feb/23/first-nations-media-has-been-caught-in-the-crossfire-of-facebooks-battle-with-australian-news

Moreton-Robinson, A. (2004). The possessive logic of patriarchal white sovereignty: The High Court and the Yorta Yorta decision. *Borderlands Ejournal, 3*(2). http://borderlands.net.au/vol3no2_2004/moreton_possessive.htm

Newcomb, S. T. (2011). The UN declaration on the rights of Indigenous peoples and the paradigm of domination. *Griffith Law Review, 20*(3), 578–607.

Nicoll, F. (2008). Consuming pathologies: the Australian against Indigenous sovereignties. In A. Moreton-Robinson, M. Casey, & F. Nicoll (Eds.), *Transnational whiteness matters* (pp. 57–79). Lexington Books.

Noble, S. U. (2018). *Algorithms of oppression: how search engines reinforce racism.* New York University Press.

Nolan, D., Waller, L., Latimore, J., Simons, M., & Mccallum, K. (2020). Analysing the Indigenous news network in action: IndigenousX, The Guardian and the Wakul App. In S. Maddison & S. Nakata (Eds.), *Questioning Indigenous-settler relations: Interdisciplinary perspectives* (pp. 69–86). Springer.

O'Neil, M., & Jensen, M. J. (2020). *Australian perspectives on misinformation.* News & Media Research Centre, University of Canberra. https://apo.org.au/sites/default/files/resource-files/2020-11/apo-nid309148_0.pdf

OECD. (2019). *Linking Indigenous communities with regional development, OECD rural policy reviews.* OECD Publishing. https://doi.org/10.1787/3203c082-en

Patten, J. T., & Ferguson, W. (n.d.). *Aborigines claim citizen rights! a statement of the case for the aborigines progressive association.* The Publicist. https://nla.gov.au/nla.obj-241787110/view?partId=nla.obj-241788701

Phillips, D. (2003). Aboriginality is about culture, not colour. In Aboriginal Community Elders Service & K. Harvey (Eds.), *Aboriginal elders' voices: Stories of the 'tide of history', Victorian Indigenous elders' life stories & oral histories* (pp. 93–105). East Brunswick.

Porter, A. (2015). Riotous or righteous behaviour? Representations of subaltern resistance in the Australian mainstream media. *Current Issues in Criminal Justice, 26*(3), 289–304.

Porter, L., Rickards, L., Verlie, B., Bosomworth, K., Moloney, S., Lay, B., Latham, B., Anguelovski, I., & Pellow, D. (2020). Climate justice in a climate changed world. *Planning Theory & Practice, 21*(2), 293–321.

Posetti, J., & Matthews, A. (n.d.). *A short guide to the history of 'fake news' and disinformation: A learning module for journalists and journalism educators.* International Center for Journalists. https://www.icfj.org/sites/default/files/2018-07/A%20Short%20Guide%20to%20History%20of%20Fake%20News%20and%20Disinformation_ICFJ%20Final.pdf

Queensland Human Rights Commission. (2020, May 28). Commission urges strong consultation with Queensland's Indigenous communities to find workable, fair and locally driven Covid-19 protections. Retrieved August 1, 2020, from https://www.qhrc.qld.gov.au/__data/assets/pdf_file/0003/26508/2020.05.27-Commission-urges-strong-consultationwith-Queensland.pdf

Randell-Moon, H. (2006). 'Common values': Whiteness, Christianity, asylum seekers and the Howard government. *Critical Race and Whiteness Studies, 2*(1), 1–14. https://acrawsa.org.au/wp-content/uploads/2017/12/CRAWS-Vol-2-No-1-2006.pdf

Randell-Moon, H. (2017). Thieves like us: The British monarchy, celebrity and settler colonialism. *Celebrity Studies, 8*(3), 393–408.

Randell-Moon, H. (2019a). Introduction. In H. Randell-Moon (Ed.), *Incarceration, migration and Indigenous sovereignty: Thoughts on Existence and resistance in racist times* (2nd printing). Dubbo: Space, Race, Bodies. https://www.spaceracebodies3.com/Incarceration,%20Migration%20and%20Indigenous%20Sovereignty.pdf

Randell-Moon, H. (2019b). Stereotype threat. In R. Hobbs & P. Mihailidis (Eds.), *The international encyclopedia of media literacy education*. Hoboken.

Rekhari, S. (2009). Indigenous communities and new media: questions on the global Digital Age. *Journal of Information, Communication & Ethics in Society, 7*(2/3), 175–181.

Rennie, E., & Yunkaporta, T. (2016, November 29). Aboriginal communities embrace technology, but they have unique cyber safety challenges. *The Conversation*. https://theconversation.com/aboriginal-communities-embrace-technology-but-they-have-unique-cyber-safety-challenges-69344

Rice, E. S., Haynes, E., Royce, P., & Thompson, S. C. (2016). Social media and digital technology use among Indigenous young people in Australia: a literature review. *International Journal for Equity in Health, 15*(81). https://doi.org/10.1186/s12939-016-0366-0

Ryan, L. (2013). The black line in Van Diemen's land: Success or failure? *Journal of Australian Studies, 37*(1), 3–18.

Saini, A. (2019). *Superior: The return of race science.* 4th Estate.

Shaw, G., Brereton, M., & Roe, P. (2014, December). Mobile phone use in Australian Indigenous communities: future pathways for HCI4D. *OzCHI '14: Proceedings of the 26th Australian Computer-Human Interaction Conference on Designing Futures: the Future of Design* (pp. 480–483).

Social Ventures Australia. (2017, November). *More than radio—a community asset: Social return on investment analyses of Indigenous broadcasting services.* https://firstnationsmedia.org.au/sites/default/files/files/ibs_sroi_report-corrected.PDF

Standfield, R., Peckham, R., & Nolan, J. (2014). Aunty Pearl Gibbs: Leading for Aboriginal rights. In J. Damousi, K. Rubenstein, & M. Tomsic (Eds.), *Diversity in leadership: Australian women, past and present* (pp. 53–67). ANU E-Press.

Stanley, F., McAullay, D., & Eades, S. (2020, April 24). Urban Aboriginal people face unique challenges in the fight against coronavirus. *The Conversation.* Retrieved August 1, 2020, from https://theconversation.com/urban-aboriginal-people-face-unique-challenges-in-the-fight-against-coronavirus-136050

Stevens, L. (2017). *'Me write myself': The free Aboriginal inhabitants of Van Diemen's land at Wybalenna, 1832–47.* Monash University Publishing.

Stoneham, M. J., Goodman, J., & Daube, M. (2014). The portrayal of Indigenous health in selected Australian media. *The International Indigenous Policy Journal, 5*(1). https://ojs.lib.uwo.ca/index.php/iipj/article/view/7426/6070

Sweet, M., Geia, L., Dudgeon, P., & McCallum, K. (2015). #IHMayDay: tweeting for empowerment and social and emotional wellbeing. *Australasian Psychiatry, 23*(6), 636–640.

Sweet, M., McCallum, K., & Geia, L. (2016, September 21). Acknowledge the brutal history of Indigenous health care—for healing. *The Conversation.* https://theconversation.com/acknowledge-the-brutal-history-of-indigenous-health-care-for-healing-64295

Taylor, P., & Jackson, S. (2021, August 14). Race to vaccinate on Covid's new frontline. *The Australian*, 4.

tebrakunna country, Lee, E., & Eversole, R. (2019). Rethinking the regions: Indigenous peoples and regional development. *Regional Studies, 53*(11), 1509–1519.

Thomas, A. (2020). The princess and the protestors: The 1972 Larrakia Petition and discourses of failure in Aboriginal protest. In A. Thomas, A. Jakubowicz, & H. Norman (Eds.), *Does the media fail Aboriginal political aspirations? 45 years of news media reporting of key political moments* (pp. 37–56). AIATSIS Research Publications.

Thomas, A., Jakubowicz, A., & Norman, H. (Eds.). (2020). *Does the media fail Aboriginal political aspirations? 45 years of news media reporting of key political moments.* AIATSIS Research Publications.

Townsend, P., Halsey, J. R., & Guenther, J. (2016). Mobile learning congruencies with Aboriginal and Torres Strait Islander cultural philosophies. In J. Orrell & D. D. Curtis (Eds.), *Publishing higher degree research: Making the transition from student to researcher* (pp. 25–32). Sense Publishers.

Tucker, W. H. (n.d.). The ideology of racism: Misusing science to justify racial discrimination. *UN Chronicle*. https://www.un.org/en/chronicle/article/ideology-racism-misusing-science-justify-racial-discrimination

United Nations. (n.d.-a). Goal 1: End poverty in all its forms everywhere. https://www.un.org/sustainabledevelopment/poverty/

United Nations. (n.d.-b). Goal 2: Zero Hunger. https://www.un.org/sustainabledevelopment/hunger/

United Nations. (n.d.-c). 4 quality education. https://www.un.org/sustainabledevelopment/education/

United Nations. (n.d.-d). United nations declaration on the rights of Indigenous peoples. https://www.un.org/development/desa/indigenouspeoples/wp-content/uploads/sites/19/2018/11/UNDRIP_E_web.pdf

United Nations, Department of Economic and Social Affairs, Indigenous Peoples. (n.d.). Indigenous peoples and the 2030 agenda. https://www.un.org/development/desa/indigenouspeoples/focus-areas/post-2015-agenda/the-sustainable-development-goals-sdgs-and-indigenous.html

United Nations Permanent Forum on Indigenous Issues. (2010, January 14). State of the world's Indigenous peoples. https://www.un.org/esa/socdev/unpfii/documents/SOWIP/press%20package/sowip-press-package-en.pdf

United Nations Permanent Forum on Indigenous Issues. (n.d.). United nations permanent forum on Indigenous issues, together we achieve—backgrounder. https://www.un.org/development/desa/indigenouspeoples/wp-content/uploads/sites/19/2018/04/Indigenous-Languages.pdf

Wahlquist, C. (2019, December 12). Channel seven settles defamation case with Aboriginal community over Sunrise segment. *The Guardian*. https://www.theguardian.com/media/2019/dec/12/channel-seven-settles-defamation-case-with-aboriginal-community-over-sunrise-segment

Walter, M. (2016). Data politics and Indigenous representation in Australian statistics. In T. Kukutai & J. Taylor (Eds.), *Indigenous data sovereignty: Toward an agenda (pp. 79–98)*. ANU e-Press. http://press-files.anu.edu.au/downloads/press/n2140/pdf/ch05.pdf

Walter, M. (2020, November 23). Indigenous data sovereignty, Indigenous research summit, School of Indigenous Australian Studies, Charles Sturt University.

Warren, M. (2020). 'When the moon shall become as large as the Sun': Unsettled settlers and the early Sydney press. *History Australia, 17*(1), 115–133.

Watson, I. (2002). Aboriginal Laws and the Sovereignty of *Terra Nullius*. *borderlands e-journal*, *1*(2). http://www.borderlands.net.au/vol1no2_2002/watson_laws.html

Watson, I. (2007). Aboriginal women's laws and lives: How might we keep growing the law? *Australian Feminist Law Journal*, *26*(1), 95–107.

Watson, I. (2009). Aboriginality and the violence of colonialism. *Borderlands e-journal*, *8*(1), 1–8. http://www.borderlands.net.au/vol8no1_2009/iwatson_aboriginality.pdf

Watson, I. (2018). Aboriginal relationships to the natural world: colonial 'protection' of human rights and the environment. *Journal of Human Rights and the Environment*, *9*(2), 119–140.

Williamson, B. (2021, August 16). The COVID-19 crisis in western NSW Aboriginal communities is a nightmare realised. *The Conversation*. https://theconversation.com/the-covid-19-crisis-in-western-nsw-aboriginal-communities-is-a-nightmare-realised-166093

CHAPTER 6

Tracking the Diffusion of Disinformation on the SDGs Across Social Media Platforms

Bashir Sa'ad Abdullahi and Habeeb Idris Pindiga

Abstract Mass awareness of the Sustainable Development Goals (SDGs) is crucial to the successful attainment of the SDGs (Grover et al., *Journal of Enterprise Information Management*, 2021). While the traditional mass media have not done a very good job of communicating the SDGs (Janoušková et al., *Sustainability (Switzerland), 11*, 1–20, 2019), social media platforms have been hailed as veritable platforms to educate the public about the SDGs and thereby help achieve social and behavioural changes needed to attain the goals (ElAlfy et al., *Sustainable Development, 28*, 1418–1430, 2020). However, the ease of access to social media platforms, such that anyone can create just any message and share it with millions of

B. Sa'ad Abdullahi (✉)
Communications and Media Research Institute (CAMRI),
University of Westminster, London, UK
e-mail: b.abdullahi@westminster.ac.uk

H. I. Pindiga
School of Media, Communication and Sociology, University of Leicester,
Leicester, UK
e-mail: hip2@leicester.ac.uk

J. Servaes, M. J. Yusha'u (eds.), *SDG18 Communicaton for All, Volume 2*, Sustainable Development Goals Series,
https://doi.org/10.1007/978-3-031-19459-7_6

people across the globe, has given rise to disinformation communities taking advantage of public ignorance and anxieties (Ha et al., *American Behavioral Scientist, 65*, 290–315, 2021; Kornbluh, *SDGs: Building Back Better*, 57–59, 2020; Meel & Vishwakarma, *Expert Systems with Applications, 153*, 1–26, 2020; Yusha'u & Servaes, *The Palgrave handbook of international communication and sustainable development*, Springer International Publishing, 2021c). Such disinformation is inhibiting effective communication aimed at behavioural changes needed to achieve the SDGs (Waszak et al., *Health Policy and Technology, 7*, 115–118, 2018). Indeed, the spread of COVID-19 in early 2020, and the subsequent widespread disinformation surrounding it, heightened the public vulnerability to become victims of disinformation, including on the SDGs (Mensah et al., *The Palgrave handbook of international communication and sustainable development*. Springer International Publishing, 2021).

This chapter tracks the major and recurring disinformation trends about SDGs on social media platforms and how COVID-19 exacerbated the trends of disinformation on SDGs. Studies have shown that development issues, in particular those pertaining to SDG3 (Health) and SDG13 (Climate action), are prone to disinformation (Communications, N., *Nature Communications, 8*, 1–2, 2017; Ha et al., *American Behavioral Scientist, 65*, 290–315, 2021). Using sampled social media posts from Twitter, along with insights from documented cases around the world, this chapter highlights the impact of disinformation on the attainment of the SDGs, arguing that such disinformation is undermining the implementation of the SDGs. This chapter further makes recommendations on how effective communication by all stakeholders can help tackle the damage disinformation is doing to the journey towards attaining the SDGs.

Keywords Disinformation trends • Social media • SDG 3 • SDG 13 • Covid19

Introduction

To successfully achieve the Sustainable Development Goals (SDGs), there is need for ensuring mass awareness of the SDGs (Grover et al., 2021). Academic research has shown that the concepts of the SDGs have been poorly communicated to the masses by the mass media (Janoušková et al., 2019). By contrast, social media platforms have been hailed as veritable platforms to educate the public about the SDGs and thereby help achieve social and behavioural changes needed to attain the goals (ElAlfy et al., 2020). There has been increase in research on discourse of the SDGs-related issues on social media platforms, as the platforms have been recognized as podiums where such discourse is increasingly taking place (Shi et al., 2020). However, social media platforms have created filter bubbles and echo chambers. The ease of access provided by the social media platforms for anyone to create problematic information and share it to millions of people across the globe has given rise to disinformation communities taking advantage of the ignorance of the public and feeding on their basic anxieties (Ha et al., 2021; Kornbluh, 2020; Meel & Vishwakarma, 2020; Yusha'u & Servaes, 2021c). Disinformation is inhibiting effective communication aimed at behavioural changes needed to achieve the SDGs (Waszak et al., 2018). The attainment of the SDGs is threatened by the widespread fake news, and the mechanisms to detect and reign in the spread of disinformation particularly related to SDGs are inadequate and therefore increase the public vulnerability to become victims of disinformation including on the SDGs (Mensah et al., 2021). Just as the spread of COVID-19 highlighted the need for further mainstreaming the role of communication for development and social change in the attainment of the SDGs, it also gave birth to additional challenges and complications that further hardened the task of communication for development and behavioural change (Yusha'u & Servaes, 2021b).

Studies have established that negative sentiments of discourse on social media affect decisions of individuals pertaining to some SDGs (Salathé & Khandelwal, 2011). A review of the literature on disinformation and the SDGs indicates that development issues pertaining to SDG3 (Health) and SDG13 (Climate action) are prone to disinformation (Communications, 2017) and received the attention of disinformation researchers. However, some SDGs receive less attention of researchers compared to others (Pindiga & Sa'ad Abdullahi, 2021), and this gives rise to a gap in the literature about disinformation on SDGs which this chapter aims to bridge. In addition, Yusha'u and Servaes (2021b) highlighted the need for an online tracker to monitor disinformation shared about SDGs. This chapter provides an overview of major and recurring disinformation about the SDGs shared on social media platforms, thereby offering a foundation for the development of the suggested tracker. This chapter further highlights the impact of disinformation on SDGs, especially during the COVID-19 pandemic, and how that inhibits development communication from achieving the desired behavioural change that could help facilitate the attainment of the SDGs.

This chapter addresses the following questions:

1. What are the major and recurring disinformation trends about SDGs shared on social media platforms?
2. How has COVID-19 exacerbated the trends of disinformation on SDGs?
3. What is the impact of disinformation on the attainment of the SDGs?

The answers to these questions would aid our further understanding of the impact of the diffusion of disinformation and conspiracy theories on the attainment of the 2030 SDGs. In the subsequent sections this chapter first provides a background and context on communication for development and social change as it relates to the use of digital media. Next, it reviews the major literature covering the impact of disinformation, highlighting various instances of how disinformation negatively affected the implementation of the SDGs. This is followed by a brief on the methodology, the findings and discussions, and finally the conclusion section that also provides some recommendations.

Communication for Development and Social Change: Background and Context

The rise of disinformation is increasingly threatening the field of communication for sustainable development and social change. This is due to the role of fake news in the pollution of believability and credibility of messages, especially on social media platforms where multitude of people now consume their information. This tendency is making the work of development communicators more complex. While they contend with designing and implementing strategies to get across their development communication messages with the hope of achieving social change, they now must contend with a muddled communication atmosphere where audiences are increasingly becoming polarized and are at times suspicious of messages from politicians, journalists and established global institutions operating in the global communication and sustainable development domain. Traditionally, global institutions, in-country institutions and politicians play vital roles in driving development communication towards the attainment of sustainable developments. But the rise in the disinformation discourse is gradually discrediting those voices. Digital disinformation also causes "detrimental societal effects" (Shu et al., 2020, p. 13) and negatively impacts various programmes and measures designed to remedy societal ills.

One of the major areas threatened by the rise of disinformation is the area of development communication around the 17 goals of the SDGs. These goals touch on various facets of human life and therefore hardly escape various forms of disinformation, fake news and misinformation spread on traditional and social media platforms. For example, one of the aims of SDG16 (Peace, justice and strong institutions) is to help "promote peaceful and inclusive societies for sustainable development, provide access to justice for all and build effective, accountable and inclusive institutions at all levels" (UNDEF, 2021), and in turn help reduce or eliminate the perceived distrust of the democratic institutions in the concerned countries. However, the increase in disinformation and its discourse in the media, especially on social media, is intensifying the distrust in democratic institutions and by extension most development communication emanating from those institutions. These institutions continue to battle misinformation and disinformation with regards to myriad of issues that give them their legitimacy. Some proponents of disinformation push conspiracy theories suggesting that some of the global actions taken by global institutions like the United Nations to tackle global challenges facing humanity, like the 2030 Agenda for Sustainable Development, are ploys to entrench 'deep-state' and achieve a centralized global system of controlling humanity by the year 2030.

The COVID-19 pandemic vividly illustrates this tendency. The pandemic led to a global shutdown and was described as an unprecedented challenge and danger to global health. A section of the global populace took it upon themselves to discredit communication emanating from politicians and democratic institution to help combat coronavirus due to the deep-seated distrust of the multilateral and political/democratic institutions. Some of the disinformation disseminators base their distrust of the institutions on the fact that many politicians and institutions habitually lie to the public and fail to fulfil various promises made during political campaigns and/or launch of global programmes. Another area that faces a rise in disinformation that affects development communication is the domain of empirical scientific evidence suggesting the prevalence of some societal challenges like climate change and related issues, and the required measures to combat them. The proponents of these conspiracy theories varied from influential politicians in power who want to remain in office and continue to push ideologies and agendas that resonate with their supporters, to opposition politicians seeking power and would make all sorts of claims in their quest to win elections. Others include digital media influencers, some journalists and website operators pushing click-bait and sensational headlines, and ordinary social media users who spread disinformation for various reasons.

All the aforementioned disinformation challenges further highlight the danger posed by disinformation to the attainment of the SDGs. They also point to the need for a concerted effort in the Sustainable Development Goals domain to craft a push back mechanism and a 'bullet proof' strategy to shield SDGs from the effect of disinformation in the form of SDG18 Communication for All Goal, with one or more of its targets focusing on combatting disinformation, as suggested by Yusha'u (2021).

Key Literature on the Impact of Disinformation on SDGs

The SDGs are a set of 17 goals with 169 targets agreed upon by leaders of countries and global institutions. The goals include ending poverty, achieving zero hunger, improved good health and wellbeing, attaining quality education for all, tackling climate change and sustainable peace, justice and strong institutions, among others. The SDGs agenda is a successor programme to the UN's Millennium Development Goals (MDGs) which could not achieve its aim by its end date of 2015. As a result of the non-realization of the MDGs, world leaders agreed to introduce new sets of goals (the SDGs) designed to succeed where previous ones failed.

However, the new set of goals now face new challenges that are threatening to make them also fail. This challenge manifests in the form of disinformation, fake news and conspiracy theories which are stifling the institutional communication aimed at sensitizing the global community to partner towards the attainment of the goals. As captured by Oxford University's Martin Programme on Misinformation, Science and Media, "Long-held scientific consensus on vital issues such as climate change or the vaccines is increasingly contested, heavily debated on social media and even in the mainstream news media" (Programme, n.d.).

The disinformation and fake news around the SDGs intensified in the wake of COVID-19 pandemic that brought the life to a halt in most parts of the world, reduced economic progress, swelled unemployment, and increased poverty and hunger (Nations, 2020). Most of the disinformation on SDGs was prevalent on social media platforms. A publication by the World Health Organization (WHO) on how to manage the impact of disinformation around COVID-19 pandemic tagged as 'infodemic' highlighted how disinformation impacts various sectors related to SDGs:

> While the virus itself physically invades and threatens our health, the COVID-19 infodemic erodes the very social cohesion that sustains health systems and institutions that support well-being. ... In tandem with the virus, it (infodemic) has the power to harm anyone in its way, especially those who are strapped for resources. Or those who lack basic health, digital and media literacy. Or those who are oppressed by injustice and inequity. (Organization, 2021, p. 9)

The preceding excerpt highlights the negative impact of disinformation on SDGs3, 4, 10, 16, among others.

DiCicco and Agarwal (2020, p. 325) highlighted that "Misinformation has affected society from political campaigns, vaccinations, pesticides and GMOs in Agriculture, and many other areas". These areas are all issues and topics related to the SDGs. A European Parliament study on the impact of disinformation and strategic political propaganda disseminated through online social media sites on the rule of law in the EU and its Member States highlighted that "disinformation and propaganda campaigns ... (interferes) with democratic processes through the manipulation of public opinion, as well as the international and national legislative and self-regulatory initiatives" (Judit, 2019, p. 11). Such interference that sometimes inspires some individuals to question the integrity of election and democratic process in general constitutes a threat and possible inhibition to the attainment of SDG16 on sustainable peace, justice and strong institutions. This is elucidated on by the report:

> Disinformation and propaganda events interfere with democracy in two ways: (i) they dominate and distort the public discourse and corrupt the process of democratic decision-making, and (ii) when this process leads to political success, the political force that won the elections through manipulation might capture the state and deconstruct the constitutional system. (Judit, 2019, p. 11)

Another section of the SDGs that witnesses recurring disinformation is the SDG on Climate action. Connolly et al. (2019, p. 472) asserted that "exposure to conspiracy theories about climate change or vaccines can reduce people's intention to limit their carbon footprint or to vaccinate themselves or a child against disease".

COVID-19 pandemic highlights visibly the impacts of disinformation on the attainment of SDG3. In their analysis of the academic literature on fake news during COVID-19 pandemic, Alias (2020) highlighted that disinformation misled people from around the world to consume chloroquine, cow urine, hot water, whiskey, honey and neat alcohol, believing that doing this would cure COVID-19 or prevent it entirely.

One of the major weapons used by the global community to fight the spread of COVID-19 pandemic is the administration of vaccines. But the discovery of the COVID-19 vaccines gave birth to widespread anti-vaccination disinformation campaigns on social media platforms. Although the issue of vaccine hesitancy predates the COVID-19 pandemic, it acquired intensity and vigour partly due to the mandates for people to get vaccinated against the virus in many parts of the world.

One of the key goals of the SDGs is to ensure global peace and security. However, disinformation and computational propaganda intrudes into the workings of global peace. This was evident in the case of Pakistan's Defence Minister who issued a nuclear retaliation warning in response to a 'fake news' story, and the Qatari state news agency hack that led to an escalation of tension in the Middle East between Qatar and some of its Arab neighbours. That Qatar incident nearly became the first 'fake news' war to transform into a physical conflict (Posetti & Matthews, 2018).

Ensuring freedom of expression and protecting free press are part of the goals and targets of the SDGs, but disinformation and computational propaganda negatively impacted the freedom of speech and press by polluting the information ecosystem with false narratives, fake news and propaganda, and also subjecting journalists to slander and false attacks on social media platforms. To illustrate this point, Posetti and Matthews (2018) highlighted that the

> prolific online harassment of independent investigative journalist Rana Ayyub elicited a call from five United Nations special rapporteurs for the Indian government to provide protection, following the mass circulation of false information aimed at countering her critical reporting. (Posetti & Matthews, 2018, p. 15)

The foregoing analysis highlights the negative impacts of disinformation, conspiracy theories and fake news on key issues on the SDGs agenda.

Theoretical Framework and Methodology

As indicated in the introduction of this chapter, one of the objectives of this chapter is tracking the major and recurring disinformation trends about SDGs on social media platforms, and how COVID-19 exacerbated the trends of disinformation on SDGs. The authors decided to appropriately use social media data with the support of secondary data to investigate the phenomenon, answer the research questions and achieve the aim of the study. They obtained and scrutinized data from social media platform in addition to obtaining interpretations for such data from other sources.

Social media data is becoming more and more central to researchers in the sense that people's behaviours and interactions are changing at a lightning speed and are moving online especially on social media where most disinformation on the SDGs now take place. For researchers to have full pictures and achieve complete understanding, they need to go to where the actions are taking place and therefore need to access and study social media data. As observed by Shu et al. (2020, p. 18), "social media enables users to be connected and interact with anyone, anywhere and anytime, which also allows researchers to observe human behaviors in an unprecedented scale with new lens."

Given that most disinformation and the sharing of conspiracy theories on SDGs now take place on social media platforms, it means that to investigate the case study of this chapter, there is need to involve social media data in the effort to answer the research question and arrive at answers and conclusions.

Data generated from social media is usually voluminous, raw and complex to analyse. Some of the difficulties and challenges involved in modelling social media data, ranging from the influence of algorithms on user behaviour which makes it difficult to theorize about, and the constant change of meaning in social media conversations over time. This makes it necessary to develop special technical analysis methods to make meaning out of the high volumes of data generated from social media platforms (Budak et al., 2021). There is also the question of whether to use inductive or deductive modelling in social media research. Inductive modelling explores the data and uses it in developing new theories, while deductive approach uses existing models to test hypothesis (Budak et al., 2021). The smrconverge group seems to favour the inductive approach, explaining that "Part of the task of researchers in a relatively new field is simply to get a sense of the data, after all. We are only beginning to understand what social media data look like and how they can be analysed ... (therefore) the potential for deductive modelling is relatively limited" (Budak et al., 2021, p. 17). This study therefore adopted the inductive approach in handling the social media data.

In terms of methodological paradigm for this chapter, there are digital media researchers who campaign for the adoption of a new 'digital positivism' as a methodological paradigm to situate digital media research. This paradigm is about "quantification, mathematics, and calculation, focusing on explaining the world based on the analysis of big stocks and flows of data" (Fuchs, 2019). However, Fuchs (2019, p. 12) argues that "the problem is that the analysis of big data does not tell us everything that matters. It cannot properly study human motivations, feelings, experiences, norms, morals, values, interpretations, concerns, fears, hopes, etc."

Adopting digital positivism would therefore make digital media studies to revolve only around computer science studies and relegate critical, theoretical and philosophical understandings associated with other fields like social sciences and humanities. This will deprive the field of the understanding of the deep meaning of phenomenon associated with the interpretative perspective of the social science and humanities field.

This study's aims include tracking the diffusion of disinformation on the SDGs across social media platforms and appraising the role of the disinformation in inhibiting effective communication aimed at behavioural changes needed to achieve the SDGs. Therefore, adopting digital positivism may not afford the researchers to critically interrogate the diffusion of disinformation on the digital media related to SDGs. The research also supports the position of Fuchs (2019, p. 13) on the central nature of the social and digital media data to this and other digital media studies:

> I am rather arguing for the development and use of alternative, critical digital methods that are more qualitative than quantitative, are combined with traditional, use small datasets instead of big datasets, are critical theory-based, creative, experimental, participatory, investigate power structures and aim at contributing to the creation of a commons-based society.

Therefore, this study would be situated within the critical theory methodology paradigm.

The study will use analysis of social media data to answer its research questions. It will employ the use of technology and computer programming as part of its method of gathering data to source and analyse contents of some of the disinformation and conspiracy theories shared on the social media platforms specifically on Twitter microblogging site. The study will be limited to Twitter platforms because checks reveal that most conspiracy theories about SDGs started from posts on the platform and most of the sharing of the disinformation around the issue took place on social media platforms, especially on the Twitter microblogging site. This in addition to the fact that Twitter is (open source) accessible and provides access to researchers to collect publicly available tweets, compared to some other social media platforms.

Social Media Data

To conduct research on social media data, researchers still employ the agelong existing media research methodologies, but with some twist to cater for the new developments introduced by the social media data characteristics and challenges. These challenges, as suggested by De Choudhury et al. (2010, p. 34), include "data acquisition bottleneck and information analysis complexity".

A look at the volume of social media messages produced daily indicates that billions upon billions of data is produced daily by billions of users of various social media platforms in the world. For example, a look at Facebook, the world's largest and most popular social media network (Judit, 2019), indicates that the platform has over 3 billion users who share billions of messages on the platform everyday (Facebook, 2021), while Twitter's Q2 2021 shareholder letter indicates that the company has over 200 million daily users posting billions of tweets monthly (Twitter, 2021).

However, Pasquetto et al. (2020) advanced that social media platforms do not always make it easy for researchers to obtain data for their researches; therefore, researchers are left to scramble to get whatever available data they could scrape/obtain from the platforms however incomplete it is and then build their studies based on such available data. While researchers blame the social media platforms for not providing access to adequate data on their platforms, some of the platforms accuse some researchers of infringing on their users' privacy by scrapping private information without consent or respecting the privacy of the users (Clark, 2021), an allegation denied by the researchers (King & Persily, 2021). Facebook claimed to have offered researchers with various "Privacy Protective methods" to conduct their research on the platform (Clark, 2021), but researchers described those methods as very restrictive and limiting.

One key bone of contention in this context is defining what is public data in reference to social media posts. Are posts by users on social media considered public since they are already in the public domain and are therefore free to use by the researchers in their studies or not? While some argue in the affirmative, some privacy advocates suggest that although the data is in the public domain, the users who posted the messages may have done so believing that the message will only be seen by those the messages were intended for and would not end up becoming research data. Therefore, if researchers would like to use the posts, they must seek permission from the data owners for their personal conversations to be turned to social research data.

Yet another point of debate is whether studying such 'public' content constitutes studying 'human subjects' since those messages are about human beings and traditionally studying human subjects requires getting their consent and approval (Gilbert et al., 2021). This is especially because previous studies highlighted the discomfort of users when their online interactions are turned to research data.

Given the insights from this debate, the authors of this chapter are of the view that the data used for the study obtained from social media platforms is in the public domain and that studying such content does not constitute studying a human subject. This study, therefore, identified Twitter platform as source for its social media data for the study due to popularity of the platform globally and because the platform was used to spread disinformation and conspiracy theories on SDGs the case study of this chapter. Furthermore, disinformation researchers have expressed preference for the platforms in collecting data for their research despite some reservations.

Sampling

Billions of posts (text, photo, video, graphics, etc.) are posted to social media daily by billions of users. This presents big challenges for social media researchers on how to wade through and analyse such voluminous content that get churned out in billions every day. While there are various technological tools to aid the analysis of millions of nodes produced by social media posts during data analysis, it is still impracticable for researchers with time and resources constraints to study each and every piece of post contained in their study data. Researchers therefore often have no choice but to analyse a "judiciously selected 'sample' of the data" (De Choudhury et al., 2010, p. 34). There are still no universally adopted methods of sampling social media content, as different studies adopt, modify and experiment with various methods in order to achieve reliability and representativeness of the data (Mneimneh et al., 2021). Some researchers conduct their sampling based on some popular hashtags associated with the studied phenomenon.

For example, in their study of "cobranding of COVID-19 misinformation with other types of misinformation", Quinn et al. (2021) adopted hashtag sampling to select their units of analysis. This study employed the use of the following keywords 'agenda2030', 'plandemic' and 'climate-hoax' to generate the data for analysis.

Twitter Data Extraction and Analysis

Mneimneh et al. (2021) highlighted various ways that researchers could source data from social media platforms for their research. This includes research partnership with social media companies like Facebook or Twitter and accessing obtainable database of previously collected social media data by other organizations, academic institutions or research centres. The researcher also has the option of buying social media data from research vendors, or the option of the use of webscraping tools to scrape the data from social media platforms. The fifth and most popular way to collect social media data is through Application Program Interfaces (APIs). Mneimneh et al. (2021, p. 8) explain that "An API is a software interface that specifies how a computer program or application can interact with another application. APIs establish secure and standard ways for software applications to work with each other. The researcher is given a 'key' by a social media platform so he/she can access specific data. Then the user can use this key to request data from the API" (Mneimneh et al., 2021, p. 8).

This study employed the use of the fifth option described above by using the API interface to collect data from twitter platform. This method is considered the easiest and also one that avoids the major controversies surrounding use of the other methods.

To obtain the data for this study, one of the authors applied for and got a Twitter developer account and also got approval to access the Twitter academic research product track. The academic research track was developed by Twitter for researchers to "Find global data for your thesis or dissertation, gather historical or real-time data for your research lab, and study the public conversation with the API v2" (Twitter, 2021, p. 1).

The research identified some of the keywords used in spreading the conspiracy theory on SDGs. The identified keywords (agenda2030, plandemic and climatehoax) were used via the Twitter API interface (using twarc python programme) to collect publicly available historical tweets containing the selected keywords and/or hashtags used in posting about the disinformation and conspiracy theory on the Twitter about the SDGs.

Different periods were picked to search for the three keywords. For 'plandemic' keyword, the researchers adopted two periods to search for the keywords due to the significance of the subject matter and the dynamic nature of the changes in the COVID-19 pandemic's development over time. The pandemic is still ongoing, and more and more information is gathered and learnt about the virus as it progresses. The authors therefore chose 11 March 2020, when the World Health Organization (WHO) declared COVID-19 as a pandemic as a peg to pick the first tranche of Twitter samples on the keyword 'plandemic'. The sample range was 1–20 March 2020, and the search returned 1810 English language-based tweets in total. The second tranche of sample on the keyword 'plandemic' was selected in the month of January 2021 due to two key reasons. The day, 30 January 2021 marked one year since the World Health Organization (WHO) declared COVID-19 as a public health emergency, and 27 January 2021 was the day when the number of COVID-19 cases worldwide reached the milestone of 100 million. The sample included a day before and a day after both dates 26 and 31 January 2021. The search returned 5739 tweets in total.

For the keyword 'climatehoax', the authors settled for the period of the 26th UN Climate Change Conference of the Parties (COP26) from 31 October to 13 November 2021. The search returned 3518 tweets in total.

For the third keyword, the authors used Google Trends to identify when the search for Agenda2030 peaked and selected 24–30 January 2021, which was the period the keyword recorded the highest spike as at the time of sampling (beginning November 2021). Only posts in the English language were collected. The authors purposively coded sampled messages from the posts by reading through the tweets using coding query tools (Nvivo and Netlytic).

Data Presentation

The research analysed the content, characteristics and dissemination methods of disinformation and conspiracy theories shared on Twitter globally to understand their impacts on SDGs and their role in inhibiting communication for development and social change. Credible secondary data from reputable organizations were also consulted and used in analysing the outcome of the social media study. The research used content analyses method to analyse the content of some of the fake news and conspiracy theories shared on issues related to 2030 SDGs.

Analysing samples of tweets containing disinformation and conspiracy theories on Twitter and how they spread especially among closely knitted individuals and those within the same filter bubble may be difficult without the help of software and computer programmes, considering the huge volume of shared information on social media. This justifies the use of collection and analysis tools to collect and peruse the millions of conversations in order to analyse the content and identify the key actors in the spread of disinformation.

Due to time and resources constraints, some samples of the extracted Twitter data were sorted and analysed using inductive approach of framing analysis. Coding categories were created after reading through the content of sampled tweets. The authors employed the intercoder reliability system in crosschecking/confirming coding selections/decisions. Data analysis software NVivo 12 software (QSR International) and Netlytic programme were used in facilitating the coding and data analysis. Google Trends on how the disinformation cases on SDGs evolved over time was also used to track the diffusion of disinformation on the SDGs. Factchecks by agencies who subscribed to International Fact-Checking Network (IFCN) code of conduct were used as yardstick and judgement source in determining whether the text of a shared information is a disinformation and/or conspiracy theory or not. These were in addition to data from agencies like World Health Organization (WHO), the United Nations Framework Convention on Climate Change and the UN Sustainable Development Goals website.

Three broad themes of the type of disinformation spread on the SDGs emerged from the data coded, namely:

- Agenda 2030: A Globalist Agenda
- Climate Hoax: A Profitable Venture
- Plandemic: A Fake Pandemic

The broad theme about 'Agenda 2030: A Globalist Agenda' includes disinformation posts claiming that SDGs are part of a global agenda by multinational institutions working with some governments to create a new world order centrally controlled by few individuals and organizations. Some claim that it is a ploy to control information and by extension influence people's behaviour to surrender to the global agenda control. The broad theme also includes a subtheme of disinformation posts about government control, alleging that climate change, COVID-19 social distancing, and lockdown measures and campaigns are part of strategies and tactics to expand governments and control people's lives by using pseudoscience to justify the introduction of regulations and telling people what to do and what not to do to control global warming and slow down the spread of COVID-19 pandemic (Table 6.1).

The broad theme of 'Climate Hoax: A Profitable Venture' shared on the SDGs includes subthemes like fear mongering with some posts describing the SDG goal of tackling climate change as fear mongering by entrenched interests for predetermined goals. Others include mockery of the climate

Table 6.1 Sample tweets around the theme Agenda 2030: A Globalist Agenda

Themes	*Subthemes*	*Sample claims*
Agenda 2030: A Globalist Agenda	Depopulation Agenda Government/ Elite Control Conspiracy Theories	• Of course it's hard to say exactly what's going on, but it looks very much like #coronavirus is real bio-weapon that #globalistCabal created to kill many, scare rest of world shitless so they could ride in and "save" us all from (their) plague with #NWO. #Cabalavirus • Cities are the foot soldiers of the Agenda2030 nnListen to DAVOS Live as they are given their marching orders by the WEF • Not About The Vaccine Or The Virus Itself, It is About The Great Reset. They Created A Virus & Control The Population Through Vaccinations. They Will Microchip The Remaining Population. Agenda2030n#NewWorldOrder • One of the reasons why they keep on pushing Smart Motorways. Next up: Travel where you are told, when you are told and at what speed you are told. All part of #Agenda21 #Agenda2030 • The Great reset scam! Your Credit Score linked with your search history. #TheGreatreset #Agenda2030 • !

change campaigns indicating that people have much more issues of immediate concern than climate change, which they do not even believe is a reality. Some even made several call-to-action posts to urge others to join them in discrediting the climate change messages. Others claim the measures taken to control climate change are measures that would benefit only the rich and disadvantage the poor. The theme also features several disinformation posts that claim that changes in the climate are natural and that the world would be just fine and no need to take any measures to control the global warming.

Furthermore, under this broad theme, there are posts that describe climate change campaigns as a ploy for expansion in taxation and disinformation posts that allege that several green measures are gambits to increase taxes on companies and individuals under the guise of green schemes. This broad theme also includes disinformation posts alleging that climate change and COVID-19 are a planned conspiracy by some companies and individuals to make profit.

Other subthemes in this category include promoting pseudoscience, with several disinformation posts alleging that some scientific facts promoted as part of the SDGs are fake and manipulated. Some of the posters tend to claim knowledge of science and assume the authority to debunk established scientific facts (Table 6.2).

The broad theme of 'Plandemic: A Fake Pandemic' includes several disinformation posts that describe the COVID-19 pandemic as a man-made disease planned to depopulate the world population, with billionaire Bill Gates as one of the sponsors of this alleged plan. However, fact checkers have debunked such disinformation. Other subthemes that emanated from perusing the disinformation tweets in this category include describing measures to curb the spread of COVID-19 as danger to the economy. Others described COVID-19 as a process manufactured by the big pharmaceutical companies to make more profit. Some of the disinformation actors described the vaccination drive to curb the spread of the pandemic as a ploy to inject people with microchips to be used in tracking and surveillance and subsequently used in curbing rights and freedoms of people (Table 6.3).

Table 6.2 Sample tweets about the theme: Climate Hoax: A Profitable Venture

Themes	*Subthemes*	*Sample claims*
Climate Hoax: A Profitable Venture	Climate Science Deniers/ Fake Science	Globalist handlers instructed all their willing sock puppets globally long ago to do &; say exactly the same. It's just the next long planned scam to collect additional tax funds for all the useless politricksters &; lobbyists to waste &; fill their deep pockets … #ClimateHoax https://t.co/HdZ4HWFPQi https://t.co/UX5LTTeb5p How scientifically &; economically clueless are the west's current leaders? The climate campaign is a hoax, perpetuated by the toothless United Nations. Money poured into its coffers is not to dabble in agendas or to redistribute wealth. Or is it just snouts in the trough? Several sun cycles and varying levels of greenhouse gases. Yes, the #ClimateHoax has nothing to do with actual climate. It's the latest way to extract money from wealthy nations to be redistributed by the UN. https://t.co/gL3T1l0P23 @ElizabethMay @morricemike Global communists want wealth distribution, elites only want your money, if you think #COP26 is about the environment, you are part of the problem #Canada #BC #Vancouver #Toronto #Ontario #Montreal #Quebec #ClimateHoax #USESkype #TaxpayerPaidVacations @ franco_nomics #hypocrites https://t.co/5UaEkZAwbA The #climatehoax isn't that climate change isn't real or humans are contributing, but it's being used to make millionaires billionaires at the cost of 100,000's (maybe millions) of lives and the wealth of the middle class. Climate policies don't just not work, they kill. https://t.co/BuUogtXcaK

Network Analysis

The authors also used network visualization to further understand the diffusion of disinformation on SDGs. 'ClimateHoax' keyword search was selected by the authors as a sample to illustrate the nature of the network of people sharing disinformation on SDGs. Figure 6.1 illustrates the social network graph generated using the Netlytic.org's analytic software. The small dots in the graph, referred to as nodes, represent each user in the conversation, while the line connecting the dots to clusters represents edges. Different colours were assigned to different clusters in the conversation around the 'ClimateHoax' discourse in the sampled data. A close perusal of the graph indicates that there are top five clusters with higher density than others as depicted in Fig. 6.2.

Table 6.3 Sample tweets about the theme: Plandemic: A Fake Pandemic

Themes	*Subthemes*	*Sample claims*
Plandemic: A Fake Pandemic	Danger to Economy	The #Plandemic of the #Swamp and Global elite's like #Soros #Gates and Co works well! THIS is PLANNED! Same as " #ClimateCrisis" https://t.co/aWcavqNHbU All the political posturing on vaccines is truly disgusting. The fact remains that ANY vaccine available today involves using murdered children before they could even be born. I renew my pledge ... I will not extend my life by USING murdered children. This is evil WAKE UP! It's funny how the #ClimateChangeHoax, #Agenda2030 the #GreatReset & a #FakePandemic work so well to usher in the destruction of our economy & society in place a fake green agenda that will further help devalue Canada's position as self sufficient and independent nation & society https://t.co/xSC0l8SWgo If anyone still needed any proof that it was all staged from Day 1. Not sure what the next scene in their script dictates but no one will get away with it. We will remember ALL the lies, ALL the crimes, ALL the destruction that has already happened and is still happening ... https://t.co/1Ipoiiem3b It,Äôs Not About The Vaccine Or The Virus Itself, It,Äôs About The ,ÄúGreat Reset,Äù . nnThey Created A Virus & Control The Population Through Vaccinations . nnThey Will Microchip The Remaining Population.nn#BillGates n#VaccineforSouthAfrica n#Agenda2030n#NewWorldOrder https://t.co/Gba6CGnowc

The clusters in the graph highlight how various individuals interact with each other on Twitter while tweeting using the hashtag #ClimateHoax. See Table 6.2 for samples of tweets shared by users in this category (Fig. 6.3).

The above graph gives a detailed view of the densest cluster in the previous clusters highlighted. The cluster revolves around a tweet by a user named @BoughtTheSwamp who appears to be a US-based Antifa activist based on the tone of his tweets and the link to the Antifa website in his bio. The tweet contained the words: "This conference is one of the most IMPORTANT meetings in history. AS ROBINETTE FALLS ASLEEP!! #ClimateHoax." The tweet also contains an attached video which shows a *Washington Post* video showing the US President Joe Biden closing his eyes

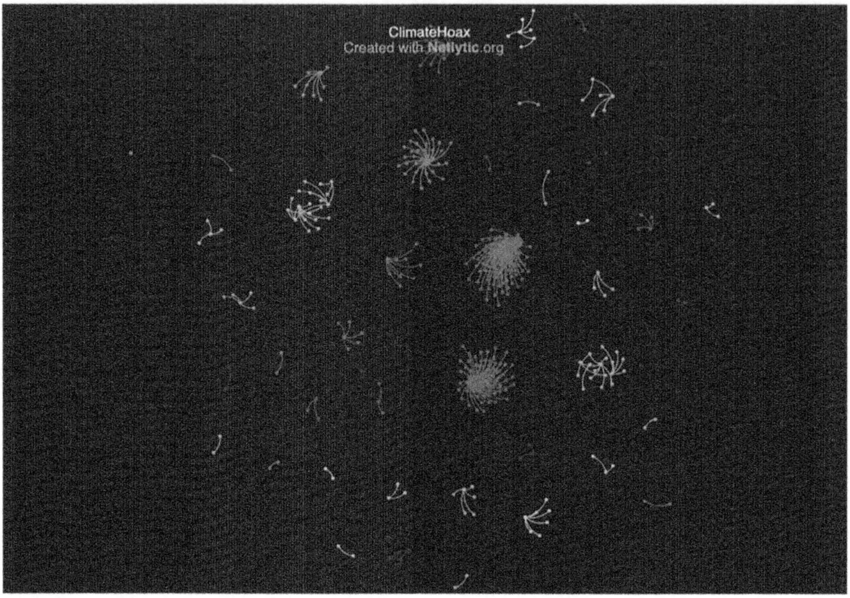

Fig. 6.1 Social network of climate hoax Twitter search

during the Glasgow leaders meeting on climate change in November 2021. He ended the tweet with the hashtag #ClimateHoax mostly used by climate change deniers to spread disinformation. The tweet was retweeted 188 times, quoted 14 times and liked 210 times.

The second cluster (pink colour) in Fig. 6.2 revolves around a tweet by user named Dr. Gina—RAV with Twitter handle @RealAmVoice. She appears to be a Fox news commentator going by her bio description and the cover image used on her profile. She self-described as a long time Trump media advisor. The tweet reads:

"Michael Bloomberg gas 6 planes, 3 helicopters, 11 houses and 42 cars. He thinks you should use public transportation to save the environment. #climatehoax #LetsGoBrandon."

The network in the third cluster (Orange colour in Fig. 6.2) revolves around a tweet by a user with handle @EnglishCartel. His tag line reads "Resist Global Communism" and the tweet reads: "#ClimateHoax #GreatReset #ClimateCrisis If you tell a lie big enough and keep repeating it, people will eventually come to believe it. (Goebbels)." The tweet was

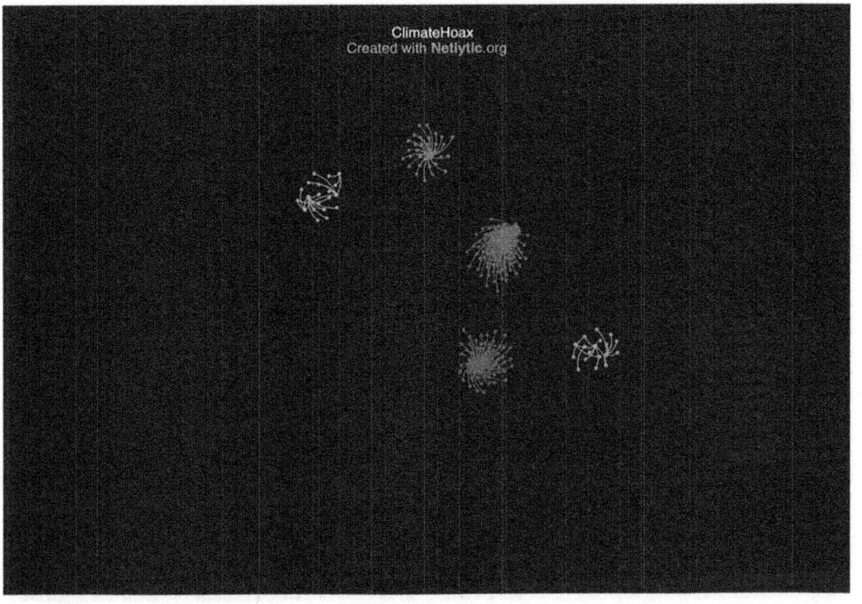

Fig. 6.2 Top five clusters with higher density

accompanied by a graphics featuring images of four men including Prince Charles and Bill Gates and also logos of some global organizations and institutions like the World Economic Forum, Council on foreign relations, Chatham House, Knights of Malta, etc. These were accompanied with the words:

"Hi, we are building a world tyranny where everyone will be our slaves with no rights, property or privacy. Seems that most of you are ok with that so thanks."

The content of the tweets at the centre of the three purposively sampled clusters highlighted above gives a flavour of the kind of disinformation messages shared by the central actors identified in the Twitter samples for this chapter. They indicate that some of the disinformation actors play on emotions and use circumstantial evidences to justify their false claims, and not only use texts to spread their disinformation but also augments it with videos and graphics.

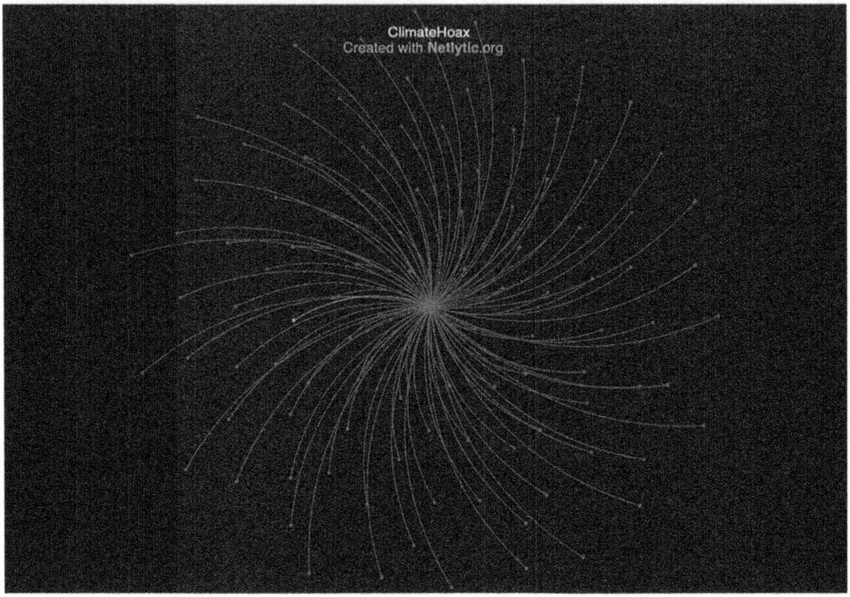

Fig. 6.3 Detailed analysis of one of the clusters

Discussions and Recommendations

This section will dissect the findings so far in relation to the research questions.

Question 1
What are the major and recurring disinformation trends about SDGs shared on social media platforms?

With regard to this research question, the Twitter data gathered and analysed revealed several main themes and subthemes of the kinds and methods of disinformation about the SDGs. These include claims that the SDGs are an agenda of the elites to depopulate the world and that they are part of an agenda devised by the government and the elite to control the 'submissive' world population. Conspiracy theories were also spread around SDG goals on health, particularly the issue of vaccination to control the spread of COVID-19 pandemic. These include the claims that vaccines are part of ploys to insert microchip into humans to achieve transhumanism in the people injected with the vaccines. Other disinformation around the health goal includes false claims that COVID-19 was a creation of the big pharmaceutical companies so that they could force everyone to take their vaccines and in the process they make humongous profit. There were also claims that COVID-19 vaccines were ploys to microchip humans and install trackers to monitor their movements and control them or that lockdown measures to control the spread of the disease introduced by various governments around the world are part of the global 2030 agenda to curb the rights and freedom of the people by the elite and government and prevent them from rising up against the governments or corporations to demand their rights.

False information around climate change goals were also shared, with claims that measures introduced to curb the global warming are dangers to the global economy or that they are ploys to transfer wealth from the rich countries to the poorer ones using the United Nations platforms.

Question 2
How has COVID-19 exacerbated the trends of disinformation on SDGs?

The primary and secondary data gathered for this study indicates that there was increase in diffusion of disinformation on SDGs-related topics due to the outbreak of COVID-19 pandemic. For example, debates and conspiracy theories around 5G technology predate the COVID-19, but conspiracy theorists and disinformation spreaders linked 5G technology to the spread of COVID-19, a situation that led to burning down of some telecom masts and the disinformation could discourage some people from embracing 5G technology. As a result of this, some countries could be forced to slow down the roll out of the 5G and that could have negative impact on the attainment of several SDGs, in particular SDGs 9, 8, 4, 3, 11 and 7.

The 5G technology could play vital role in the attainment of several SDGs. For example, during the total lockdown occasioned by COVID-19 pandemic in several countries, education of children and tertiary institutions moved online and that ensured continued efforts to attain the SDGs on education. There are ongoing developments and innovation towards popularizing telemedicine which could be enhanced by greater internet speed, which 5G technology provides. The 5G technology could play vital roles in these sectors and disinformation around the technology discourages its adoption by those who believe in such conspiracy theories.

The spread of disinformation around COVID-19 pandemic was tagged as an infodemic. In a publication titled infodemic management, the World Health Organization (WHO) defined the term infodemic as

> a tsunami of information—some accurate, some not—which spreads alongside a disease outbreak. With the speed of technology and the "plugged in" nature of our world, the COVID-19 infodemic cannot be eliminated, though it can be managed. (Organization, 2021, p. 6)

Even before the COVID-19 pandemic, issues like climate change, vaccinations, elections and security were already prone to disinformation and conspiracy theories. COVID-19 gave a boost to the spread. Some researchers believe that the global lockdown as a result of the pandemic pushed people to rely more on the internet and social media platforms and this in turn increased their exposure and in some cases participation in the dissemination of disinformation. Dow et al. (2021, p. 4) highlighted this:

> In general, the pandemic increased social media usage, such that general internet activity rose 25% in the days after lockdown … More specifically, the year 2020 saw global social media use accelerate by 13%, with 330 million new users, resulting in a total of 4.7 billion total users in April 2021 … We argue that part of the reason people consumed more social media was because of pandemic-related disruptions to their cognitive and social structures.

In a speech to the Munich Security Conference in February 2020, the head of the World Health Organization (WHO) highlighted the role of COVID-19 in exacerbating disinformation on the discourse around health issues, one of the key goals of the 2030 agenda. He also highlighted the role of social media platforms in the spread of disinformation on the phenomenon:

> We're not just fighting an epidemic; we're fighting an infodemic. Fake news spreads faster and more easily than this virus, and is just as dangerous. That's why we're also working with search and media companies like Facebook, Google, Pinterest, Tencent, Twitter, TikTok, YouTube and others to counter the spread of rumours and misinformation. (Adhanom-Ghebreyesus, 2020)

The case of Brazil's President Jair Bolsonaro provides clear evidence of how the spread of COVID-19 exacerbated trends on SDGs-related discourse, especially on the SDG goal related to improving good health and wellbeing of the populace. Through his periodic live-streamed videos on social media and other channels, Bolsonaro showed disregard to science by promoting conspiracy theories about the effects and cures of COVID-19. He made erroneous claims that 90% of people infected with COVID-19 do not show symptoms and that the virus is just a "gentle flu" that "armored glass protects against" (Ricard & Medeiros, 2020).

The social media data analysed by this study also confirm some of the findings by Ognyanova et al. (2021) in which they highlighted some of the widely spread myths about COVID-19 vaccine especially by Americans as follows:

- The COVID-19 vaccines will alter people's DNA.
- The COVID-19 vaccines contain microchips that could track people.
- The COVID-19 vaccines contain the lung tissue of aborted foetuses.
- The COVID-19 vaccines can cause infertility (Ognyanova et al., 2021, p. 5).

The 5G technology is another SDG-related subject of disinformation that COVID-19 affected. Already before COVID-19, there were controversies around the environmental and health impacts of the 5G technology; with the advent of COVID-19, the debate took on a new form (Bruns et al., 2020). Finding of this study affirms that disinformation surrounding 5G heighted with the advent of the COVID-19 pandemic.

Question 3
What is the impact of disinformation on the attainment of the SDGs?

As highlighted, disinformation could play a role in slowing down the attainment of SDGs. If we take COVID-19 as an example, lack of vaccination due to disinformation slows down the opening up of economies; global trade was shut down due to COVID-19 pandemic. This then have impacts on food production and various other sectors and if not properly addressed, could eventually have impact on the attainment of goals such as SDGs 1, 2, 8, 9 and 16. The WHO stressed this point: "Due to the COVID-19 pandemic, employers and workers alike have experienced enormous upheaval, with forced shutdowns, disintegration of customer bases, loss of income and force majeure" (Organization, 2021, p. 26).

Furthermore, continued lockdown and social distancing measures impact the implementation of various development projects to improve the health and wellbeing of people and eventually impact SDGs 4 and 6.

One of the measures advanced by experts to curtail the viral misinformation circulated by bots and 'human bots' is for the social media platforms to tweak their algorithms and police their platforms to make it difficult for bots to churn out messages at an industrial scale that sometimes cause virality of disinformation. Some of the social media platforms initially pushed back against several calls on them to take action on the misinformation shared on their platforms claiming that they are not "arbiter of truth" (Iosifidis & Nicoli, 2020, p. 74).

The social media platforms therefore came under severe criticism for 'facilitating' the viral spread of disinformation and conspiracy theories (e.g. anti-vaxers conspiracy theories), which led to the platforms to announce several actions to curtail the phenomenon. For example, in 2017, Facebook platform announced that its investigation revealed that a tiny group of people on its platform is in the habit of sharing high volume of posts every day in their efforts to make such information go viral and, in the process, end up spamming the feeds of millions of users. Facebook therefore announced that it was tweaking its algorithm to ensure that low-quality information/links shared by spammers receive low exposure and therefore reduce the possibility of them going viral (Adam Adam, 2021). As highlighted by Shu et al. (2020, p. 28), "Detecting disinformation and fake news at an early stage is desired to prevent a large amount of people to be affected."

Yusha'u and Servaes (2021a) highlighted the need for an online tracker to monitor disinformation shared about SDGs. This chapter agrees with this suggestion.

There are many models developed by disinformation researchers on how to track, detect and mitigate disinformation spreading on social media before and after using various machine learning models. This chapter recommends that instead of re-inventing the wheel, such developed models could be compiled, synthesized and tested, and effective ones be adopted as part of the suggested SDGs disinformation tracker. This chapter strongly recommends the adoption of emerging blockchain technology in tracking, detecting and mitigating the spread of disinformation on SDGs.

There is need to invest more in mass media literacy to educate the public about the dangers of disinformation, how to identify and debunk fake news, and how the public could help stem the spread of disinformation. Achieving this could help in reducing disinformation about SDGs.

Therefore, implementing an SDG18 goal with tackling disinformation as one of its targets could further accelerate the journey towards the attainment of the SDGs.

References

Adam, M. (2021). *Working to stop misinformation and false news.* Facebook for Media. https://www.facebook.com/formedia/blog/working-to-stop-misinformation-and-false-news

Adhanom-Ghebreyesus T. (2020). *Munich security conference.* World Health Organization. https://www.who.int/director-general/speeches/detail/munich-security-conference

Alias, N. R. (2020). *An Analysis of the Academic Literature on Fake News During Covid-19 Pandemic., 4*(2), 40–48.

Bruns, A., Harrington, S., & Hurcombe, E. (2020). 'Corona? 5G? Or both?': The dynamics of COVID-19/5G conspiracy theories on Facebook. *Media International Australia, 177*(1), 12–29. https://doi.org/10.1177/1329878X20946113

Budak, C., Soroka, S., Singh, L., Bailey, M., Bode, L., Chawla, N. V, Davis-kean, P. E., Choudhury, M. De, De Veaux, R., & Hahn, U. (2021). *Modeling considerations for quantitative social science research using social media data.* https://doi.org/10.31234/osf.io/3e2ux.

Clark, M. (2021). *Research cannot be the justification for compromising people's privacy.* Facebook Newsroom. https://about.fb.com/news/2021/08/research-cannot-be-the-justification-for-compromising-peoples-privacy/

Communications, N. (2017). Fake news threatens a climate literate world. *Nature Communications, 8*(1), 1–2. https://doi.org/10.1038/ncomms15460

Connolly, J. M., Uscinski, J. E., Klofstad, C. A., & West, J. P. (2019). Communicating to the public in the era of conspiracy theory. *Public Integrity, 21*(5), 469–476. https://doi.org/10.1080/10999922.2019.1603045

De Choudhury, M., Lin, Y. R., Sundaram, H., Candan, K. S., Xie, L., & Kelliher, A. (2010). How does the data sampling strategy impact the discovery of information diffusion in social media? *ICWSM 2010—Proceedings of the 4th International AAAI Conference on Weblogs and Social Media*, 34–41.

DiCicco, K. W., & Agarwal, N. (2020). Blockchain technology-based solutions to fight misinformation: A survey. In *Disinformation, misinformation, and fake news in social media* (pp. 267–281). https://doi.org/10.1007/978-3-030-42699-6_14.

Dow, B. J., Johnson, A. L., Wang, C. S., Whitson, J., & Menon, T. (2021). The COVID-19 pandemic and the search for structure: Social media and conspiracy theories. *Social and Personality Psychology Compass, 15*(9), 1–22. https://doi.org/10.1111/spc3.12636

ElAlfy, A., Darwish, K. M., & Weber, O. (2020). Corporations and sustainable development goals communication on social media: Corporate social responsibility or just another buzzword? *Sustainable Development, 28*(5), 1418–1430. https://doi.org/10.1002/sd.2095

Facebook. (2021). *About Facebook, company info*. https://about.facebook.com/company-info/?_ga=2.89318683.1227295290.1632909565-175872339.1632909565

Fuchs, C. (2019). What is critical digital social research? Five reflections on the study of digital society. *Journal of Digital Social Research, 1*(1), 10–16. https://doi.org/10.33621/jdsr.v1i1.7

Gilbert, S., Vitak, J., & Shilton, K. (2021). Measuring Americans' comfort with research uses of their social media data. *Social Media and Society, 7*(3). https://doi.org/10.1177/20563051211033824

Grover, P., Kar, A. K., Gupta, S., & Modgil, S. (2021). Influence of political leaders on sustainable development goals—Insights from twitter. *Journal of Enterprise Information Management*. https://doi.org/10.1108/JEIM-07-2020-0304

Ha, L., Andreu Perez, L., & Ray, R. (2021). Mapping recent development in scholarship on fake news and misinformation, 2008 to 2017: Disciplinary contribution, topics, and impact. *American Behavioral Scientist, 65*(2), 290–315. https://doi.org/10.1177/0002764219869402

Iosifidis, P., & Nicoli, N. (2020). The battle to end fake news: A qualitative content analysis of Facebook announcements on how it combats disinformation. *International Communication Gazette, 82*(1), 60–81. https://doi.org/10.1177/1748048519880729

Janoušková, S., Hák, T., Nećas, V., & Moldan, B. (2019). Sustainable development-a poorly communicated concept by mass media. Another challenge for SDGs? *Sustainability (Switzerland), 11*(11), 1–20. https://doi.org/10.3390/su11113181

Judit, B. (2019). *Disinformation and propaganda impact on the functioning of the rule of law in the EU and its Member States*. Issue February. QA-02-19-140-EN-N.

King, G., & Persily, N. (2021). *Unprecedented Facebook URLs dataset now available for academic research through social science one*. Social Science One.. https://socialscience.one/blog/unprecedented-facebook-urls-dataset-now-available-research-through-social-science-one.

Kornbluh, K. (2020). Fighting COVID misinformation. *SDGs: Building Back Better*, 57–59. https://www.sustainablegoals.org.uk/

Meel, P., & Vishwakarma, D. K. (2020). Fake news, rumor, information pollution in social media and web: A contemporary survey of state-of-the-arts, challenges and opportunities. *Expert Systems with Applications, 153*, 1–26. https://doi.org/10.1016/j.eswa.2019.112986

Mensah, K., Awini, G., & Mensah, G. K. (2021). Fake news and SDG16: The situation in Ghana. In *The Palgrave handbook of international communication and sustainable development* (pp. 325–344). Springer International Publishing. https://doi.org/10.1007/978-3-030-69770-9_15

Mneimneh, Z., Pasek, J., Singh, L., Best, R., Bode, L., Bruch, E., Budak, C., Davis-kean, P., Donato, K., Ellison, N., Gelman, A., Hemphill, L., Hobbs, W., Jensen, B., Karypis, G., Ladd, J., West, B. T., & Wojcik, S. (2021). *Data acquisition, sampling, and data preparation considerations for quantitative social science research using social media data*. www.smrconverge.org

Nations, U. (2020). Achieving SDGs in the wake of COVID-19: Scenarios for policymakers. *Sustainable Development Outlook 2020*. https://sdgs.un.org/publications/sustainable-development-outlook-2020-24567

Ognyanova, K., Lazer, D., Baum, M. A., Druckman, J., Green, J., Perlis, R. H., & Simonson, M. (2021). Vaccine misinformation, from uncertainty to resistance. *The COVID-19 Consortium for Understanding the Public's Policy Preferences Across States*, 1–16. www.covidstates.org

Organization, W. H. (2021). *Infodemic management: An overview of infodemic management during COVID-19*, January 2020–May 2021 (Issue May).

Pasquetto, I., Swire-Thompson, B., & Amazeen, M. A. (2020). Tackling misinformation: What researchers could do with social media data. *Harvard Kennedy School Misinformation Review*, *1*(8), 1–14. https://doi.org/10.37016/mr-2020-49

Pindiga, H. I., & Sa'ad Abdullahi, B. (2021). Communicating development: News coverage of the SDGs in the Nigerian press. In M. J. Yusha'u & J. Servaes (Eds.), *The Palgrave handbook of international communication and sustainable development* (pp. 559–583). Springer International Publishing. https://doi.org/10.1007/978-3-030-69770-9_24

Posetti, J., & Matthews, A. (2018). A short guide to the history of 'fake news' and disinformation: A new ICFJ learning module. *International Center for Journalists*, 23–25. https://www.icfj.org/news/short-guide-history-fake-news-and-disinformation-new-icfj-learning-module

Programme, O. M. (n.d.). *Misinformation, science and media*. Retrieved October 18, 2021, from https://www.oxfordmartin.ox.ac.uk/misinformation/

Quinn, E. K., Fazel, S. S., & Peters, C. E. (2021). The Instagram Infodemic: Cobranding of conspiracy theories, coronavirus disease 2019 and authority-questioning beliefs. *Cyberpsychology, Behavior and Social Networking*, *24*(8), 573–577. https://doi.org/10.1089/cyber.2020.0663

Ricard, J., & Medeiros, J. (2020). Using misinformation as a political weapon: Covid-19 and bolsonaro in Brazil. *Harvard Kennedy School Misinformation Review*, *1*(2), 1–8. https://doi.org/10.37016/mr-2020-013

Salathé, M., & Khandelwal, S. (2011). Assessing vaccination sentiments with online social media: Implications for infectious disease dynamics and control. *PLoS Computational Biology, 7*(10). https://doi.org/10.1371/journal.pcbi.1002199

Shi, W., Fu, H., Wang, P., Chen, C., & Xiong, J. (2020). #Climatechange vs. #Globalwarming: Characterizing two competing climate discourses on twitter with semantic network and temporal analyses. *International Journal of Environmental Research and Public Health, 17*(3). https://doi.org/10.3390/ijerph17031062

Shu, K., Wang, S., Lee, D., & Liu, H. (2020). Mining disinformation and fake news: Concepts, methods, and recent advancements. In *Disinformation, misinformation, and fake news in social media emerging research challenges and opportunities* (pp. 1–19). https://doi.org/10.1007/978-3-030-42699-6_1.

Twitter, I. (2021). *Twitter announces second quarter 2021 results.* Twitter Investor Relations. https://investor.twitterinc.com/home/default.aspx

UNDEF. (2021). *Democracy & the SDGs.* https://sustainabledevelopment.un.org//index.php?page=view&type=20000&nr=5780&menu=2993

Waszak, P. M., Kasprzycka-Waszak, W., & Kubanek, A. (2018). The spread of medical fake news in social media—The pilot quantitative study. *Health Policy and Technology, 7*(2), 115–118. https://doi.org/10.1016/j.hlpt.2018.03.002

Yusha'u, M. J. (2021). SDG18—The missing ventilator: An introduction to the 2030 agenda for development. In M. J. Yusha'u & J. Servaes (Eds.), *The Palgrave handbook of international communication and sustainable development* (pp. 53–75). Springer International Publishing. https://doi.org/10.1007/978-3-030-69770-9_3

Yusha'u, M. J., & Servaes, J. (2021a). Beyond the SDGs: From 2030 to 2050 agenda for development. In M. J. Yusha'u & J. Servaes (Eds.), *The Palgrave handbook of international communication and sustainable development* (pp. 605–620). Springer International Publishing. https://doi.org/10.1007/978-3-030-69770-9_26

Yusha'u, M. J., & Servaes, J. (2021b). Communication for sustainable development in the age of COVID-19. In *The Palgrave handbook of international communication and sustainable development* (Issue 2020, pp. 3–30). Springer International Publishing. https://doi.org/10.1007/978-3-030-69770-9_1.

Yusha'u, M. J., & Servaes, J. (2021c). Beyond the SDGs: From 2030 to 2050 agenda for development. In *The Palgrave handbook of international communication and sustainable development* (Vol. 73(2), pp. 605–620). Springer International Publishing. https://doi.org/10.1007/978-3-030-69770-9_26.

CHAPTER 7

SDG18: Communication for All—Including People with a Communication Disability, Children, and People Who Do Not Speak Dominant Languages

Sharynne McLeod, Sarah Verdon, and Kathryn Crowe

Abstract Everyone has the right to communicate; however, not everyone can communicate in the same way. If SDG18 truly stands for "Communication for All", then we must listen to and advocate for people whose voices are rarely heard despite their right to "freedom of opinion

---

S. McLeod (✉)
School of Education, Charles Sturt University, Bathurst, NSW, Australia
e-mail: smcleod@csu.edu.au

S. Verdon
School of Allied Health, Exercise and Sports Sciences, Charles Sturt University, Albury, NSW, Australia
e-mail: sverdon@csu.edu.au

K. Crowe
University of Iceland, Reykjavík, Iceland
e-mail: kcrowe@csu.edu.au

J. Servaes, M. J. Yusha'u (eds.), *SDG18 Communicaton for All, Volume 2*, Sustainable Development Goals Series,
https://doi.org/10.1007/978-3-031-19459-7_7

and expression" being articulated in the Universal Declaration of Human Rights and subsequent conventions and declarations. This chapter focuses on three groups of people whose voices are particularly marginalized: (1) people with communication disabilities, (2) children, and (3) people who do not speak/understand/read/write the dominant language of their community. These three groups make up a large portion of the world's population but are unheard due to their invisible disability. The intersectionality between these three groups is a particular focus of this chapter leading to a call for multilingual children with communication disability to be supported to take their place as communicators in society, to fulfill their potential as multilingual speakers, and to realize their communication rights.

Keywords Communication rights • Communication disability • Bilingual • Multilingual • Children • Speech, Language, Communication Needs (SLCN) • Intersectionality

Introduction

Communication is central to our existence (Servaes, 2017; Yusha'u & Servaes, 2021). Communication is accomplished through speech, signing, gestures, vocalizations, facial expressions, writing, images (drawings, photos, movies, graphics), and many other forms. Most people communicate effortlessly every day with those around them, as well as with those across the world. Communication can be simultaneous (e.g., face-to-face, telephone, and text) or sequential (e.g., stored in cave paintings, books, photographs, movies, and online) to be shared with the future or listened to from the past. People take for granted that they can communicate their needs, wants, and even trivial thoughts whenever they want. Communication is central to most workplaces in the twenty-first century (Ruben, 2000). Accomplishment of each of the Sustainable Development Goals (SDGs) can only be achieved through successful communication at community, national, and international levels (Yusha'u & Servaes, 2021). The recent call for SDG18—Communication for All—by Yusha'u and Servaes acknowledges the centrality of communication and has been promoted by media and communication scholars, journalists, and policy makers. The call for SDG18 has also attracted the attention of those who advocate for communication for vulnerable and marginalized people within society. Those whose voices are rarely heard despite the right to "freedom of opinion and expression" being articulated as a human right (United Nations, 1948). There are three groups of people whose voices are particularly marginalized:

- people with communication disabilities,
- children, and
- people who do not speak/understand/read/write the dominant language of their community (McLeod, 2018).

These three groups will be the focus of the current chapter, particularly the intersectionality between these three groups.

Communication is a human right (McLeod, 2018; Servaes, 2017) and is enshrined in Article 19 of the Universal Declaration of Human Rights:

> Everyone has the right to freedom of opinion and expression; this right includes freedom to hold opinions without interference and to seek, receive and impart information and ideas through any media and regardless of frontiers. (United Nations, 1948)

Article 19 is for all people, regardless of their age, status, ability, or communicative capacity, not just a right for people who can communicate effectively within their dominant culture. The right to "freedom of opinion and expression" and rights and freedoms "without distinction of … language" permeate most of the subsequent United Nations Conventions and Declarations. For example, Article 21 of the Convention on the Rights of Persons with Disabilities (United Nations, 2006) focuses on the communication rights of people with disabilities:

> Freedom of expression and opinion, and access to information.
>
> States Parties shall take all appropriate measures to ensure that persons with disabilities can exercise the right to freedom of expression and opinion, including the freedom to seek, receive and impart information and ideas on an equal basis with others and through all forms of communication of their choice, as defined in article 2 of the present Convention, including by:

a) Providing information intended for the general public to persons with disabilities in accessible formats and technologies appropriate to different kinds of disabilities in a timely manner and without additional cost;

b) Accepting and facilitating the use of sign languages, Braille, augmentative and alternative communication, and all other accessible means, modes and formats of communication of their choice by persons with disabilities in official interactions;

c) Urging private entities that provide services to the general public, including through the Internet, to provide information and services in accessible and usable formats for persons with disabilities;

d) Encouraging the mass media, including providers of information through the Internet, to make their services accessible to persons with disabilities;

e) Recognizing and promoting the use of sign languages. (United Nations, 2006, Article 21)

Children's communication rights are outlined in Articles 2, 12, 13, 29, 30, and 40 of the Convention on the Rights of the Child (United Nations, 1989). Articles 12 and 13 relate to freedom of opinion and expression:

> Article 12. 1. States Parties shall assure to the child who is capable of forming his or her own views the right to express those views freely in all matters affecting the child, the views of the child being given due weight in accordance with the age and maturity of the child…
>
> Article 13. 1. The child shall have the right to freedom of expression; this right shall include freedom to seek, receive and impart information and ideas of all kinds, regardless of frontiers, either orally, in writing or in print, in the form of art, or through any other media of the child's choice. (United Nations, 1989)

Article 40 includes "To have the free assistance of an interpreter if the child cannot understand or speak the language used" (United Nations, 1989). Similarly, the Universal Declaration on Cultural Diversity states, "All persons have therefore the right to express themselves and to create and disseminate their work in the language of their choice, and particularly in their mother tongue" (Article 5, UNESCO, 2001). Articles 13, 14, and 16 of the Declaration on the Rights of Indigenous Peoples support the revitalization, use, development, and transmission of "language, oral traditions, philosophies, writing systems and literatures" (United Nations, 2007).

Communication for All

The call for SDG18—Communication for All—is relevant to the three main groups of people whose voices are particularly marginalized not only because it is articulated in human rights conventions and declarations but also because these people make up a large portion of society. First, the prevalence of communication disability is high (McLeod, 2019). In high-income countries (HIC) such as the U.S., the prevalence of adults with speech, language, and voice disabilities was 9.9% (Stransky et al., 2018) and the U.S. Department of Education (2015) indicated that 16.4% of children with disabilities aged 6–21 years received services for primary speech or language impairments. In Australia, over a quarter (27.4%) of people with a disability experience a communication disability (Australian Bureau of Statistics, 2017a). In low- and middle-income countries (LMICs), health conditions linked to communication disability, such as oral cancer (Moore et al., 2000), may be higher than in high-income countries. A quarter (25%) of children across 63 LMICs are suspected of having developmental delay (Gil et al., 2020), and communication disability is frequently noted. However, communication disability often is invisible (McLeod et al., 2010; McLeod & McLeod, 2021). For example, children with primary communication disability (that is not caused by a medical condition) were not counted in a study of developmental disabilities in young children across 195 countries (Olusanya et al., 2018). The World Report on Disability documented that approximately 15% of the world's population have a disability; however, they indicated, "people with ... communication difficulties, and other impairments may not be included in these estimates [of disability], despite encountering difficulties in daily life" (World Health Organization and the World Bank, 2011, p. 22).

The second group of people whose voices are often marginalized are children; however, in 2016 children comprised 26% of the world's population, with a lower proportion in high-income countries (17%) and a higher proportion in low-income countries (43%) (World Bank Group, 2017). It is possible that children may form a larger part of society in the current decade since the COVID-19 pandemic primarily has impacted the health outcomes of adults (UN News, 2020). The third group of people whose voices are often marginalized are those who are multilingual or who do not speak/understand/read/write the dominant language of their community. There are 7139 known languages in the world with the most commonly spoken first languages being: Chinese, Spanish, English, Hindi, and

Arabic (Eberhard et al., 2021). Most people in the world speak more than one language and English is one of the most common second languages. Over 300 languages are spoken in countries such as the U.S. and Australia. In the U.S., 20.8% of the population speaks a language other than English at home with 12.9% speaking Spanish (Ryan, 2013). In Australia, 22.2% speaks a language other than English at home with the most commonly spoken languages after English being: Mandarin, Arabic, Cantonese, Italian, and Vietnamese (Australian Bureau of Statistics, 2017b). In Australia, a strong predictor of migrants' self-sufficiency is competence in the dominant language of the country (Blake et al., 2019) and multilingual speakers who were competent in English have higher employment, education, and income than monolingual English-speaking Australians (Blake et al., 2018). Although multilingualism has many individual, social, economic, political, and cognitive benefits (Bialystok; 2011; Pietiläinen, 2011) governments play a major role in supporting or denying communication rights relating to language and culture. For example, Simon-Cereijido (2018) outlined the impact of eliminating bilingual public education in California in 1998 (Proposition 227). Intersectionality between people with communication disabilities, children, and people who do not speak/understand/read/write the dominant language of their community will be the focus of the remainder of the chapter.

Communication for Multilingual Children

The acquisition of speech and language underpins cognitive and social development from the moment children are born. The majority of the world's children will acquire two or more languages (Tucker, 1998), each of which plays an important and unique role in facilitating engagement and interaction in different social and educational contexts. For the purpose of this chapter, multilingualism is defined as: "the ability to comprehend and/or produce two or more languages in oral, manual, or written form with at least a basic level of functional proficiency or use, regardless of the age at which the languages were learned" (International Expert Panel on Multilingual Children's Speech, 2012, p. 1). This broad definition of multilingualism encompasses spoken, written, and signed languages.

Children may become multilingual either simultaneously or sequentially. Simultaneous language learners receive frequent exposure to two or more languages regularly from birth or soon after birth (Paradis et al., 2011). Some authors (de Houwer, 1995; Paradis et al., 2011) have suggested that for a language to be considered a first language, children should have begun learning it before 3 years old. By this age, most children will have developed an understanding of the phonological, grammatical, and syntactic structures of a language, as well as an increasingly expansive vocabulary (McLeod, 2010; McLeod & Crowe, 2018). Sequential multilingualism occurs when additional languages are learned after the establishment of a first language (Tabors, 1997). In addition, subtractive multilingualism can occur, meaning that one or more languages is lost (or competency diminishes) as the child grows older. Subtractive multilingualism can occur when the children begin speaking a language that is not the dominant language of the society in which they live and then make what is referred to as a "language shift" to the language of the dominant culture (Veltman, 1983). There are many known benefits to maintaining the use of multiple languages, particularly relating to cognitive and metalinguistic competence, including increased attentional control, working memory, and abstract and symbolic representation skills (Adesope et al., 2010, Barac et al., 2014; Bialystok, 2011; Gathercole et al., 2010; Nguyen & Astington, 2014). Therefore, it is important that children are provided with opportunities and support to maintain multiple languages if they or their families wish to.

Knowledge regarding patterns of language acquisition, use, and maintenance among multilingual children in early childhood is essential for planning and implementing educational services which can support multilingual children's language development. In this chapter, we will draw upon international examples to describe and explore multilingualism for children with speech, language, hearing, and communication needs.

Multilingualism Among Children in English-Dominant Contexts

The world is becoming increasingly mobile, and, therefore, communities which were built upon a foundation of English dominance and monolingualism now face the challenge of providing health and education services to diverse multilingual populations. For example, in the U.S., 20.7% of the population over five years of age speak a language other than English at home (Ryan, 2013); in Canada, 20.6% of people speak a language other than English or French at home; and 17.5% speak at least two languages at home (Statistics Canada, 2012).

In Australia, almost one quarter of the population over the age of five years speak a language other than English at home (Australian Bureau of

Statistics, 2017b). Given that census data only include those over 5 years of age, a population study of 5107 Australian children from zero to five years was examined to identify the linguistic diversity of these children (Verdon et al., 2014a). The study revealed linguistic diversity with 15.3% of children speaking a language other than English at home by 4 to 5 years of age and no major second language identified. Children in the study spoke a range of 36 languages and individual children spoke up to 3 languages other than English (Verdon et al., 2014a). A second large-scale study, known as *Footprints in Time: The Longitudinal Study of Indigenous Children*, was undertaken to consider the linguistic diversity of Australia's Indigenous children. The children in the study were found to speak up to eight languages (McLeod, Verdon et al., 2014). In total, and 21.6% spoke more than one language at 3–5 years of age, and 19.3% spoke an Indigenous language (Verdon & McLeod, 2015). These studies show that, within English-dominant contexts, a large number of children are speaking multiple languages, and, therefore, continued support both at home and in educational settings is required to achieve competency in the languages they speak, not simply in the dominant language, English.

Language Maintenance Across Early Childhood

Children's ability to maintain speaking multiple languages when immersed in an English-dominant context across early childhood has been investigated (Verdon et al., 2014b; Verdon & McLeod, 2015). Longitudinal data from 4252 Australian children revealed that, while 86.6% of children were able to maintain speaking multiple languages across early childhood, the remaining children made a language shift to English by 4–5 years of age. Additionally, it was found that language maintenance patterns varied among different linguistic groups. For example, Arabic-speaking children in Australia were found to have higher rates of maintenance (86.0%) across early childhood, while Italian-speaking children were found to experience a far greater language shift toward English, with 48.0% of children who were learning Italian from birth speaking only English by 4–5 years of age (Verdon et al., 2014b). Among Australian Indigenous children, high rates of language maintenance were found with 76.3% of children exposed to an Indigenous language from birth continuing to speak it at 3–5 years of age (Verdon & McLeod, 2015).

The *International Classification of Functioning, Disability and Health: Children and Youth Version* (World Health Organization, 2007) advocates consideration of the whole child in context when planning for and supporting their health and wellbeing. Therefore, environmental and personal factors associated with language maintenance among multilingual children from around the world have been examined. Factors differed between Indigenous and non-Indigenous populations. Among non-Indigenous populations in Australia, Singapore, and the U.S., it has been reported that the factors related to language maintenance among children include

- exposure to languages in the home environment,
- number of generations since migration,
- language status,
- presence of speech, language, and communication needs,
- influence of peers and older siblings,
- type of childcare, and
- level of understanding of the needs of culturally and linguistically diverse children from early childhood education settings (Dixon et al., 2012; Verdon et al., 2014b; Tran, McLeod et al., 2021; Tran, Wang et al., 2021; Wong Fillmore, 1991).

Among Indigenous children in Australia, Bolivia, Canada, and Ecuador, researchers have identified that the factors associated with language maintenance include

- parent/caregiver use of the language,
- gender of the child,
- amount and type of language input at home, at school, and in the community,
- level of school-based education,
- use of Indigenous languages in educational settings, and
- residence in a remote community (Burnaby & Beaujot, 1986; Hornberger & King, 1996; Simpson & Wigglesworth, 2008; Verdon & McLeod, 2015).

The studies mentioned above included typically developing children as well as children with speech, language, and communication needs (SLCN). In the following sections, specific considerations for children with SLCN are discussed.

Communication for Children with Communication Disability

Communication disability in children is also known as "speech, language and communication needs (SLCN)" and includes any difficulty in a person's "ability to receive, send, process, and comprehend concepts or verbal, nonverbal and graphic symbol systems" (American Speech-Language-Hearing Association, 1993, p. 1). Difficulties may range in severity from mild to profound and can be either developmental (e.g., language delay) or acquired (e.g., from a traumatic brain injury) of known (e.g., hearing loss) or unknown causes. SLCN can affect a person's speech (articulation or phonology), language (semantics, morphology, syntax, discourse), fluency (stuttering), voice, or social communication.

There are a high number of children with SLCN across the world (McLeod, McAlister et al., 2014). A systematic review of the literature undertaken by Law et al. (2000) found that the prevalence of children with SLCN (within studies published in English conducted across the world) ranged from 2.0% to 24.6%, depending on the assessment measure and the type of impairment. A large-scale longitudinal study of over 14,500 school-aged Australian children demonstrated that SLCN were more prevalent than most other areas of learning need (e.g., behavior, vision, intellectual impairment, physical/medical, and speaking English as an additional language) with the exception of learning disabilities (McLeod & McKinnon, 2007). Another study considering parent- and teacher-reported concern of 1205 preschool-aged children showed that children's expressive speech and language skills were more likely to be identified as areas of concern than any other area (e.g., behavior, gross and fine motor, school readiness skills) (McLeod et al., 2018).

A range of risk and protective factors relate to children's SLCN. For example, in a population study of 4983 Australian 4- to 5-year-olds, risk and protective factors were identified for parent-reported concern about expressive and receptive language skills, receptive vocabulary skills, and attendance at speech and language therapy services. Risk factors across these areas included being male, having ongoing hearing problems, and having a reactive temperament (Harrison & McLeod, 2010). In contrast, having a more sociable temperament and higher levels of maternal wellbeing were protective factors (Harrison & McLeod, 2010). While child factors (e.g., sex and hearing loss) and maternal factors (e.g., maternal education and wellbeing) are commonly reported, fewer studies have previously considered temperament or self-regulation as relating to SLCN (Conture et al., 2013). Having parents who spoke a language other than English in the home was a risk factor for receptive vocabulary skills in English, but protective for expressive speech and language difficulties (in any language), and for attendance at speech and language therapy services.

Having SLCN in childhood can impact children's educational, social, and occupational outcomes. While natural history studies indicate that not all people with SLCN continue to have difficulties throughout life (Law et al., 2000; Roulstone et al., 2009), others have ongoing difficulties. For example, a review by McCormack et al. (2009) identified that many people with a history of speech impairment were reported to have ongoing difficulties: learning to read/reading, learning to write/writing, focusing attention/thinking, calculating, speaking, writing messages, holding a conversation, being mobile, undertaking self-care, relating with persons in authority, having informal relationships with friends and peers, having relationships with parents and siblings, undertaking school education, and acquiring, keeping, and terminating a job. These difficulties were often reported in childhood, but some studies have documented ongoing difficulties into adolescence and adulthood (e.g., Felsenfeld et al., 1994; Johnson et al., 2010; Lewis et al., 2015).

Communication for Multilingual Children with Communication Disability

Children who speak more than one language may (or may not) have SLCN, regardless of the number of languages they speak. The presence of SLCN is not a result of being multilingual; rather, it is because they are having difficulties in their first (and subsequent) language(s). Therefore, it is important to consider children's speech and language skills using a 2 × 2 quadrant (see Table 7.1). The development of this quadrant was informed by the work of McLeod et al. (2016), who examined the skills and outcomes for 3240 Australian children both with and without SLCN at ages 4–5 years, 6–7 years, and 8–9 years. They found that at 4–5 years, there was minimal evidence of "double delay" (Paradis, 2010, p. 237); predominantly that multilingual children with SLCN knew significantly fewer English vocabulary items but performed equally well or better than English-only children with SLCN on measures of school readiness (i.e., early numeracy, literacy, and fine motor skills). By 6–7 and 8–9 years, the gap closed: the defining factor regarding their outcomes at school was

Table 7.1 Quadrant for the comparison of monolingual versus multilingual children with typical speech, language, and communication versus children with speech, language, and communication needs (SLCN)

	Monolingual	*Multilingual*
Typical speech, language, and communication	Monolingual children with typical speech, language, and communication	Multilingual children with typical speech, language, and communication skills
Speech, language, and communication needs (SLCN)	Monolingual children with SLCN	Multilingual children with SLCN

Note: The shaded area indicates that McLeod et al. (2016) demonstrated that children's academic outcomes were not impacted by multilingualism. They were impacted by whether or not the children had been identified with SLCN. There was no evidence of "double disability"

their speech and language competency at 4–5 years. The multilingual children (+/-SLCN) had similar language and literacy, mathematical thinking, and social skills to those who only spoke English (+/-SLCN). Outcomes at school (when 6–7 and 8–9 years) in the areas of literacy, numeracy, and behavior were more related to whether or not children had SLCN at 4–5 years of age rather than the children's multilingual status, demonstrating that it is the presence of a SLCN that negatively impacted children's outcomes at school, not their multilingualism.

Multilingual Children with Hearing Loss

Many children with hearing loss also develop and learn languages within multilingual communities (Crowe & McLeod, 2014). Due to the language learning difficulties associated with childhood hearing loss, parents and professionals consider how children with hearing loss will communicate very early in their development (Hardonk et al., 2010). These decisions relate to which communication modes and spoken or signed languages may best suit the child, the family, and the child's participation in their environment (Crowe, Fordham et al., 2014; Crowe, McLeod et al., 2014). Communication mode describes the modality in which communication occurs and may include:

- oral: speech and listening (e.g., spoken languages such as English, Arabic, and Cantonese),

- manual: visual communication through the air (e.g., signed languages), or
- mixed: speech and listening + visual communication (e.g., cued speech).

Limited information is available concerning the ways in which young children with hearing loss communicate and their extent of multilingualism (Leigh & Crowe, 2015). Among U.S. preschool and school-aged children with hearing loss, English has been identified as the most frequently used language at home (82%), followed by Spanish (22%) and American Sign Language (6%), indicating that some of these children are multilingual (Gallaudet Research Institute, 2011). Mahon et al. (2011) reported that 28% of 147 children who received cochlear implants at one center in London were from multilingual families where English was an additional language, a figure that is reflective of the demography of all children in London. Crowe et al. (2012) reported that, for a population-based sample of 3-year-old Australian children with hearing loss, the majority of children used oral communication (75%), with fewer using mixed (24%) or manual (1%) communication. In the home environment, 12.7% were multilingual, whereas 19.9% of their mothers and 21.2% of their fathers were multilingual. The most frequently reported spoken language used by Australian children with hearing loss was English (94%) followed by Arabic (4.5%), Cantonese (2.3%), Vietnamese (1.5%), and Spanish (1.0%) (Crowe et al., 2012). Guiberson (2013) described a cohort of 71 parents of Spanish children with hearing loss. Within this cohort, 38% of parents had chosen to raise their children using more than one spoken language.

The availability of universal newborn hearing screening in many high-income countries means that the parents of many children with hearing loss must make decision about how their children will communicate long before the exact impact of the hearing loss on communication can be accurately determined. These are decisions that may be re-evaluated as their children develop and more is known about their communication strengthens and difficulties (Young, 2002). For example, families may initially choose to speak with their child in Spanish and English but may consider that the addition of sign language may facilitate greater communication in the early years. Parents' decisions about their children's communication (i.e., communication mode, language choice, and multilingualism) have been reported to be influenced by many factors, including audiological characteristics, child and family preferences, advice from professionals, and maximizing future academic and vocational potential (for review, see Crowe et al., 2014). There are anecdotal reports that spoken language multilingualism may be actively discouraged by professionals working with the families of children with hearing loss (e.g., Waltzman et al., 2003). However, there is still no clear evidence as to which communication strategy will lead to the best outcomes for any child with hearing loss (Spencer & Marschark, 2010).

Supporting Communication for Multilingual Children with Communication Disability

The development and maintenance of languages among children promotes a strong sense of self and cultural identity (Puig, 2010), which in turn has many cognitive and social benefits (Adesope et al., 2010). Conversely, the loss of languages may negatively impact upon family communication, the transmission of cultural wisdom and esteem at both the community and individual level (Wong Fillmore, 1991). Therefore, it is important that services be provided to support multilingual children in their acquisition and maintenance of languages.

To be effective in supporting multilingual children's development, it is essential that health and education professionals engage in culturally competent practice, that is, practice that "acknowledges and incorporates—at all levels—the importance of culture, assessment of cross-cultural relations, vigilance toward the dynamics that result from cultural differences, expansion of cultural knowledge, and adaptation of services to meet culturally unique needs" (Betancourt et al., 2003, p. 294). To guide professionals' holistic consideration of the needs of the children and families with whom they work, Verdon et al. (2016) developed a set of six principles for culturally competent practice. These six principles are:

1. Identification of culturally appropriate and mutually motivating therapy goals
2. Knowledge of languages and culture
3. Use of culturally appropriate resources
4. Consideration of the cultural, social and political context
5. Consultation with families and communities
6. Collaboration with other professionals. (Verdon et al., 2016, p. 81)

Each of these concepts is expanded in the following sections.

Appropriate Intervention Targets

A position paper by the International Expert Panel on Multilingual Children's Speech (2012) stated that children have the right "to communicate effectively and intelligibly in the languages spoken within their families and communities, in the context of developing their cultural identities" (p. 2). Therefore, it is essential that all stakeholders—including parents, professionals working with children, and the children themselves—be consulted to develop speech, language, and communication goals that meet children's individual social, cultural, and academic needs (McLeod, Baker et al., 2017).

Professional Knowledge, Training, and Preparation

Specialist training of health and education professionals to develop the ability to work in culturally competent ways with multilingual children and their families is essential (International Expert Panel on Multilingual Children's Speech, 2012). A number of studies investigating practice with multilingual children have cited a lack of multilingual professionals as a major barrier to providing appropriate services for supporting multiple language acquisition and maintenance (Espinosa, 2005; Guiberson & Atkins, 2012; Kritikos, 2003; Williams & McLeod, 2012). However, it has also been acknowledged that, even if the number of multilingual practitioners available was sufficient, they would still not possess knowledge about every culture and language (as well as individual combinations of these) among the children they serve (Verdon et al., 2014). Therefore, the development of cultural competence among professionals is key to the provision of culturally and linguistically appropriate services for multilingual children (Espinosa, 2005; Harry, 1997; Verdon et al., 2014). To increase cultural competence, professionals need to reflect on their own practice and identify their own culture, values, and potential biases, as well as inform themselves about the culture of the children and families with whom they are working. This can be achieved via both pre-service training and professional development courses for working cross-culturally and also through accessing the online resources.

Resources

When speech-language pathologists provide assessments and intervention for multilingual children suspected of having SLCN, narrow, traditional forms of assessment, such as using standardized tests based on English competency, are inappropriate and ineffective for identifying children's true capabilities (McLeod & Verdon, 2014). Rather, contextual and assessment information needs to be collected from numerous sources including parents, teachers, children, and direct assessment (McLeod, Verdon et al., 2017). To facilitate culturally and linguistically appropriate approaches to working with children's with SLCN, a number of resources for supporting multilingual speech and language acquisition in national and international contexts are being developed and shared (e.g., Multilingual Children's Speech website—http://www.csu.edu.au/research/multilingual-speech).

Context

An understanding of the cultural, social, and political context is essential for engaging in culturally competent practice. For example, in some contexts, policies can impede practitioners from supporting children's home languages and may only provide resources for supporting the development of English (Verdon et al., 2015a). It is therefore important that professionals play an active role in lobbying governments, policy makers, and employers to "acknowledge and support the need for culturally competent and safe practices and equip health and education professionals with additional time, funding, and resources in order to provide equitable services for multilingual children" (International Expert Panel on Multilingual Children's Speech, 2012, p. 2).

Working with Families and Communities

In recent decades, an important shift in services for children with SLCN has occurred from a provider-centered model to a family-centered model (Watts Pappas & McLeod, 2009). In order to engage in a family-centered model of practice, early childhood education researchers have emphasized the importance of breaking down cultural barriers and stereotypes between professionals and families from diverse backgrounds (Harry, 1997). Encouragingly, it has been found that, even if parents' and early childhood professionals' ethnicity and beliefs regarding child-rearing differ, children can still achieve positive social and cognitive outcomes in early childhood education and care settings as long as sensitive and stimulating care is provided (Burchinal & Cryer, 2004). When working with multilingual children, culturally sensitive practice can be facilitated by spending time with families and gaining an understanding of needs, goals, and aspirations for their children so that professionals and families can be on the same page when moving forward with the provision of services (Verdon et al., 2016). Parents should be acknowledged as the experts on their own child and therefore should feel valued and heard as vital collaborative partners in the provision of services for multilingual children (Verdon et al., 2015b).

Interdisciplinary Collaboration

Given that language permeates all areas of children's development, an interdisciplinary approach by health and education professionals is key for holistic consideration of children's needs in order to achieve the best possible outcomes in all domains of their lives. Collaboration among professionals including educators, speech-language pathologists, audiologists, psychologists, occupational therapists, social workers, medical personnel, interpreters, cultural mediators, educational support staff, and others may be necessary in order to facilitate children to fulfill their potential as competent communicators and active participants in their communities.

As outlined above, many multilingual children living in English-dominant contexts experience a language shift to English monolingualism during early childhood when entering educational settings where English is the language of instruction. Thus, educational environments, including both early childhood education and care settings and formal school settings play a key role in the support of language maintenance for both typically developing multilingual children and those with SLCN. Collaboration between education and health professionals and interpreters and bicultural support workers can aid in bridging cultural and linguistic barriers to facilitate both the maintenance of home language and culture in conjunction with supporting children to acquire the skills necessary to be successful in English-based educational environments.

Conclusion

In summary, this chapter has presented an intersectional case study of supporting communication for multilingual children with communication disability. There are numerous social and academic benefits to supporting both the maintenance of home languages and culture in addition to supporting children to be competent communicators in the dominant language of a society. While many multilingual children are able to acquire languages either simultaneously or sequentially without difficulty, some multilingual children have SLCN. Interdisciplinary support can holistically cater for children's individual needs in ways that are culturally appropriate, motivating, and accessible to their families. Interdisciplinary practice has the ability to cross boundaries of languages, cultures, and professions by drawing on the strengths of professionals from a range of domains. In doing so these children can take their place as communicators in society to be supported to fulfill their potential as multilingual speakers and realize their communication rights.

References

Adesope, O. O., Lavin, T., Thompson, T., & Underleider, C. (2010). A systematic review and meta-analysis of the cognitive correlates of bilingualism. *Review of Educational Research, 80*(2), 207–245.

American Speech-Language-Hearing Association. (1993). *Definitions of communication disorders and variations.* http://www.asha.org/policy/RP1993-00208/

Australian Bureau of Statistics. (2017a). *4430.0—Disability, ageing and careers, Australia: Summary of findings, 2015: Australians living with communication disability.* http://www.abs.gov.au/AUSSTATS/abs@.nsf/Lookup/4430.0Main+Features872015?OpenDocument

Australian Bureau of Statistics. (2017b). *Quickstats.* http://www.abs.gov.au/websitedbs/D3310114.nsf/Home/2016%20QuickStats

Barac, R., Bialystok, E., Castro, D. C., & Sanchez, M. (2014). The cognitive development of young dual language learners: A critical review. *Early Childhood Research Quarterly, 29*(4), 699–714.

Betancourt, J. R., Green, A. R., Carrillo, J. E., & Ananeh-Firempong, O. (2003). Defining cultural competence: A practical framework for addressing racial/ethnic disparities in health and health care. *Public Health Reports, 118*(4), 293–302.

Bialystok, E. (2011). Reshaping the mind: The benefits of bilingualism. *Canadian Journal of Experimental Psychology, 65*(4), 229–235.

Blake, H. L., Bennetts Kneebone, L., & McLeod, S. (2019). The impact of oral English proficiency on humanitarian migrants' experiences of settling in Australia. *International Journal of Bilingual Education and Bilingualism, 22*(6), 689–705. https://doi.org/10.1080/13670050.2017.1294557

Blake, H. L., McLeod, S., Verdon, S., & Fuller, G. (2018). The relationship between spoken English proficiency and participation in higher education, employment and income from two Australian censuses. *International Journal of Speech-Language Pathology, 20*(2), 202–215. https://doi.org/10.1080/17549507.2016.1229031

Burchinal, M. R., & Cryer, D. (2004). Diversity, child care quality, and developmental outcomes. *Early Childhood Research Quarterly, 18*(4), 401–426.

Burnaby, B., & Beaujot, R. (1986). *The use of Aboriginal languages in Canada: An analysis of 1981 census data*. Social Trends Analysis Directorate and Native Citizens Directorate, Department of the Secretary of State.

Conture, E. G., Kelly, E. M., & Walden, T. A. (2013). Temperament, speech and language: An overview. *Journal of Communication Disorders, 46*(2), 125–142.

Crowe, K., Fordham, L., McLeod, S., & Ching, T. Y. C. (2014). 'Part of our world': Influences on caregiver decisions about communication choices for children with hearing loss. *Deafness and Education International, 16*(2), 61–85.

Crowe, K., & McLeod, S. (2014). A systematic review of cross-linguistic and multilingual speech and language outcomes for children with hearing loss. *International Journal of Bilingual Education and Bilingualism, 17*(3), 287–309.

Crowe, K., McLeod, S., & Ching, T. Y. C. (2012). The cultural and linguistic diversity of 3-year-old children with hearing loss. *Journal of Deaf Studies and Deaf Education, 17*(4), 421–438.

Crowe, K., McLeod, S., McKinnon, D. H., & Ching, T. Y. C. (2014). Speech, sign, or multilingualism for children with hearing loss: Quantitative insights into caregivers' decision-making. *Language, Speech, and Hearing Services in Schools, 45*, 234–247.

de Houwer, A. (1995). Bilingual language acquisition. In P. Fletcher & B. MacWhinney (Eds.), *The handbook of child language* (pp. 219–250). Blackwell.

Dixon, L. Q., Wu, S., & Daraghmeh, A. (2012). Profiles in bilingualism: Factors influencing kindergarteners' language proficiency. *Early Childhood Education Journal, 40*(1), 25–34.

Eberhard, D. M., Simons, G. F., & Fennig, C. D. (2021). *Ethnologue: Languages of the world* (24th ed.) SIL International. http://www.ethnologue.com

Espinosa, L. M. (2005). Curriculum and assessment considerations for young children from culturally, linguistically, and economically diverse backgrounds. *Psychology in the Schools, 42*(8), 837–853.

Felsenfeld, S., Broen, P. A., & McGue, M. (1994). A 28-year follow up of adults with a history of moderate phonological disorder: Educational and occupational results. *Journal of Speech and Hearing Research, 37*, 1341–1353.

Gallaudet Research Institute. (2011). *Regional and national summary report of data from the 2009–10 annual survey of deaf and hard of hearing children and youth.* Gallaudet Research Institute, Gallaudet University.

Gathercole, V. C. M., Thomas, E. M., Jones, L., Guasch, N. V., Young, N., & Hughes, E. K. (2010). Cognitive effects of bilingualism: Digging deeper for the contributions of language dominance, linguistic knowledge, socio-economic status and cognitive abilities. *International Journal of Bilingual Education and Bilingualism, 13*(5), 617–664.

Gil, J. D., Ewerling, F., Ferreira, L. Z., & Barros, A. J. (2020). Early childhood suspected developmental delay in 63 low- and middle-income countries: Large within- and between-country inequalities documented using national health surveys. *Journal of Global Health, 10*(1), 010427. https://doi.org/10.7189/jogh.10.010427

Guiberson, M. (2013). Survey of Spanish parents of children who are deaf or hard of hearing: Decision making factors associated with communication modality and bilingualism. *American Journal of Audiology, 22*(1), 105–119.

Guiberson, M., & Atkins, J. (2012). Speech-language pathologists' preparation, practices, and perspectives on serving culturally and linguistically diverse children. *Communication Disorders Quarterly, 33*(3), 169–180.

Hardonk, S., Bosteels, S., Desnerck, G., Loots, G., Van Hove, G., Van Kerschaver, E., Vanroelen, C., & Louckx, F. (2010). Pediatric cochlear implantation: A qualitative study of parental decision-making processes in Flanders. *Belgium. American Annals of the Deaf, 155*(3), 339–352.

Harrison, L. J., & McLeod, S. (2010). Risk and protective factors associated with speech and language impairment in a nationally representative sample of 4- to 5-year-old children. *Journal of Speech, Language, and Hearing Research, 53*(2), 508–529.

Harry, B. (1997). Leaning forward or bending over backwards: Cultural reciprocity in working with families. *Journal of Early Intervention, 21*(1), 62–72.

Hornberger, N. H., & King, K. A. (1996). Language revitalisation in the Andes: Can the schools reverse language shift? *Journal of Multilingual and Multicultural Development, 17*(6), 427–441.

International Expert Panel on Multilingual Children's Speech. (2012). *Multilingual children with speech sound disorders: Position paper.* Research Institute for Professional Practice, Learning and Education (RIPPLE), Charles Sturt University. http://www.csu.edu.au/research/multilingual-speech/position-paper

Johnson, C. J., Beitchman, J. H., & Brownlie, E. B. (2010). Twenty-year follow-up of children with and without speech-language impairments: Family, educational, occupational, and quality of life outcomes. *American Journal of Speech-Language Pathology, 19*(1), 51–65.

Kritikos, E. P. (2003). Speech-language pathologists' beliefs about language assessment of bilingual/bicultural individuals. *American Journal of Speech-Language Pathology, 12*(1), 73–91.

Law, J., Boyle, J., Harris, F., Harkness, A., & Nye, C. (2000). Prevalence and natural history of primary speech and language delay: Findings from a systematic review of the literature. *International Journal of Language and Communication Disorders, 35*(2), 165–188.

Leigh, G., & Crowe, K. (2015). Responding to cultural and linguistic diversity among deaf and hard of hearing learners. In H. Knoors & M. Marschark (Eds.), *Teaching deaf learners* (pp. 69–92). Oxford University Press.

Lewis, B. A., Freebairn, L., Tag, J., Ciesla, A. A., Iyengar, S. K., Stein, C. M., & Taylor, H. G. (2015). Adolescent outcomes of children with early speech sound disorders with and without language impairment. *American Journal of Speech-Language Pathology, 24*(2), 150–163.

Mahon, M., Vickers, D., McCarthy, K., Barker, R., Merritt, R., Szagun, G., Mann, W., & Rajput, K. (2011). Cochlear-implanted children from homes where English is an additional language: Findings from a recent audit in one London centre. *Cochlear Implants International, 12*(2), 105–113.

McCormack, J., McLeod, S., McAllister, L., & Harrison, L. J. (2009). A systematic review of the association between childhood speech impairment and participation across the lifespan. *International Journal of Speech-Language Pathology, 11*(2), 155–170.

McLeod, S. (2010). Laying the foundations for multilingual acquisition: An international overview of speech acquisition. In M. Cruz-Ferreira (Ed.), *Multilingual norms* (pp. 53–71). Peter Lang Publishing.

McLeod, S. (2018). Communication rights: Fundamental human rights for all. *International Journal of Speech-Language Pathology, 20*(1), 3–11. https://doi.org/10.1080/17549507.2018.1428687

McLeod, S., Baker, E., McCormack, J., Wren, Y., Roulstone, S., Crowe, K., Masso, S., White, P., & Howland, C. (2017). Cluster-randomized controlled trial evaluating the effectiveness of computer-assisted intervention delivered by educators for children with speech sound disorders. *Journal of Speech, Language, and Hearing Research, 60*(7), 1891–1910. https://doi.org/10.1044/2017_JSLHR-S-16-0385

McLeod, S., & Crowe, K. (2018). Children's consonant acquisition in 27 languages: A cross-linguistic review. *American Journal of Speech-Language Pathology, 27*(4), 1546–1571. https://doi.org/10.1044/2018_AJSLP-17-0100

McLeod, S., Crowe, K., McCormack, J., White, P., Wren, Y., Baker, E., Masso, S., & Roulstone, S. (2018). Preschool children's communication, motor and social development: Parents' and educators' concerns. *International Journal of Speech-Language Pathology, 20*(4), 468–482. https://doi.org/10.1080/17549507.2017.1309065

McLeod, S., Harrison, L. J., Whiteford, C., & Walker, S. (2016). Multilingualism and speech-language competence in early childhood: Impact on academic and social-emotional outcomes at school. *Early Childhood Research Quarterly, 34*, 53–66. https://doi.org/10.1016/j.ecresq.2015.08.005

McLeod, S., McAllister, L., McCormack, J., & Harrison, L. J. (2014). Applying the World Report on Disability to children's communication. *Disability and Rehabilitation, 36*(18), 1518–1528.

McLeod, S., & McKinnon, D. H. (2007). The prevalence of communication disorders compared with other learning needs in 14,500 primary and secondary school students. *International Journal of Language and Communication Disorders, 42*(S1), 37–59.

McLeod, S., & McLeod, J. (2021, in press). Communication rights moderated through hierarchies of disability and childhood. In S. Meyers, M. McCloskey, G. Petri (Eds.). *Hierarchies of disability human rights*. Routledge.

McLeod, S., Press, F., & Phelan, C. (2010). The (in)visibility of children with communication impairment in Australian health, education, and disability legislation and policies. *Asia Pacific Journal of Speech, Language, and Hearing, 13*(1), 67–75. https://doi.org/10.1179/136132810805335173

McLeod, S., & Verdon, S. (2014). A review of 30 speech assessments in 19 languages other than English. *American Journal of Speech-Language Pathology, 23*(4), 708–723.

McLeod, S., Verdon, S., & Bennetts Kneebone, L. (2014). Celebrating Indigenous Australian children's speech and language competence. *Early Childhood Research Quarterly, 29*(2), 118–131.

McLeod, S., Verdon, S., & International Expert Panel on Multilingual Children's Speech. (2017). Tutorial: Speech assessment for multilingual children who do not speak the same language(s) as the speech-language pathologist. *American Journal of Speech-Language Pathology, 26*(3), 691–708. https://doi.org/10.1044/2017_AJSLP-15-0161

Moore, S., Johnson, N., Pierce, A., & Wilson, D. (2000). The epidemiology of mouth cancer: A review of global incidence. *Oral Diseases, 6*, 65–74. https://doi.org/10.1111/j.1601-0825.2000.tb00104.x

Nguyen, T.-K., & Astington, J. W. (2014). Reassessing the bilingual advantage in theory of mind and its cognitive underpinnings. *Bilingualism: Language and Cognition, 17*, 396–409.

Olusanya, B. O., Davis, A. C., Wertlieb, D., Boo, N. Y., Nair, M. K. C., Halpern, R., Kuper, H., Breinbauer, C., de Vries, P. J., Gladstone, M., Halfon, N., Kancherla, V., Mulaudzi, M. C., Kakooza-Mwesige, A., Ogbo, F. A., Olusanya, J. O., Williams, A. N., Wright, S. M., Manguerra, H., et al. (2018).

Developmental disabilities among children younger than 5 years in 195 countries and territories, 1990–2016: A systematic analysis for the Global Burden of Disease Study 2016. *The Lancet Global Health, 6*(10), e1100–e1121. https://doi.org/10.1016/S2214-109X(18)30309-7

Paradis, J. (2010). The interface between bilingual development and specific language impairment. *Applied Psycholinguistics, 31*, 227–252.

Paradis, J., Genesee, F., & Crago, M. (2011). *Dual language development and disorders: A handbook on bilingualism and second language learning* (2nd ed.). Paul H. Brookes.

Pietiläinen, J. (2011). Public opinion on useful languages in Europe. *European Journal of Language Policy, 3*(1), 1–14. https://doi.org/10.3828/ejlp.2011.2

Puig, V. I. (2010). Are early intervention services placing home languages and cultures 'at risk'? *Early Childhood Research and Practice, 12*(1), 1–19.

Roulstone, S., Miller, L. L., Wren, Y., & Peters, T. J. (2009). The natural history of speech impairment of 8-year-old children in the Avon longitudinal study of parents and children: Error rates at 2 and 5 years. *International Journal of Speech-Language Pathology, 11*(5), 381–391.

Ruben, R. J. (2000). Redefining the survival of the fittest: Communication disorders in the 21st century. *Laryngoscope, 110*(2 part 1), 241–245.

Ryan, C. (2013). *Language use in the United States: 2011*. US Census Bureau.

Servaes, J. (2017). All human rights are local. The resiliency of social change. In H. Tumber & S. Waisbord (Eds.), *The Routledge companion to media and human rights* (pp. 136–146). Routledge.

Simon-Cereijido, G. (2018). Bilingualism, a human right in times of anxiety: Lessons from California. *International Journal of Speech-Language Pathology, 20*(1), 157–160. https://doi.org/10.1080/17549507.2018.1392610

Simpson, J., & Wigglesworth, G. (2008). *Children's language and multilingualism: Indigenous language and use at home and school*. Continuum.

Spencer, P. E., & Marschark, M. (2010). *Evidence-based practice in educating deaf and hard-of-hearing students*. Oxford University Press.

Statistics Canada. (2012). *Linguistic characteristics of Canadians: Language, 2011 census of population*. (Report 98-314-X2011001). Ottawa, Canada: Minister of Industry, Statistics Canada. http://www12.statcan.gc.ca/census-recensement/2011/as-sa/98-314-x/98-314-x2011001-eng.cfm

Stransky, M. L., Jensen, K. M., & Morris, M. A. (2018). Adults with communication disabilities experience poorer health and healthcare outcomes compared to persons without communication disabilities. *Journal of General Internal Medicine, 33*(12), 2147–2155. https://doi.org/10.1007/s11606-018-4625-1

Tabors, P. O. (1997). *One child, two languages: A guide for preschool educators of children learning English as a second language*. Paul H. Brookes.

Tran, V. H., McLeod, S., Verdon, S., & Wang, C. (2021). Vietnamese-Australian parents: Factors associated with language use and attitudes towards home language maintenance. *Journal of Multilingual and Multicultural Development, Advance online publication.* https://doi.org/10.1080/01434632.2021.1904963

Tran, V. H., Wang, C., McLeod, S., & Verdon, S. (2021). Vietnamese–Australian children's language proficiency and use. *International Journal of Bilingualism, 25*(6), 1735–1763. https://doi.org/10.1177/13670069211034587

Tucker, G. R. (1998). A global perspective on multilingualism and multilingual education. In J. Cenoz & F. Genesee (Eds.), *Beyond bilinguals: Multilingualism and multilingual education* (pp. 3–15). Multilingual Matters.

U.S. Department of Education. (2015). 42nd Annual Report to Congress on the Implementation of the Individuals with Disabilities Education Act, 2020. https://www2.ed.gov/about/reports/annual/osep/2020/parts-b-c/42nd-arc-for-idea.pdf

UN News. (2020): *Startling Disparities in Digital Learning Emerge As COVID-19 spreads: UN Education Agency.* https://news.un.org/en/story/2020/04/1062232 01/05/2021

UNESCO. (2001). *Universal declaration on cultural diversity.* Retrieved from http://portal.unesco.org/en/ev.php-URL_ID=13179&URL_DO=DO_TOPIC&URL_SECTION=201.html

United Nations. (1948). *Universal declaration of human rights.* http://www.un.org/en/universal-declaration-human-rights/

United Nations. (1989). *Convention on the rights of the child.* https://www.unicef.org/crc/

United Nations. (2006). *Convention on the rights of persons with disabilities.* https://www.un.org/development/desa/disabilities/convention-on-the-rights-of-persons-with-disabilities.html

United Nations. (2007). *Declaration on the rights of indigenous peoples.* http://www.ohchr.org/EN/Issues/IPeoples/Pages/Declaration.aspx

Veltman, C. J. (1983). *Language shift in the United States* (Vol. 34). Walter de Gruyter.

Verdon, S., & McLeod, S. (2015). Indigenous language learning and maintenance among young Australian Aboriginal and Torres Strait Islander children. *International Journal of Early Childhood, 47*(1), 153–170.

Verdon, S., McLeod, S., & McDonald, S. (2014). A geographical analysis of speech-language pathology services to support multilingual children. *International Journal of Speech-Language Pathology, 16*(3), 304–316.

Verdon, S., McLeod, S., & Winsler, A. (2014a). Linguistic diversity among Australian children in the first five years of life. *Speech, Language, and Hearing, 17*(4), 196–203.

Verdon, S., McLeod, S., & Winsler, A. (2014b). Language maintenance and loss in a population study of young Australian children. *Early Childhood Research Quarterly, 29*, 168–181.

Verdon, S., McLeod, S., & Wong, S. (2015a). Supporting culturally and linguistically diverse children with speech, language, and communication needs: Overarching principles, individual approaches. *Journal of Communication Disorders, 58*, 74–90.

Verdon, S., McLeod, S., & Wong, S. (2015b). Reconceptualising practice with multilingual children with speech sound disorders: People, practicalities and policy. *International Journal of Language and Communication Disorders, 50*, 48–62.

Verdon, S., Wong, S., & McLeod, S. (2016). Shared knowledge and mutual respect: Enhancing culturally competent practice through collaboration with families and communities. *Child Language Teaching and Therapy, 32*(2), 205–221. https://doi.org/10.1177/0265659015620254

Waltzman, S. B., McConkey Robbins, A., Green, J. E., & Cohen, N. L. (2003). Second oral language capabilities in children with cochlear implants. *Otology and Neurotology, 24*(5), 757–763.

Watts Pappas, N., & McLeod, S. (Eds.). (2009). *Working with families in speech-language pathology*. Plural Publishing.

Williams, C. J., & McLeod, S. (2012). Speech-language pathologists' assessment and intervention practices with multilingual children. *International Journal of Speech-Language Pathology, 14*(3), 292–305.

Wong Fillmore, L. (1991). When learning a second language means losing the first. *Early Childhood Research Quarterly, 6*(3), 323–346.

World Bank Group. (2017). *Population ages 0–14 (% of total)*. https://data.worldbank.org/indicator/SP.POP.0014.TO.ZS?end=2016&start=2016&view=map

World Health Organization. (2007). *International classification of functioning, disability and health: Children and youth version: ICF-CY*. Author.

World Health Organization, & The World Bank. (2011). *World report on disability*. World Health Organization.

Young, A. (2002). Factors affecting communication choice in the first year of life: Assessing and understanding an on-going experience. *Deafness and Education International, 4*(1), 2–11.

Yusha'u, M. J., & Servaes, J. (2021). *The Palgrave Handbook of International Communication and Sustainable Development*. Palgrave Macmillan.

CHAPTER 8

COVID-19, Intimate Partner Violence, and Immigrant Women: SDG 18 and Overcoming Communication Barriers to Attain Goal 5

Satarupa Dasgupta

Abstract Gaining gender parity and empowerment of women across the globe is one of the 17 Sustainable Development Goals (SDGs). Women's equality is an integral aspect of inclusive and sustainable development, and the success of all SDGs depends on the achievement of Goal 5—the attainment of gender equality. Unfortunately, the targeted elimination of many of the structural barriers that restrict women's rights in private and public spheres has halted due to the COVID-19 pandemic. On October 28, 2020, an article in NPR noted that "[w]omen are seeing the fabric of their lives unravel during the coronavirus pandemic … the pandemic is wreaking havoc on households, and women are bearing the brunt of it". Disease outbreaks have traditionally exacerbated gender inequality and increased

S. Dasgupta (✉)
Communication Arts, Ramapo College of New Jersey, Mahwah, NJ, USA
e-mail: sdasgupt@ramapo.edu

J. Servaes, M. J. Yusha'u (eds.), *SDG18 Communicaton for All, Volume 2*, Sustainable Development Goals Series,
https://doi.org/10.1007/978-3-031-19459-7_8

vulnerabilities borne by women, besides derailing hard-won progress. During lockdowns necessitated by the pandemic, women are at greater risk of domestic violence perpetrated by intimate partners and family members. Concurrently, women also suffer from decreased access to violence prevention and support services. Additionally, they are also disproportionately disadvantaged by reduced access to sexual and reproductive health services. Hard-fought gains for women's rights are also under threat across the globe.

Intimate partner violence (IPV) is a serious national concern that has the potential to be exacerbated in scope and impact by the COVID-19 pandemic. Public safety measures adopted during COVID-19—including physical distancing, self-quarantining, and "safer-at-home" mandates intended to prevent widespread infection—decimated economic choices and left many IPV victims trapped in close contact with their abusers. Among immigrant victims of IPV in US, disclosure, support-seeking behavior, and resource uptake were remarkably low in pre-COVID-19 times. Yet, the impact of COVID-19 on intimate partner violence (IPV) support services programs catering to immigrant groups in US is a topic that remains largely unexplored. The current paper delineates the impact of COVID-19 on the support-seeking and service utilization among immigrant victims of IPV living in the US. It incorporates the conceptual framework of intersectionality, which recognizes that women of color experience life and negotiate a pandemic through multiple systems of oppression.

Immigrant women experience the same stressors and trauma of IPV as women born in the US, but they face the added burdens of immigration status and negotiate the challenges of the pandemic differently. The IPV experiences of immigrant women in the US during COVID-19 can be exacerbated by a set of factors that are peculiar to their immigrant status. These may include limited English language proficiency, unique sociocultural and religious norms, changing legal status due to immigration, lack of family support, stigma of IPV, uncertain or undocumented immigration status and threats of deportation as a means of control by the abuser, and increasing social isolation. Despite IPV program growth, service gaps remain and have been magnified by COVID-19. This is especially true for immigrant women who are a marginalized and vulnerable survivor population in the US.

The effects of the COVID-19 pandemic can reverse the limited progress made on gender equality and women's rights globally. For immigrant women in the US the coronavirus outbreak can aggravate existing inequalities besides restricting an already limited access to essential support services across every sphere—from health to economy, to security and social protection. It is essential to create targeted responses to mitigate the impact of the COVID-19 crisis on immigrant women and to ensure that the long-term recovery benefits them and creates a path toward achievement of Goal 5. The chapter expects to add to research on a proposed SDG 18 which will create a framework of accessible communication strategies for all. The latter in turn can precipitate a reimagined IPV service delivery—rooted not only in the traditionalist feminist paradigm but also in the context of intersectionality that strives to address the unique experiences of immigrant battered women. The proposed SDG 18 (Communication for all) can play an important role in overcoming barriers toward attainment of Goal 5 among immigrant women in the US, by highlighting on intersecting issues of displacement and marginalization during and after the pandemic.

Keywords Gender equality • Intimate partner violence • Immigrant women • Pandemic • Crisis communication • Intersectionality

Introduction

Gaining gender parity and empowerment of women across the globe is one of the 17 Sustainable Development Goals (SDGs). The Sustainable Development Goals (SDGs) were launched in 2016 to expand the scope of the Millennium Development Goals generated in 2000 (UN 2030 agenda). Women's equality is an integral aspect of inclusive and sustainable development. The success of all SDGs—including the proposed SDG 18 (Communication for all)—depends on the achievement of Goal 5 which is the attainment of gender equality. SDG 5 which addresses gender equality and empowerment of women is comprehensive and ambitious (United Nations, 2016). SDG 5 emphasizes the need to dissipate the impediments to gender equality, including structural and contextual barriers including economic disparities, social norms, and practices. "Recognized as a core tenet of the 2030 Agenda, gender equality is both a stand-alone goal of sustainable development and a cross-cutting priority for achieving all the SDGs" (United Nations, 2016). However, to make SDG 5 attainable by 2030, appropriate and accessible healthcare services and support services need to be generated. The SDGs are "systemic in nature, complexly interrelated and materialize at the interface between public–private and profit–nonprofit interests" (van Tulder, 2018, p. 36). The guiding principle of the 2030 Agenda insists that no one must be left behind which in itself poses a societal challenge.

Unfortunately, the targeted elimination of many of the structural barriers that restrict women's rights in private and public spheres has been disrupted due to the COVID-19 pandemic. Disease outbreaks have traditionally exacerbated gender inequality and increased vulnerabilities borne by women, besides derailing hard-won progress. During lockdowns necessitated by the pandemic, women are at greater risk of domestic violence perpetrated by intimate partners and family members. Concurrently, women also suffer from decreased access to violence prevention and support services, and sexual and reproductive health services. The pandemic has caused hard-fought gains for women's rights to be under threat across the globe.

Intimate partner violence (IPV) is a serious national concern that has the potential to be exacerbated in scope and impact by the COVID-19 pandemic. Public safety measures adopted during COVID-19—including physical distancing, self-quarantining, and "safer-at-home" mandates intended to prevent widespread infection—decimated economic choices and left many IPV victims trapped in close contact with their abusers. Among immigrant victims of IPV in the US, disclosure, support-seeking behavior, and resource uptake were remarkably low in pre-COVID-19 times. Yet, communication barriers and challenges, and the impact of COVID-19 on intimate partner violence (IPV) support services programs catering to immigrant groups in the US, are topics that remain largely unexplored.

The chapter looks at the incidence of IPV among immigrant populations, pre-pandemic strategies of IPV response including culture-specific support services, and barriers to disclosure and support-seeking among immigrant victims of IPV. For this purpose, the chapter delineates extant literature to gain an understanding of IPV, help-seeking strategies, and service uptake among immigrant victims of violence. The outlined literature also looks at the impact of COVID-19 on IPV victims and repercussions from the pandemic on COVID-19 responses. The chapter delineates the notion of SDG 18 (Communication for all) in reducing the impact of COVID-19 and minimizing communication barriers to improve support-seeking and service utilization among immigrant victims of IPV living in the US. For this purpose, the chapter gauges the importance of remote and technology-based responses in IPV mitigation services and explores the way ahead. In order to explore the concept of SDG 18, it looks at communication frameworks within the context of intersectionality, which recognizes that women of color experience life and negotiate a pandemic through multiple systems of oppression.

The effects of the COVID-19 pandemic can reverse the limited progress made on gender equality and women's rights globally. For immigrant women in the US the coronavirus outbreak can aggravate existing inequalities besides restricting an already limited access to essential support services across every sphere. It is essential to create targeted responses to mitigate the impact of the COVID-19 crisis on immigrant women, and to ensure that the long-term recovery benefits them and creates a path toward achievement of Goal 5. The chapter expects to add to research on a proposed SDG 18 which will create a framework of accessible communication strategies for all. The latter in turn can precipitate a reimagined IPV service delivery—rooted not only in the traditionalist feminist paradigm but also in the context of intersectionality—that strives to address the unique experiences of immigrant battered women. The proposed SDG 18 (Communication for all) can play an important role in overcoming barriers toward attainment of Goal 5 among immigrant women in the US, by highlighting on intersecting issues of displacement and marginalization during and after the pandemic.

Background Information

On April 26, 2020, Garima Kothari, an Indian restaurateur in Jersey City and a finalist for MasterChef India, was battered to death by her husband—an investment banker—who then committed suicide by jumping in the Hudson River. Kothari had opened a restaurant in Jersey City in February 2020, but was forced to close the restaurant approximately a month later due to COVID-19. Kothari was five months pregnant when she was killed. Approximately, a year later in northern New Jersey, Indian IT professional Balaji Rudrawar violently stabbed his wife Aarti to death, before killing himself in another murder suicide incident. Aarti was seven months pregnant when she died.

Garima and Aarti are not isolated cases; they are two of the many immigrant women victims of intimate partner violence (IPV), the prevalence of which has surged during COVID-19, across the world and in the US. Yet help-seeking by victims of violence has dropped by 50% (Fielding, 2020). IPV has been called "a pandemic within a pandemic" (Evans et al., 2020, p. 2302). People of all races, cultures, genders, sexual orientations, socioeconomic classes, and religions experience IPV. However, "such violence has a disproportionate effect on communities of color and other marginalized groups" (Evans et al., 2020, p. 2302).

What Is IPV?

IPV is violence that can occur within the context of dating, intimate, and romantic relationships. IPV can comprise physical violence (like punching, kicking, and hitting), sexual violence (including rape, non-consensual sexual contact, coercive reproduction, and verbal sexual abuse), psychological violence (including emotional and verbal abuse), and economic and financial abuse (Campbell, 2002; Graham et al., 2019). IPV has negative physical and psychological health consequences. Prior research indicates that victims of IPV suffer from chronic pain, gastrointestinal disorders, and gynecological ailments, and have significantly increased rates of physical injury, depression, posttraumatic stress disorder (PTSD), substance abuse, suicide ideations and attempts, and sexually transmitted infections (Ackard & Neumark-Sztainer, 2002; Reuter et al., 2017).

Strategies in IPV Response

Liang et al. (2005) offered a framework that analyzes IPV victims' cognitive process leading to the intentional action of looking for help. According to Liang et al. (2005), the help-seeking process consists of three steps: problem recognition, the decision to seek support, and selecting a services provider. The research on help-seeking and service provision tends to focus on models within the framework of clinical or social work settings. For instance, there are several IPV screening tools used by clinicians such as the Abuse Assessment Screen, the Computer Based IPV Questionnaire, the HITS (Hurt, Insult, Threaten, and Scream) Domestic Violence Screening Tool for men and women, and Women Abuse Screening Tool (Dicola & Spaar, 2016). There is limited research available on communication strategies or channels that are utilized by IPV victims for help-seeking or those used by service providers. Similarly, insufficient research has been done to analyze communication strategies or channels utilized by immigrants or by culture-specific organizations to cater to their needs.

Despite IPV program growth, service gaps remain for immigrant women who are a marginalized and vulnerable survivor population in the US (Evans et al., 2020). In order to understand the impact of IPV on immigrant victims, the following section analyzes extant literature on barriers to support-seeking and service utilization among immigrant victims of violence, and explores the importance of culture-specific IPV response and support services.

Barriers to Disclosure of Violence, Help-Seeking, and Service Uptake Among Immigrant Victims of Violence

Yet, among immigrant victims of IPV in the US, help-seeking and resource uptake are remarkably low even in pre-pandemic times (Hurwitz et al., 2006). Immigrant women go through the same stressors and trauma of IPV as women born in the US, but their experiences can be exacerbated by a set of factors that are peculiar to their immigrant status. These may include limited English language proficiency, unique sociocultural and religious norms, changing legal status due to immigration, lack of family support, stigma of IPV, uncertain or undocumented immigration status, threats of deportation used as means of control by the abuser, and increasing social isolation.

Occasionally there are cultural barriers to disclosure and support-seeking among immigrant victims. For instance, Tripathi and Azhar (2020) point out that immigrant communities like South Asians tend to value community well-being over individual welfare (Tripathi & Azhar, 2020). Consequently, the principle of collective identity shapes moral values and sociocultural norms across a very diverse South Asian immigrant diaspora (Varughese, 2017). Rigid gender roles and patriarchy result in women assuming subservient roles in families irrespective of their financial contribution.

> The division of labor within South Asian families is such that women are responsible for caregiving roles while men are expected to head the household. ... This division of labor often makes women feel that their emotional or mental health concerns are trivial in comparison to the pragmatic tasks of earning an income and financially managing a household. Women may be viewed by members of the South Asian community as being physically and intellectually inferior to men, leading their emotional, financial and health needs to be less prioritized over their male counterparts. (Tripathi & Azhar, 2020, p. 2)

Often, IPV is normalized and framed as being a part of the marital experience for the immigrant women (Dasgupta, 2007). Consequently, victims may not even consider themselves being abused due to culturally prescribed rigid gender roles and familial obligations (Tripathi & Azhar, 2020; Ahmad et al., 2004). Stigmatization and ostracization—in case of disclosure of abuse—by extended family members or community members who act as extended family by proxy can also prevent victims from divulging their experiences (Tripathi & Azhar, 2020; Yoshioka et al., 2003). The lives of immigrants in the US are often marked by precarity, instability, racial stereotyping, and lack of social support. For the immigrant women who are victims of IPV the lack of family support combined with social isolation often leads to mental health issues—like anxiety and depression—that can compromise daily well-being (Tripathi & Azhar, 2020).

Financial dependence on the violent spouse is also one of the primary barriers against help-seeking. A significant number of foreign women immigrate to the US on spousal visas—like the H4—that renders them dependent on their spouses and legally prevents them from seeking employment within the US (Kelkar, 2012). The battered woman is often forced to stay with her spouse, as she is often without an alternative source of economic support.

For many immigrant women in the US, limited English proficiency can be an obstacle in seeking services. Victims with limited language proficiency might be reluctant or unable to access mainstream social or legal services (Douglas & Hines, 2011). They may even be unaware of their legal rights (Douglas & Hines, 2011). Tripathi and Azhar (2020) delineate the case of South Asian immigrant women who "experience stress caused by intersectional experiences of gender, immigrant status, and culture" (pp. 2–3). The women trapped in abusive relationships face "additional legal and integration barriers. …These systemic barriers coupled with patriarchal traditions make it difficult for the women facing IPV to seek assistance from both formal and informal sources" (Tripathi & Azhar, 2020, pp. 2–3).

Disclosure of sexual abuse by family members, romantic partners, or spouses is negligible among many immigrants (Dasgupta, 2007). The concept of marital rape is occasionally absent in many cultures, as a result of which women believe they do not have the right to complain about sexual violence perpetrated by their intimate partners (Gelles, 1997). Consequently, they are much less likely to disclose intimate partner sexual abuse and seek help. In addition, a high value is often ascribed to women's sexual purity, an understanding of which is conflated with premarital virginity and post-marital sexual fidelity. Disclosure of premarital sexual abuse or spousal sexual abuse can be constructed as a moral transgression especially when sexual purity is culturally depicted as a feminine virtue which preserves the honor of men, family, and community (Dasgupta, 1996). "As the dominant cultural rhetoric upholds the subordination of women by men as an integral part of the gendered construction of family, the socialization of both males and females in context of sexual relations within marriage emphasizes the suppression of women's sexual needs and rights. Given the notions of masculinity and femininity, men assume it is their responsibility and marital right to take control of sexual interaction and affirm their sexual prowess" (Abraham, 1998, p. 599). Marital rape thus can become ethically permissible as consent to marriage is constructed as consent to sexual intercourse. Consequently, intimate partner sexual abuse is often not recognized as abuse among many immigrant communities in the US, and disclosure and reporting remain minimal.

Culture-Specific Support Services Providing Organizations: Why Are They Important?

Help-seeking strategies by IPV victims are generally dichotomized as either informal or formal sources of help (Liang et al., 2005). Informal networks include family, friends, and community members, and formal networks include support-providing organizations, courts, law enforcement, legal services, and so on. Previous research shows that immigrant victims of violence are more likely to access services from culture-specific organizations that also offer linguistically relevant services (Upadhyay et al., 2002; Hurwitz et al., 2006). The US has an extensive network of mainstream (i.e., not culturally specific) agencies who provide most of the essential support services to violence victims. However, these mainstream agencies frequently find it difficult to reach out to immigrant victims due to multiple, co-occurring barriers—such as linguistic barriers and organizations' lack of familiarity with the living circumstances of the community (Upadhyay et al., 2002). Hence, culture-specific support services organizations are essential for effective IPV service delivery and for effectively meeting the needs of immigrant populations. There are many organizations and support groups across the US that provide culture-specific support services to immigrant women who are victims of IPV. The services provided by these organizations include domestic violence and sexual assault support services, crisis counseling, mental health service provision, legal help, advocacy, emergency shelter, court accompaniment, and other essential services—including linguistically appropriate support services and language translation and interpretation—as needed by victims with limited English proficiency.

SDG 18 and the Importance of Communication for All

The SDGs strive to address universal challenges including poverty, inequality, climate change, environmental degradation, peace, and justice, among others. The United Nations General Assembly passed a new Resolution on September 25, 2015, entitled "Transforming Our World, the 2030 Agenda for Sustainable Development", as "a plan of action for people, planet, and prosperity" (UNGA, 2015, p. 1). This resolution aimed to create updated goals for the SDGs including lessons learned from the Millennium Development Goals which incorporated the 17 Sustainable Development Goals and 169 targets (UNGA, 2015, p. 1). The updated goals strive to achieve gender equality and the empowerment of women and girls across the globe. "They are integrated and indivisible and balance the three dimensions of sustainable development: the economic, social and environmental" (Poole, 2018, p. 316).

As Servaes (2017) notes, SDGs need to be positioned within the broader context of development and communication perspectives in order to be sustainable. Servaes also provides a strong argument for the inclusion of culture and communication in the formulation of SDGs. Yusha'u (2021) also argues for emphasizing communication for development as an essential element in designing SDGs by noting that otherwise it is fairly difficult to achieve the targets set in the global goals. As Yusha'u elaborates, "As the COVID-19 pandemic indicates, the communication infrastructure available the world over served as the 'ventilator' that provided the needed life support for the global economy during the pandemic. Almost all institutions in many countries worked from home, and education and health activities were facilitated remotely. … The entire global population relied on the mass media for information and guidance on how to tackle the pandemic" (Yusha'u, 2021, p. 53). Yusha'u and Servaes

(2021) conclude that communication for development and social change need to serve as the framework of SDGs in order to achieve the 2030 Agenda for Development. They suggest that some of the communication for development strategies—as recommended by development institutions such as the World Bank, WHO, UNICEF, and IFRC—need to be implemented in times of pandemics such as COVID-19.

Thus, the notion of SDG 18 (Communication for all) is essential for reducing the impact of COVID-19 and minimizing communication barriers to improve support-seeking and service utilization among immigrant victims of IPV living in the US. In order to explore the concept of SDG 18, one has to look at various aspects of the pandemic's repercussions, communication frameworks within the context of intersectionality, the importance of strengthening IPV mitigation services, the role of Information and Communication Technologies (ICTs) in IPV response, and technology-based IPV interventions.

COVID-19 and IPV

Extant research indicates that adverse situations like a pandemic tend to place IPV victims at greater risk. While both men and women are victims of IPV, statistics indicate women are at higher risk of IPV and are more likely to be killed by abusive male partners. Public safety measures adopted during COVID-19—including physical distancing, self-quarantining, and "safer-at-home" mandates intended to prevent widespread infection—left many IPV victims trapped in close contact with their abusers and isolated from networks of support (Foster & Fletcher, 2020; Moreira & da Costa, 2020; Zero & Geary, 2020). The pandemic exacerbated financial stress by precipitating job loss and unemployment, especially among women of color and migrant communities (Kantamneni, 2020). The social isolation and stay-at-home directives reduced access of IPV victims to essential support services and resources such as alternative sources of housing like shelters and safe havens (Evans et al., 2020). Many domestic violence shelters closed or started operating at reduced capacity, and walk-in facilities for victims for most support providers were suspended. As noted previously, support-seeking during the pandemic drastically decreased (Fielding, 2020). While there were multiple factors precipitating decreased support-seeking, a primary cause was the fact that the victims were forced to share the same living space with the abusers which made making phone calls or communicating through alternative means impossible.

Challenges for Help-Seeking and the Importance of SDG 18 and the "communication" Aspect of Response Services

The abrupt transition to remote support services due to COVID-19 presented its own challenges to service providing organizations (Pfitzner et al., 2020). There are varied communication strategies for help-seeking that victims utilize, but as noted before, the pandemic has rendered help-seeking risky and sparse. The communication strategies for providing support to IPV victims by service providers have also been restructured by the pandemic, along with the discontinuation of some of the established practices. A focus on the communication aspect in IPV response research can be used to understand help-seeking patterns as well as service provision models and channels, and finally, patterns of service uptake by IPV victims belonging to immigrant and ethnocultural groups. This is where the importance of the notion of SDG 18 and "communication for all" needs to be emphasized.

In pre-pandemic times, help-seeking communication strategies included making phone calls to service providers, communicating through emails, doing individual walk-ins to a service provider's office, accompany a friend/community member to a service provider's office, using web-based forms to reach out to providers, and so on (Slakoff et al., 2020). Due to the pandemic, there has been a disruption of regular means of communication and discontinuation or minimization of face-to-face communication and walk-ins. Importantly, "services for violence prevention and intervention were already struggling to meet needs before the arrival of COVID-19" (Gunraj & Howard, 2020). Since the most dangerous time for a battered female is when she tries to leave the relationship (National Coalition Against Domestic Violence, 2020), the closing of shelters and lack of emergency accommodation space put victims at an even greater risk. For immigrant women—lacking family, friends, or community support—closed shelters signify the lack of a safe physical space.

In the COVID-19 era, the capacities of service providing organizations have been further curtailed, and outreach to victims was significantly reduced. A pandemic involving stay-at-home orders and social distancing can make dissemination of information on available services a complex affair. For organizations supporting immigrant victims, additional obstacles—such as cultural and linguistic barriers—can render such outreach even more convoluted. Most providers have tried to employ creative ways to pivot their services and endeavored to redesign almost every aspect of their operations due to the pandemic. Essential services such as crisis intervention, counseling, legal help, and so on had to be provided remotely, with limited in-person communication. As a result of restrictions on public gatherings and limitations on services deemed "non-essential", the service provision model by most organizations was disrupted. Consequently, there were "difficulties connecting with survivors due to abusers being home, limited time for phone conversation, difficulty delivering food with controlling partners, and inability to transport survivors in their cars" (Sabri et al., 2020, p. 1302).

Communication tools, technologies, and strategies are indispensable for IPV response services. Many service providers had to use novel technological tools such as multimedia messaging apps, live-chat options and web-based video chat systems, digital document filing systems, and so on (Slakoff et al., 2020). However, for immigrant victims, virtual platforms of service provision can present multiple difficulties. Linguistic barriers can get magnified with technological advances. Also, victims may not have access to the Internet, may lack familiarity with and understanding of latest digital tools, and also might prefer to engage in face-to-face interactions. Additionally, technological abuse—when abusers place tracking apparatus on their partners' devices—has been on the rise (Emezue, 2020).

Complexities and Repercussions from the Pandemic for IPV Victims

Financial difficulties resulting from job loss as well as fear of job loss and potential financial hardship have been identified as one of the factors for aggravating conflict in families and increasing the severity of IPV. "Most survivors and service providers mentioned the effects of unemployment on the ability to have basic needs met in the family (rent, food, childcare) and husbands losing their jobs and taking out on their wives" (Sabri et al., 2020, p. 1296). For immigrants, job loss can also result in loss of immigrant status which creates its own complex fallouts. Loss of health insurance due to employment disruption or loss of immigration status can suspend healthcare seeking and make COVID-19 infection an added burden for immigrant battered victims. The pandemic also exacerbated mental health consequences among IPV victims which include posttraumatic stress disorder (PTSD), depression, anxiety, and eating disorders. During the pandemic, IPV has been a cause of mortality due to suicide and homicide (Evans et al., 2020, p. 2302). Among immigrant groups there is often prevalent cultural stigma surrounding mental health, and support-seeking is actively discouraged by family and community. Consequently—among immigrant victims of IPV suffering from mental health consequences—resource uptake is remarkably low (Sabri et al., 2020).

The financial hardships, complexities in the immigration process, social distancing, and stay-at-home directives precipitated by COVID-19 increased the frequency and severity of IPV for immigrant women who were already in abusive relationships. Also, research shows that during the pandemic victims reported an increase of stalking and monitoring behavior of abusive partners (Sabri et al., 2020). "Stalking included watching women's every move in the house and monitoring who they talk to outside of the household. … Control strategies included financial control, trying to get survivors pregnant, controlling when survivors can leave the house, means to managing childcare, and limited access to services" (Sabri et al., 2020, p. 1300).

Immigrant victims face multiple and complex barriers when trying to leave an abusive partner. Financial exigencies, job loss, and lacking resources to relocate due to the pandemic have been some of the primary reasons for victims hesitant toward leaving an abusive partner. For undocumented victims the stalling in immigration processes due to the pandemic has rendered it almost impossible to leave an abusive relationship especially when the perpetrator use threats of deportation as means of control (Campbell, 2002). Divorce procedures have been halted by the pandemic, and complexities in custodial arrangement of children for immigrant victims also render the latter reluctant to leave a relationship. Support from other community members—who sometimes take the role of family in the latter's absence in a foreign land—had also been completely disrupted by the pandemic.

Need for an Intersectional Approach for Analyzing Communication Frameworks for Immigrant Victims' Response to Violence

While exploring the communication aspect of help-seeking and service uptake by immigrant women in the US, it is essential to contextualize such study by the framework of intersectionality. Intersectionality posits that multiple social identities like race, ethnicity, gender, sexual orientation, socioeconomic condition, immigration status, and so on, which are embodied within individuals, intersect at the micro level of personal experience to reflect multiple interlocking systems of privilege and oppression at the macro, social-structural level (Crenshaw, 1989). Intersectionality assumes that social identities are affected by structures of power, and thus refers to the multiple and complex ways in which systems of oppression and inequality connect. IPV victims with marginalized social positions often face structural racism and discrimination at multiple levels that further shape their daily survival strategies. Intersectionality can provide a framework for understanding marginalization, critique, resistance, and transformation of the status quo, and helps to include context and history that situate social identities (Greenwood, 2008; Suter, 2018). Immigrant women of color experience and respond to IPV while already being disadvantaged by multiple circumstances—sociocultural norms, legal status, religion, language proficiency, education, and economic factors. Recognizing these intersections will provide a better understanding of the impact of COVID-19 on immigrant IPV victims. Intersectionality theory also adds further complexity and nuance to understanding the spectrum of actions that immigrant violence victims take, as a response to IPV. By examining IPV through an intersectional lens, researchers and service providers will be better able to adapt support strategies for victims with multiple marginalized identities like immigrant women of color.

Strengthening IPV Mitigation Services

There is a current need for innovative and creative safety strategies for improving IPV awareness, providing education and counseling, and enhance outreach. An important aspect of IPV mitigation service is devising safety strategies for protection at home, since future waves of the pandemic will result in many women being home all day with their abusers. Important components of IPV education and counseling can incorporate "discussing safety strategies, identifying relationship red flags, and providing de-escalation techniques for partners. … Implementing strategies to stay safe and decreasing likelihood of conflict with the abuser are suggested for survivors with limited ability to leave" (Sabri et al., 2020, p. 1303). Outreach to victims also need to be modified and strategized including "putting DV information in public spaces such as grocery stores, covertly providing information to survivors during basic needs provision or in bags of food during distribution and distributing surveys to understand survivor needs" (Sabri et al., 2020, p. 1303). Outreach to IPV victims can also be conducted in innovative ways such as putting information on resources and support services in strategic areas of grocery stores, parks, and religious buildings. Resource provision specific to immigrant victims such as delivery of culturally specific meals—to counter food and resource control by abusive partners—is also needed (Sabri et al., 2020).

Technology-Mediated Forms of IPV Intervention

The notion of SDG 18 and "communication for all" is reinforced in the practicability of Information and Communication Technologies (ICTs) which offer access to relevant information in real time and allow tailoring of services to specific cases of abuse (Hamm, 2001). Like the utilization of telemedicine has shifted healthcare provision to adept to patient needs during the pandemic, it is essential to popularize and diversify virtual and technology-based IPV services especially in view of the impact of COVID-19 on mainstream communication processes and interpersonal interactions. It is also important to find ways to remotely connect with IPV victims who face difficulties in using or even accessing virtual platforms. Sabri et al. (2020) note that future virtual services need to include online support groups, remote mental health services, and online personal check-ins. Also, text messages, videoconferencing through applications like Zoom, low-data messaging platforms like WhatsApp and WeChat, and emails can be utilized by service providers to interact with help-seekers, check-in, and deliver support (Sabri et al., 2020).

"Online DV organizations also provide other advocates with health and support information in order to better facilitate and provide a solution to victims/survivors of DV and other related types of sensitive healthcare issues. … The amount of information available online is also used to provide online training for individuals and organizations that deal with violence against women (VAW)" (Olaniran, 2021, p. 31). Technology has also provided innovative strategies for abusers to perpetrate physical and non-physical forms of violence against their partners—an emerging trend is the utilization of communication technology for this purpose (Powell & Henry, 2018). Social media, email, and smart phones have been used to stalk and harass former partners through techniques such as unwanted phone calls, sharing images (e.g., revenge porn), unwanted texting, and hacking (Powell & Henry, 2018). Such forms of abuse can be perpetrated at a regular level without the physical presence of the abuser (Olaniran, 2021). "Surveillance apps have been used to enable perpetrators to monitor and stalk either current or former partner. … New spyware that can be linked to mobile phones is readily available and allows the perpetrator to read partner's email and monitor all other electronic devices. The spyware can identify a victim's current location and can be set up to mirror the phone or a personal computer where the perpetrator can watch everything the victim is doing" (Olaniran, 2021, p. 35). Tracking devices can also be attached to a victim's vehicle so that she can be easily stalked (Olaniran, 2021; Powell & Henry, 2018). In such situations, the victim is often unaware of the illegal tracking. Such technology-mediated forms of abuse and intimidation are also easily available for the perpetrators, and regular improvements and innovations enhance their accessibility and impact. "Technology-mediated violence against women can traumatize and isolate women, because online interactions relate to daily part of life. The Internet and mobile phones are used to maintain social contact, but due to tech stalking, women may have to change their online persona or withdraw their digital presence to stop their abuser" (Powell & Henry, 2018). The scope of technological abuse has proliferated during the pandemic; hence, technological and communication strategies need to be implemented and made accessible for victims to generate IPV response interventions.

In order to manage such technology-mediated violence, several digital intervention apps and safety decision aids for IPV victims have been devised. Some of them were developed in pre-pandemic times—like the myPlan app (Emezue, 2020; Glass et al., 2015), I-DECIDE (Emezue, 2020; Hegarty et al., 2019), and iSafe (Emezue, 2020; Koziol-McLain et al., 2018). Twenty-four hours crisis hotlines using telephones and web-based messaging systems also need to be in place to cater to needs of victims. These technology-based tools are often free and have been tested for efficacy among IPV victim groups. "Substantively, digital interventions provide safer options for leaving or navigating an abusive relationship (i.e., safety planning). These interventions also offer risk and danger assessment, psychoeducation, referral to trusted care, and can be tailored to unique social ecologies in ways that mitigate user burden and maximize safety. In this COVID-19 era, these digital interventions have become of value to socially and physically isolated people who experience abuse, especially while survivors are sequestered at home with abusive partners" (Emezue, 2020, p. e19831).

National domestic violence coalitions and networks like the National Network to End Domestic Violence (NNEDV), the National Coalition Against Domestic Violence, and the National Domestic Violence Hotline have published several tech safety guidelines. "These tech safety guidelines have become useful evaluative tools as survivors, service providers, bystanders, and advocates decide on which digital solution is best for whom, signaling emerging best practices. … With concerns for safety, several guidelines are in place to ensure these online spaces remain confidential, private, and secure" (Emezue, 2020, p. e19831).

Need and Potential for Further Research

COVID-19 dramatically underscores the need to accelerate progress toward achievement of SDGs, including SDG 5 addressing gender inequality and empowerment. Women comprise the majority of population lacking access to essential services particularly women belonging to marginalized groups and those residing in low- and middle-income countries. Such a lack of access to essential resources constrains the ability of women to protect themselves from the pandemic and exacerbates the secondary impacts of the disease outbreak and response. Especially increasing IPV rates, gaps in response services, and additional care and domestic burden due to COVID-19 limit women's social engagement, political participation, and achievement of SDG 5. The COVID-19 pandemic potentially restricts women's lives, to engage in the response to the pandemic and the success of all SDGs, including SDG 5.

The notion of SDG 18 or communication for all becomes essential as we delineated how communication strategies form an integral part of IPV response. Yet future implementation of SDG 18 is fraught with complexities as there has been little research on communication processes inherent in help-seeking and service provision within the context of IPV. Most research on IPV tends to focus on the public health aspect of the outcomes of violence, or the clinical and social work facet of help-seeking and service provision. There is scope of future research on communication strategies and channels utilized by victims and service providers. An exploration of communication strategies in help-seeking and service provision will also provide guidance for developing effective response and recovery approaches as well as best practices expanding the range of viable support options available to IPV victims—particularly immigrant women and women of color. It would also further the understanding of the relationships between the COVID-19, IPV, and battered immigrant women's responses to multiple crises during the pandemic. Such research can enable the researchers, victim advocates, clinicians, and social workers to re-evaluate their response strategies to alleviate the multiple stressors faced by immigrant victims of violence. It is also essential to identify key areas for future studies to help inform on how to best formulate and disseminate culturally specific support services. Interdisciplinary collaborations and multisector partnerships—involving scholars, researchers, advocates, and practitioners—represent a critical next step to advance social justice in the field of culturally contextualized IPV support services for immigrant victims.

There has also been a notable lack of research in examining the intersecting systems of oppression faced by IPV victims belonging to immigrant and ethnocultural groups. Even more understudied is the impact of COVID-19 on exacerbating the vulnerabilities of immigrant women. Future studies need to address the gaps in current research and demonstrate that communication techniques and response strategies can play a crucial role in victim advocacy for sexual and gender-based violence—especially among underserved immigrant communities. The current study and future research can add to the repository of knowledge that aspires for a reimagined IPV service delivery rooted not only in the traditionalist feminist paradigm but also in the conceptual framework of intersectionality that addresses the unique experiences of immigrant battered women.

As Sen (2015) noted, "SDG 5 proposes a range of targets to end discrimination, violence and harmful practices, recognize and value unpaid care work, participation and leadership in decision-making, and universal access to sexual and reproductive health and reproductive rights". But "How SDG 5 and its proposed targets will finally translate into indicators, and whether these will be effective and usable for monitoring (where the rubber hits the road) remains to be seen" (Sen, 2015). Ultimately, the notion of SDG 18 (Communication for all) is essential for countering the impact of COVID-19 and reducing communication barriers to improve service utilization among immigrant victims of IPV living in the US, thus ensuring the success of SDG 5. The future implementation of SDG 18 can contribute to a research agenda on the intersecting issues of displacement and marginalization, as well as contestation and empowerment for immigrant victims of IPV during and after the pandemic.

References

Abraham, M. (1998). Alienation and marital violence against South Asian immigrant women in the United States. In D. Kaleki-Fishman (Ed.), *Designs for alienation: Exploring diverse realities* (pp. 175–196). University of Jyvaskyla.

Ackard, D. M., & Neumark-Sztainer, D. (2002). Date violence and date rape among adolescents: Associations with disordered eating behaviors and psychological health. *Child Abuse & Neglect, 26*(5), 455–473.

Ahmad, F., Riaz, S., Barata, P., & Stewart, D. E. (2004). Patriarchal beliefs and perceptions of abuse among South Asian immigrant women. *Violence Against Women, 10*(3), 262–282.

Campbell, J. C. (2002). Health consequences of intimate partner violence. *The Lancet, 359*(9314), 1331–1336.

Crenshaw, K. (1989). Demarginalizing the intersection of race and sex: A black feminist critique of antidiscrimination doctrine, feminist theory and antiracist politics. *The University of Chicago Legal Forum, 140*, 139–167.

Dasgupta, S. D. (1996). Feminist consciousness in women centered Hindi films. *Journal of Popular Culture, 30*(1), 173–189.

Dasgupta, S. D. (Ed.). (2007). *Body evidence: Intimate violence against South Asian women in America*. Rutgers University Press.

Dicola, D., & Spaar, E. (2016, October 15). Intimate partner violence. American Family Physician, *94*(8), 646–651. PMID: 27929227.

Douglas, E. M., & Hines, D. A. (2011). The reported availability of us domestic violence services to victims who vary by immigration status, primary language, and disability. *Partner Abuse, 2*(4), 427–451.

Emezue, C. (2020). Digital or digitally delivered responses to domestic and intimate partner violence during COVID-19. *JMIR Public Health and Surveillance, 6*(3), e19831.

Evans, M. L., Lindauer, M., & Farrell, M. E. (2020). A pandemic within a pandemic—Intimate partner violence during Covid-19. *New England Journal of Medicine, 383*(24), 2302–2304.

Fielding, S. (2020). In quarantine with an abuser: Surge in domestic violence reports linked to coronavirus. *The Guardian, 3.*

Foster, H., & Fletcher, A. (2020). Women's safety NSW update: Impacts on COVID-19 on domestic and family violence in NSW. Retrieved July, 5, 2020.

Gelles, R. J. (1997). *Intimate violence in families*. Sage.

Glass, N., Clough, A., Case, J., Hanson, G., Barnes-Hoyt, J., Waterbury, A., Alhusen, J., Ehrensaft, M., Grace, K. T., & Perrin, N. (2015). A safety app to respond to dating violence for college women and their friends: The MyPlan study randomized controlled trial protocol. *BMC Public Health, 15*(1), 1–13.

Graham, L. M., Jensen, T. M., Givens, A. D., Bowen, G. L., & Rizo, C. F. (2019). Intimate partner violence among same-sex couples in college: A propensity score analysis. *Journal of Interpersonal Violence, 34*(8), 1583–1610.

Greenwood, R. M. (2008). Intersectional political consciousness: Appreciation for intragroup differences and solidarity in diverse groups. *Psychology of Women Quarterly, 32*(1), 36–47.

Gunraj, A., & Howard, J. (2020). *Why is the COVID-19 pandemic linked to more gender-based violence. Canadian Women.*

Hamm, S. (2001). Information communications technologies and violence against women. *The Society for International Development, 44*(3), 36–41. https://doi.org/10.1057/palgrave.development.1110259

Hegarty, K., Tarzia, L., Valpied, J., Murray, E., Humphreys, C., Taft, A., Novy, K., Gold, L., & Glass, N. (2019). An online healthy relationship tool and safety decision aid for women experiencing intimate partner violence (I-DECIDE): A randomised controlled trial. *The Lancet Public Health, 4*(6), e301–e310.

Hurwitz, E. J. H., Gupta, J., Liu, R., Silverman, J. G., & Raj, A. (2006). Intimate partner violence associated with poor health outcomes in US South Asian women. *Journal of Immigrant and Minority Health, 8*(3), 251–261.

Kantamneni, N. (2020). The impact of the COVID-19 pandemic on marginalized populations in the United States: A research agenda. *Journal of Vocational Behavior, 119*, 103439.

Kelkar, M. (2012). South Asian immigration in the United States: A gendered perspective. *Harvard Journal of Asian American Policy Review, 22*, 55–60.

Koziol-McLain, J., Vandal, A. C., Wilson, D., Nada-Raja, S., Dobbs, T., McLean, C., Sisk, R., Eden, K. B., & Glass, N. E. (2018). Efficacy of a web-based safety decision aid for women experiencing intimate partner violence: Randomized controlled trial. *Journal of Medical Internet Research, 20*(1), e8.

Liang, B., Goodman, L., Tummala-Narra, P., & Weintraub, S. (2005). A theoretical framework for understanding help-seeking processes among survivors of intimate partner violence. *American Journal of Community Psychology, 36*(1–2), 71–84.

Moreira, D. N., & da Costa, M. P. (2020). The impact of the Covid-19 pandemic in the precipitation of intimate partner violence. *International Journal of Law and Psychiatry, 71*, 101606.

National Coalition Against Domestic Violence. (2020). *Why do victims stay?* Retrieved August 6, 2021, from https://ncadv.org/why-do-victims-stay

Olaniran, B. A. (2021). ICTs and Domestic Violence (DV): Exploring Intimate Partner Violence (IPV). *International Journal of Big Data and Analytics in Healthcare (IJBDAH), 6*(2), 31–44.

Pfitzner, N., Fitz-Gibbon, K., & True, J. (2020). Responding to the 'shadow pandemic': Practitioner views on the nature of and responses to violence against women in Victoria, Australia during the COVID-19 restrictions.

Poole, A. K. (2018). The UN sustainable development goals and the biocultural heritage lacuna: Where is goal number 18?. In *From biocultural homogenization to biocultural conservation* (pp. 315–331). Springer.

Powell, A., & Henry, N. (2018). *Digital harassment and abuse of adult Australians: A summary report.* RMIT University.

Reuter, T. R., Newcomb, M. E., Whitton, S. W., & Mustanski, B. (2017, January). Intimate Partner Violence Victimization in LGBT Young Adults: Demographic Differences and Associations with Health Behaviors. *Psychology of Violence, 7*(1), 101–109. https://doi.org/10.1037/vio0000031. Epub 2016 Jan 25. PMID: 28451465; PMCID: PMC5403162.

Sabri, B., Hartley, M., Saha, J., Murray, S., Glass, N., & Campbell, J. C. (2020). Effect of COVID-19 pandemic on women's health and safety: A study of immigrant survivors of intimate partner violence. *Health Care for Women International, 41*(11–12), 1294–1312.

Sen, G. (2015). Goal 5–Achieving gender equality and empowering women and girls: Is SDG 5 missing something? *UN Chronicle, 51*(4).

Servaes, J. (2017). Introduction: From MDGs to SDGs. In *Sustainable Development Goals in the Asian Context* (pp. 1–21). Springer.

Slakoff, D. C., Aujla, W., & PenzeyMoog, E. (2020). The role of service providers, technology, and mass media when home isn't safe for intimate partner violence victims: best practices and recommendations in the era of CoViD-19 and beyond. *Archives of Sexual Behavior, 49*(8), 2779–2788.

Suter, E. A. (2018). The promise of contrapuntal and intersectional methods for advancing critical interpersonal and family communication research. *Communication Monographs, 85*(1), 123–139.

Tripathi, S., & Azhar, S. (2020). A systematic review of intimate partner violence interventions impacting South Asian Women in the United States. *Trauma, Violence, & Abuse*. https://doi.org/10.1177/1524838020957987

United Nations. (2016). *Transforming our world: the 2030 Agenda for Sustainable Development.* https://sdgs.un.org/2030agenda.

Upadhyay, U. D., Vyas, A. N., Ghosh, A., & Akram, S. A. (2002). *Brown paper: The health of South Asians in the United States.* The South Asian Public Health Association (SAPHA).

Van Tulder, R. (2018). *Business and the sustainable development goals: A framework for effective corporate involvement.* Rotterdam School of Management, Erasmus University.

Varughese, J. (2017). Historical & cultural factors in ethnic identity formation of Asian–Indian Immigrants: Understanding the context of care. In J. Varughese (Ed.), Counselling Asian Indian immigrant families: A pastoral psychotherapeutic model (pp. 21–54). Palgrave Macmillan.

UNGA. (2015). United Nations General Assembly resolution 70/1, transforming our world: the 2030 agenda for sustainable development, A/79/L.1 undocs.org/A/RES/70/1.

Yoshioka, M. R., Gilbert, L., El-Bassel, N., & Baig-Amin, M. (2003). Social support and disclosure of abuse: Comparing South Asian, African American, and Hispanic Battered Women. *Journal of Family Violence, 18*, 171–180.

Yusha'u, M. J. (2021). SDG18—The missing ventilator: An introduction to the 2030 agenda for development. In *The Palgrave handbook of international communication and sustainable development* (pp. 53–75). Palgrave Macmillan.

Yusha'u, M. J., & Servaes, J. (2021). Communication for sustainable development in the age of COVID-19. In *The Palgrave handbook of international communication and sustainable development* (pp. 3–30). Palgrave Macmillan.

Zero, O., & Geary, M. (2020). COVID-19 and intimate partner violence: A call to action. *Rhode Island Medical Journal, 103*(5), 57–59.

CHAPTER 9

The Importance of Sustainable Communication in the Covid-19 Period: The Case of Turkey

Nurcan Törenli and Zafer Kıyan

Abstract In the present study, the crisis communication model adopted by the Ministry of Health, the manager of the COVID-19 pandemic in Turkey, is analyzed based on chronological developments that were criticized and discussed during the beginning, emergence, and chronicity of the pandemic. The study argues that an effective crisis communication strategy, required during the COVID-19 pandemic, could not be adopted due to the communication problems across the social stakeholders in Turkey. This miscommunication stemmed from Ministry of Health's

The present study benefited from the TUBITAK (The Scientific and Technological Research Council of Turkey) project "Crisis Communication: Preventive Communication Approaches Based on the Lessons Learned During the Covid-19 Pandemic" (No: 120K634).

N. Törenli (✉) • Z. Kıyan
Faculty of Communication, Ankara University, Ankara, Turkey
e-mail: torenli@ankara.edu.tr

J. Servaes, M. J. Yusha'u (eds.), *SDG18 Communicaton for All, Volume 2*, Sustainable Development Goals Series,
https://doi.org/10.1007/978-3-031-19459-7_9

flawed strategy and the value paradox due to the neglect of social reaction, demands, concerns, and requirements. Those responsible for the crisis management attempted to spread messages not only through conventional media but also through social media to achieve media diversity. However, these messages were not only repetitive and similar, but they aimed to influence rather than interact. Therefore, the value and credibility of these messages gradually decreased across the public that was significantly affected by the crisis. Furthermore, the Ministry of Health did not provide accurate, adequate, and timely information to the citizens, leading to the interruption of mutual and solidaristic communication between the ruler and the ruled. Turkish COVID-19 experience presented in the present study is a significant example that demonstrated how the provision of sustainable development goals—especially the elimination of poverty (SGD1) and hunger (SGD2), health and welfare (SGD3), and gender equality (SGD5)—could be interrupted and how the disruption of the communications during the crisis would complicate normalization for social stakeholders in the absence of an accurate and realistic communication strategy. For this purpose, the main outline of an effective crisis communication model is also presented in the study.

Keywords COVID-19 pandemic • Crisis communications • Sustainable development • Social integration • Communication

Introduction

The difference between the COVID-19 pandemic and other crises was the impossibility of solving the unprecedented psychological, social, and economic problems (induced by the pandemic) merely through technical and administrative skills. The nature of the COVID-19 crisis that destroyed not only the material but also the human resources of the societies required effective communication strategy along with other drastic measures. Thus, communications during crisis should be perceived as a realistic and strategic approach to create a partnership for solution between those who experience the problem and those who should solve the problem.

The COVID-19 pandemic has completely and irreversibly altered social life. In the process, even some of the most developed societies struggled miserably to control COVID-19 effectively during certain periods. Thus, it was paramount for each society to seek and find ways and methods, determine, and implement priorities to maximize its ability to produce solutions. Two key concepts in this process include social integration and communication. Since the COVID-19 pandemic is an extraordinary case in social life, it is not possible for citizens to overcome this problem on their own. It is necessary to ensure and maintain social integration through communication.

The first responsibility of public authorities is to ensure social integration in the environment of chaos and panic during crises induced by pandemics such as the COVID-19. The severity of the problems experienced in times of crisis varies not only between the societies but also within the society. The close correlation between communication and social integration is significant in these periods. The collection and processing of the data during the chaotic and panicky environment and the timely and adequate delivery of the solutions that were developed based on the collected data requires an effective organization of communications, which can be considered a crisis communication strategy, where all communication channels between the stakeholders should be kept open to ensure social integration. Keeping the communication channels open is also significant for the determination and implementation of the measures that would minimize the costs of the crisis. Sustainability of social integration requires communication to function as a participatory-negotiatory cultural infrastructure (Polk & Servaes, 2015).

Society is a dialectic whole where conflict, change, and development are determined by dynamic processes. With this approach, the role of communication in ensuring and sustaining social integration, which becomes even more fragile in extraordinary periods such as crises, becomes indispensable. As Servaes and Lie (2015, p. 127) emphasized, communication could not be considered as an instrumentally neutral phenomenon in crises where development and social change are suspended. On the contrary, since human beings need to change and develop to exist, interpersonal and human-nature interaction is a minimum requirement. Thus, the phenomenon of crisis, which prevents sustainable development and social change, requires an approach to communication as socialization.

Ways and methods employed to determine the policies that aim to overcome the crisis and to find solutions to the problems associated with the crisis are mostly identified by developmental theories. The adoption and implementation of the policies based on theoretical knowledge and public approval have been largely powered by the process philosophy in sustainable development communication (Servaes & Malikhao, 2007, p. 4). The success of the policies developed by crisis management depends on the functionality of the communication models they adopt for social acceptance.

The most needed remedy during the COVID-19 pandemic was a mutual and consistent communication between the crisis management and the victims of the crisis. The present study findings reveal that the conditions in Turkey were far from this premise. During the COVID-19, communications were broken between those who managed the crisis and those who were affected by the crisis, as well as among those who managed the crisis in Turkey. This increased the normalization efforts and related public spending that prevented the achievement of sustainable development goals. Particularly, the reluctance of the Ministry of Health in establishing solution partnerships with social stakeholders, and its unilateral approach that ignored social reactions, demands, concerns, and needs nullified the expected benefits of social integration.

As such, the Turkish experience was a significant case that demonstrated how sustainable development goals could be interrupted when communication was conceived not only as a means but also as an end, as often emphasized by Servaes (2000, 2016, 2020). The COVID-19 experience is a significant example that demonstrated how the provision of sustainable development goals, especially the elimination of poverty (SGD1) and hunger (SGD2), health and welfare (SGD3), gender equality (SGD5) could be interrupted and how the disruption of the communications during the crisis would complicate normalization for social stakeholders in the absence of an accurate and realistic communication strategy.

In the current study, descriptive research method was employed to determine the developments that led to the loss of communication between the social stakeholders during the COVID-19 pandemic, and to reveal possible interrelations between the events. Thus, the crisis communication model, adopted by the Ministry of Health, was analyzed chronologically based on the developments in the beginning, emergence, and chronicity of the pandemic. The analysis was based on the publicly criticized approaches, understanding, public communication methods, and crisis management strategies of the Ministry of Health and publicized in the traditional and social media. Furthermore, the testimony and expertise of the authors, who exchanged views with both academic and public actors who experienced the crisis, were also scrutinized in the study. This approach aimed to improve the reliability of the findings via data triangulation (Merriam & Tisdell, 2016).

From Developmental Communications to Sustainable Developmental Communications: The Changing Role and Meaning of Communication

Communication is a dominant topic in the development and sustainable development literature. This corresponds to two separate conceptions in the development and sustainable development literature. The development literature adopts the instrumentalist approach, where the assignment of the roles and functions of communication is deterministic. On the other hand, in the sustainable development literature, a conceptual-factual approach is more prominent since communication is primarily considered as a socialization process. In these two approaches, the communication concept not only reflects the discussion of the development problem, but also clarifies how and for what purpose communication should be employed to determine an accurate and effective strategy to avoid the developments that actually hinder social development, such as crises. There is a greater need for a strategy that realistically blends the instrumental and conceptual-factual dimensions of communication to overcome the crisis such as COVID-19 pandemic that has devastating effects on human and natural resources of the society. Thus, the classification of Servaes (2016, p. 701–702) could be quite beneficial. In this classification, communication for development, sustainable development, and social change were discussed in the literature based on three paradigms and two communication models where theory and practice are consistent: The modernization paradigm and the dependency paradigm, which are consistent with the top-down diffusion model, and the multiplicity paradigm, which is consistent with bottom-up participation model. In the classification, the modernization and dependency paradigms are described as traditional approaches, and the multiplicity paradigm is described as an alternative approach.

As emphasized by Servaes (2016, p. 701), the modernization paradigm could be considered as a 3rd World project by the West. The modernization paradigm, which is based on a one-way instrumental relationship between social development and communication in terms of sending a message between the receiver and the sender, reflects a traditional approach that aims for economic development under underdevelopment conditions (Servaes & Malikhao, 2007, p. 7). The paradigm is consistent with the assignment of significant instrumental roles and functions to communication and the model of dissemination of innovations selected as the communication model for the paradigm that works from top to bottom. In other words, the main mechanism that would lead to social change and development in the modernization paradigm entails the communication tools. Reforms and innovations determined by the public authority are adopted by and popularized across the social classes via the communication tools. As indicated by Hugill (2003, p. 103), in the diffusion model, which could be considered as a pioneering approach in the development literature in early twentieth century, the dissemination of innovations was discussed based on a communicative approach; however, the theory was based on the mathematical diffusion model that was founded on the spread of epidemics. In the model, mass media such as radio and television are prominent due to the size of their coverage area and the fact that they transmit messages from top to bottom based on the same content. Especially in the rural development approach, the messages conveyed by the mass media contribute significantly to the adoption of innovations and new ideas by the members of the society, and prevalence of these innovations and new ideas within a short time (Beam, 1992, p. 112). During the 1960s, the role of mass media, which was the dominant communication method of the period, became more prevalent for modernization. For instance, in Everest Rogers's 1962 book *Diffusion of Innovations* and *Modernization Among Peasants*, published in 1969, mass media was considered significant due to the diffusion of the innovations from the center to the periphery (Stevenson, 2003). On the other hand, Daniel Lerner's 1958 study, "The Passing of Traditional Society: Modernizing the Middle East," emphasized the contribution of mass media to the transition to a modern personality by increasing empathy and mobility across people (Başaran, 2010; Jinqiu & Xiaoming, 2005).

The main criticism of the modernization paradigm was the acceptance of change and development as a natural-universal phenomenon that could be experienced in every land via communication means due to the instrumentalist perspective of the paradigm. Since communication is conceived as a developmental instrument in the paradigm, the issue that communication is the process of socialization itself, as indicated by the concepts of participation and negotiation, has been neglected (Hudson, 1983). Another criticism was the prioritization of the instrumental benefits of communication by the power elites, who desire the state to control the media, instead of prioritizing the general social benefits. For example, in the 1970s, the criticism that one-way mass media, such as the radio, did not include interaction that would allow social integration and general benefits, was strengthened by international organizations such as the UNESCO, International Telecommunication Union (ITU), World Bank, and OECD Development Center (Samarajiva & Shields, 1990). This criticism laid the foundations of a new approach, which allowed an information flow not only from top to bottom but also from the bottom to top; thus, allowing the contribution of local elements. As mentioned by Samarajiva and Shields (1990, p. 91), the studies conducted based on this new approach, which could be christened as telecommunications and developmental communication, focused on the opportunities offered by the tools that allow two-way communication such as the telephone. Although there were instrumental differences within the approach, the interest in the conceptual-factual aspect of communication and the content of the messages were weak. The main interest was to popularize communication networks that carry more channels and for a longer period of time. Samarajiva and Shields (1990, p. 92) argued that this approach was based on the acceptance that both individual and social development could be achieved by feeding more data through interactive channels.

The dependency paradigm was founded on the criticism of the universalist view of the modernization paradigm. Similar to the modernization paradigm, the dependency paradigm was also considered within the traditional approach with a top-down dissemination model (Servaes, 2016, p. 703). However, the dependency paradigm was differentiated from the modernization paradigm, which was deadlocked after the devastation of World War II due to its emphasis on the prioritization of the social benefits of the communication technology developments. Mattelart (1994, p. 148) indicated that the developmental literature underwent a post-war transformation due to the extraordinary devastation of the war. Accordingly, the economic-political polarization in the bipolar world led to a competition between the traditional paradigms. This competition was mainly between the modernist-universalist development approach and a communication for a development based on the general benefit and resources of the society approach (Servaes & Malikhao, 2007). Despite this divergence, the dependency paradigm also adopted the top-down model of diffusion.

The dependency paradigm, in contrast to the technological deterministic development communication approach of the modernization paradigm (Riaz, 1997), perceives development as a problem of emancipation of underdeveloped countries from the Western world. Stokke (1991) emphasized that the problem of emancipation in the dependency paradigm includes a strong criticism of both condoning the destruction of the natural environment in development-industrialization-based modernization and ignorance of the needs of future generations to save the present. Similarly, Servaes and Lie (2015) underlined the fact that the struggle against colonial and dictatorial powers lies at the heart of the dependency paradigm. As such, the addiction paradigm includes the main elements of the communication approach for sustainable development. In their description of the sustainable development approach, Mansell and Wehn (1998, p. 239) emphasized the principled stance of each nation in the employment of communication technologies primarily for broad social benefits for its citizens based on the specific historical, economic, and political conditions.

In parallel to the modernization and dependency paradigm, another significant approach was the multiplicity paradigm in recent studies. Unlike the modernization and dependency paradigms, the multiplicity paradigm was an alternative perspective that employed the bottom-to-top participatory communication model. Multiplicity paradigm is an approach that emphasizes the forgotten social-human aspect of change and development and prioritizes cultural freedoms (Servaes & Malikhao, 2007, p. 7). Cultural freedoms, which are the focus of the multiplicity paradigm, are considered as the fundamental tool of socialization, radical changes, and integration that will ensure development, especially for the development of the cultural and political identity of the society (Samarajiva & Shields, 1990). The recognition of cultural freedom would secure alternative lifestyles in human development and encourage creativity, experiences, and diversity (Servaes & Malikhao, 2007, p. 7).

The multiplicity paradigm approaches the development based on the perspective of sustainability and flexibility and could also be interpreted as a synthesis of traditional approaches. In this synthesis of alternative approaches, the global destruction induced by the neoliberal policies was taken into account. In the 1987 Brundtland report published by the World Commission on Environment and Development, which was established in 1983 to investigate the failure of strategies to eliminate environmental pollution, poverty, and hunger, sustainable development was defined as fulfillment of the needs of the current generation without compromising the needs of future generations (1987, p. 43) and inspired the multiplicity paradigm. The significant emphasis in this definition was the commonality of the sustainable development for both current and future generations. Thus, the proposed solutions should be fair for the future generations that are not represented today. This perspective includes the essence of the communication approach for sustainable development: Solutions should be determined via a participatory-negotiatory dialogue on the widest possible scale and updated based on each new development.

Based on the theoretical and practical preferences of traditional and alternative approaches, it could be suggested that crisis communication occurs within the multiplicity paradigm and bottom-to-top participatory communication model. Servaes and Lie (2015, p. 132) argued that crisis communication is a thematic sub-discipline in communication approaches for sustainable development such as communications in health or environment. The authors (2015, p. 132) described the crisis communication to include studies on how government institutions and organizations assess and manage risks and crises and how they communicate with the stakeholders and citizens during a crisis.

As stressed in the above-mentioned definition, two issues are significant in crisis and risk communication. The first is to assess and manage crises and risks, and the second entails the communications with the society and the citizens. As witnessed during the COVID-19 pandemic, the social actors who assessed and managed the crisis and risks were those who were also responsible for communication, namely, state institutions and organizations. Since it is also the focus of the present study, the communications with the society and the citizens, who are the victims of the crisis, should be emphasized. Thus, the call for the completion of the communication targets (SGD18 on communication for all), a missing sustainable development goal, is quite significant. This call becomes even more important when it is considered that a crisis like the COVID-19 pandemic that introduced unprecedented difficulties and problems is a direct threat to social change and sustainable development. Unless citizens are free to identify the problems that most deeply affect their lives, not only in times of crisis but also in ordinary times, it would not be possible for them to convert their requirements into social demands and participate in policy making processes. Therefore, the fulfillment of the communications goal, a missed sustainable development target, would guarantee the nullification of the moves of public authorities to use crises as a reason to suspend cultural freedoms. In an environment of ambiguous social demand, the political approaches of the public authority to sustainable development would be detached from reality and the solutions for the problems could be determined based on political priorities that prioritize limited benefits rather than social ones. As previously emphasized, the nature of the COVID-19 crisis, which destroyed not only the material but also human resources, requires an effective crisis communication approach that focuses on cultural freedom and a coexistence and solidarity culture across all social stakeholders. Thus, the direction of the will of the public authority is quite important. In that case, communication for all should be defined as the 18th goal in the United Nations' list of sustainable development targets, and this should be accepted as a common goal by the international community. This development would exert a strong pressure on member state public authorities to concentrate social change on social benefits based on the desires and needs of the citizens.

The Course of the COVID-19 Pandemic in Turkey

The COVID-19 pandemic evolved into a crisis that deeply affected social life in Turkey as well as the rest of the globe. The crisis took different forms during different stages such as the development, emergence, and chronicity (Fink, 1986). In Turkey, the Ministry of Health adopted various practices based on the form of the crisis.

The attitude of the Ministry of Health during the development phase of the crisis did not reflect the seriousness of the problem. In fact, the precautions implemented by the Ministry of Health in the quarter until March 11, 2020, which was the beginning of the emergence phase, remained at best symbolic. For example, a scientific committee was established to manage the COVID-19 pandemic by the Ministry of Health quite late on January 10, 2020. The policy of screening of the passengers who arrived from China, quarantining of those with risk, and initiating infrared scanning and disinfection at airports and customs were adopted as late as January 24, 2020. The surge in the infection led to the suspension of flights to China and then to Iran on February 3, 2020, and also the flights to Italy, South Korea and Iraq were then suspended on February 25, 2020. The disinfection of public spaces and public transportation vehicles started as late as March 8, 2020. Although misinformation is a critical factor that elevates the challenges that communications should overcome for development and social change, the first case was announced in Turkey on March 11, 2020, as COVID-19 cases increased rapidly globally between January 2020 and the first week of March, leading to initial doubts as to whether the number of cases was hidden.

The Ministry of Health had started to share official COVID-19 data on March 11, 2020, which represented the beginning of the outbreak phase in Turkey. On March 12, 2020, spectators were banned in sports competitions and the travel of public employees abroad was subjected to special permission. The education was suspended in all schools and distance education was adopted only on March 25, 2020. The government waited until April 2020 for significant decisions such as closing the entertainment venues, banning congregation in mosques, a curfew for individuals over 65 and under 20, limits on the working hours of groceries, and restrictions in domestic airline transportation. Furthermore, these restrictions were implemented at a time when almost half of the settlements were quarantined and before the general curfew was implemented across the country. Thus, it could be suggested that the course of the emergence stage of the COVID-19 pandemic was quite ironic in Turkey. Between the time when the first case was announced and March 31, 2021, the total number of reported cases and the number of death increased to 13,531 and 214 respectively. It was interesting that the total number of tests conducted during this period remained at only 92,403.

The developments witnessed during the phase when the epidemic became rampant were similar to the administrative failures of the first two phases. In this stage, the cost of living with the crisis became even more dire for the citizens. For example, major problems were experienced in the distribution of masks. The Ministry of Health discussed the protective capacity of the masks for days; then sale of the masks was banned on April 6, 2020. Although it was announced that the masks would be sent to everyone free of charge via e-Government, this did not work, and the sale of the masks was allowed again. The 48-hour nationwide curfew was declared by the Ministry of Interior on April 10, 2020, only two hours before the start of the curfew, and people swarmed groceries, leading to an atmosphere of chaos and panic.

On the other hand, although it was announced that the transition to the normalization would be conducted gradually during May, June, and July in 2020, travel restrictions and curfews were lifted in June itself, and as the restaurants, cafés, movie theaters, theaters, and wedding halls reopened, the number of cases peaked. In this dramatic outlook, it became clear that the daily official count of COVID cases as announced by the Ministry of Health was not real. In fact, the Ministry of Health had to change these figures in mid-July 2020 and it started reporting the number of patients instead of the number of cases. Not only this, it stopped reporting ICU and intubated patients, and started reporting the number of severe patients and the rate of pneumonia, which did not make much sense for ordinary citizens. The vaccination drive was initiated only on

December 11, 2020, and was managed poorly without raising awareness among the citizens about the significance of vaccination in preventing the infection.

The Turkish Ministry of Health Crisis Communication Strategy During the COVID-19 Pandemic

Based on the perspective of developmental communications, the main problem associated with the COVID-19 pandemic in Turkey was the neglect of the two significant components of crisis communication. These components, namely the assessment and management of the crisis and the risks and communication of these to the society and citizens, actually constitute the backbone of an integrated crisis communication model. This backbone serves to ensure and sustain social integration with a participatory and solidarity approach in extraordinary times such as crises. It also ensures the mutual interaction between the government and citizens within the regular social relationships.

The indifference of the Ministry of Health to the social demands and the critics during the different stages of the pandemic disabled the first of the above-mentioned components. Furthermore, the Ministry of Health adhered to the modernization paradigm and top-down approach to communications, disabling the second component and cutting off the communications with the citizens. M.D.,[1] who was appointed as a member of the Board of Science established by the Ministry of Health during the COVID-19 pandemic, discussed the above-mentioned developments as follows:

> Several strata are affected by the pandemic within a short time. Social strata, health industry, social security, judicial services, law enforcement, economy, manufacturing. ... In other words, it affected life at large. Therefore, an institution or organization does not have a function in the control of the pandemic, you would successfully emerge from a pandemic only when you can include all layers of the society—for example, minibus drivers, metro drivers, ticketers, security guards, marketers, construction workers, manufacturers, and the whole industry. (MD, personal communication, December 12, 2020)

[1] The name is abbreviated as requested by the interviewee.

Due to the adoption of this paradigm and the communication model, the Ministry of Health declared that it considered crisis communication as a temporary solution during crisis periods and an issue that could be avoided with measures that only aim to save the day rather than a strategic solution. The measures implemented by the Ministry of Health during the three-month period between the development and emergence of the pandemic were symbolic rather than qualitative.

However, as indicated by the concepts of sustainability and flexibility, mutual interaction between the crisis managers and those affected by the crisis could be ensured by the preference of the bottom-to-top participatory (communication) model. Furthermore, it is necessary to establish a participatory solidaristic interaction and communication between the crisis managers and local governments, professional associations, non-governmental organizations, political parties, and other stakeholders. However, the Ministry of Health had a negative attitude toward the local government aid campaigns for citizens affected by the crisis; thus, obstructing both institutional solidarity and social solidarity that aimed to establish a bond of sympathy with those affected by the crisis. The President of the Ankara Medical Chamber, Dr. Ali Erkoç, explained the neglect of civil society with several examples:

> Pandemic boards were established in cities during the pandemic. However, associations of health professionals or related specialist associations were excluded from these boards. Quite an anti-democratic structure was established. Unfortunately, there is no chance of participative decisions or a democratic approach. At the center, a decision is made by the Ministry of Health or the Provincial Health Directorate, but these decisions were not announced. The impact of which is never discussed. There is no non-governmental organization in that board, the decisions pretend that there is. As a result, the pandemic process should be more transparent, more participatory, more democratic. (A. Erkoç, personal communication, December 03, 2020)

Another important factor in the crisis and risk assessment, management, and communications is to ensure that the statements are accurate and satisfactory, and the media preferred by the citizens are employed. Thus, social media, especially Twitter, has been the most preferred medium of communication by both the Ministry of Health and the citizens affected by the crisis since the emergence of COVID-19 pandemic. The Ministry of Health started to post COVID-19 data on the official Twitter account on daily basis after March 11, 2020, the date of the first COVID-19 case. However, even the first post lacked geographical location of the case. This led to doubts among the citizens about the accuracy and reliability of the Ministry of Health posts. Furthermore, the reports about COVID-19 cases in various cities were only posted after March 2021, a year after the first case, gradually turning the suspicion among the citizens into distrust.

The Ministry of Health could not exhibit the requirements to overcome the crisis of trust and to improve the weakness in social integration during the chronic period of the pandemic. The Ministry of Health discontinued the distinction between the cases and patients on November 25, 2020. The dramatic increase in the data provided in the same statement actually justified the suspicions about the accuracy of the previous data regarding the number of cases and deaths. In other words, it became obvious that the data provided by the state were misleading since the beginning of the pandemic and that the real figures were hidden, and these views were not a speculation as claimed by the public authorities. This development totally destroyed the credibility of the crisis management among the citizens. Also, the neglect of the dramatic developments during the COVID-19 pandemic by the Ministry of Health and the underestimation of the pandemic even during the chronic period alleviated the above-mentioned case. Ankara Medical Chamber President Dr. Ali Erkoç confirmed this as follows: "The citizens significantly panicked during the initial days. However, the policies and attitudes adopted by the Ministry of Health or the political authority, unfortunately, weakened this perception across the citizens. Citizens do not take the pandemic seriously, unfortunately, they do not follow the pandemic regulations in daily life" (A. Erkoç, personal communication, December 03, 2020). Furthermore, the Minister of Health tweeted the following on 28.01.2022: "The virus has weakened. There is no need to worry about the increasing figures. We will continue our normal lives and protect our elders and those with chronic diseases and implement personal precautions. Let us not neglect our vaccines. We have our powerful Turcovac."[2]

On the same day, 93,586 new cases were identified in Turkey, while 210 people lost their lives. These developments demonstrated that the

[2] https://twitter.com/drfahrettinkoca/status/1487106007553785858?cxt=HHwWhIC-uZ3CoaMpAAAA

Ministry of Health lost the opportunity to assess and manage the crisis and risks, and failed to establish communications with the citizens.

An important factor in an integrated crisis communication strategy is the interaction between crisis managers and those affected by the crisis based on the participatory communication model. Thus, instead of using the bidirectional communication opportunities inherent in social media, the Ministry of Health preferred the unidirectional communication model of the traditional media, thereby disconnecting communication with the citizens. Since the unidirectional employment of social media that allows the integration of the tool and the environment due to the habit of traditional media employment that focuses on the tool, transformed communicative activity into a daily-statement routine, ignoring the dynamics, awareness, and sympathy-forming capacity of the new medium. M.D., a member of the Scientific Board, emphasized this problem clearly as follows:

> The inclusion of sociologists and communication scientists in crisis management from the start could have had significant contributions. If sociologists, communication scientists, healthcare professionals, and those who worked in the field were included from the beginning, before the pandemic started in the country, these problems would not have experienced. Thus, it was necessary to focus on the rehabilitation of the psychology of the society via periodic measurements. How should you communicate with ordinary citizens, how could you persuade them, I cannot do this alone as a health professional. Sociologists and communication scientists should do this. (M. D., personal communication, December 12, 2020)

Furthermore, the strategy ignored the role of social media in improving the trust and social integration (Liu et al., 2016) as a communication model that minimizes uncertainty (bottom-up) about the statements.

Since the social media messages posted by the Minister of Health were based on assumptions and sensory information instead of first-hand data, they were ineffective in preventing speculations with negative crisis management outcomes and nurtured the insecurity risk across the citizens. In his Twitter post on 06.08.2020, the Minister of Health neither clarified the allegations nor informed the citizens about the reality and opened the door for further speculations that could lead to social chaos by stating the following: "We do not have a full capacity urban hospital or any hospital. The allegations are unfounded. Those who propagate these baseless claims should take precautions as if the hospitals are full. Maybe this would be the only benefit of the allegations."[3] Since mutual interaction weakens when information is transmitted by only the crisis managers, the fact that speculations or fake news would continuously be in the circulation was neglected. The adoption of a similar attitude in vaccinations led to an unawareness across the society, the targeted vaccination rates were not achieved, and the resistance of the anti-vaccine groups could not be resolved. Another factor that fed these developments was the fact that the Ministry of Health was almost entirely the only source in social media, which led to a state of communicative introversion. The Minister of Health only once referred to the World Health Organization website in his messages about COVID-19.

Another significant factor for integrated crisis communication strategy is flexibility and sustainable coordination between the crisis managers. Turkey missed this opportunity as well. A multi-head administration emerged that included the Presidency, the Ministry of Health, the Ministry of Interior, and the Directorate of Communications on the assessment and management of the crisis. For example, the Minister of Interior attempted to resign when the first curfew turned into a chaos; however, the request was rejected by the president to prevent the perception of the resignation as a political failure of the government. On the other hand, the Scientific Board, which aimed to play an active role in eliminating the panic that emerged during the developmental phase of the pandemic, did not have the opportunity to communicate directly with the citizens since it was established within the Ministry of Health. Thus, the citizens were in the dark about the decisions of the crisis managers on healthcare problems.

In general, the approach of the public actors, especially the Ministry of Health, toward communication was centralized that predominantly aimed to control the society during the COVID-19 pandemic. These public actors relaxed the measures during the holidays, for the wedding ceremonies, and public rituals such as sending off transcripts based on the abovementioned centralist approach and lost their credibility due to decisions such as randomly banning and allowing in-classroom education, workplaces, and accommodation facilities for economic reasons. The public was informed about these and similar cases by the statements of various nongovernmental organizations, especially the Turkish Medical Association. In the interview conducted with the Ankara Medical Chamber President

[3] https://twitter.com/drfahrettinkoca/status/1291270092068663298

Dr. Ali Erkoç, he attributed the crisis management problems to the centralized management approach:

> After all, it was not reasonable and logical to keep a village primary school in Samsun, a rather small city, closed while the pandemic was rampant in crowded cities like Ankara and Istanbul. In other words, you cannot manage every location with central decisions. ... It is not right. So, local governments have a significant effect on this. Quarantine decisions should be taken by the local governments, by explaining it to everyone, to the local people transparently. Unfortunately, this did not happen, it was managed with a central approach, it was managed by a single authority, so unfortunately, we were not very successful. (A. Erkoç, personal communication, December 03, 2020)

Despite these warnings, the attitude of the relevant public actors did not change, and the most needed accurate and reliable data were not provided to the citizens affected by the crisis.

Conclusion

The study aimed to draw attention to the fact that the effective crisis communications strategy required during the COVID-19 pandemic was not adopted due to the communication problems between the social stakeholders in Turkey. As emphasized in the study, since the communication model adopted by the Ministry of Health was ex parte and ignored the public reaction, demands, concerns, and fears, it was far from fulfilling the needs of those affected by the crisis. Furthermore, the concerns and fears of the citizens affected by the crisis were used to cover up the crisis management failures or to make it look like normal. In other words, communications aimed at social control, not social dialogue.

On the other hand, the Ministry of Health did not provide accurate, adequate, and timely information that allows a mutual and solidaristic interaction between the government and the people, leading to the disconnection of the communication. M.D., member of the Scientific Board, emphasized the erosion of the language employed in crisis communication:

> Success in pandemic should be based on robust scientific foundations, managerial practices, public acceptance for these practices, and adequate rhetoric on infection control across the social classes. Crisis communication should

> be conducted based on the dynamics-spirit of the process without eroding the process. If you always say the same things, these would not be credible. (M.D., personnel communication, December 12, 2020)

On the other hand, the involvement of the main solution partners, both in the determination and solution of the problems with different degrees of severity, was prevented for political reasons. As a result, citizens tended to not comply with the restrictions during the pandemic, the number of cases exhibited generally a high trend, despite periods of short-term decrease. In an environment where the number of individuals who "preferred to die of the disease instead of starvation" has increased as stated by the Science Board member M.D. (M.D., personal communication, December 12, 2020), the COVID-19 pandemic became unmanageable, leading to long quarantines in Turkey, which in turn led to isolation, pessimism, and indifference among the people.

In the case of Turkey, the main reason for the lack of communication between the social stakeholders was the traditional instrumentalist attitude that aims social control, which was adopted by the Ministry of Health in the crisis communications strategy. Both the instrumental communications approach and the failure to implement participatory-negotiatory decision-making and implementation policies in this approach were significantly consistent with the characteristics of the modernization paradigm and its communications model. While it is essential for the official statements to refer to experts and reliable sources in times of crisis to raise awareness and to introduce the desired behavioral changes (Christensen & Lægreid, 2020; Duffy & Chan, 2019), the Ministry of Health, in contrast, preferred an introvert approach. It is not also possible to argue that the public authority responsible for crisis management adopted an encouraging attitude toward the employment of social media to reinforce the democratic culture. On the contrary, the public authority tried to narrow the virtual public space for individual representation and free ideas on social media by hiding behind the chaos induced by the crisis. However, for an effective crisis communication strategy, it should have employed the social media to organize large masses and increase participation, which should be supported by the persuasive power of traditional media. However, those responsible for crisis management considered those affected by the crisis not as solution partners but as the source of the problems.

The lack of communication induced by this introversion and lack of dialogue not only weakened the confidence of those affected by the crisis in public authorities, but also triggered a crisis of legitimacy and trust that led to significant risks for future generations. The collection and analysis of social data that would reveal the communications dimension of the crisis was repressed by an environment where citizens experienced difficulties in expressing their emotions about the problems and their magnitude. However, as emphasized by Servaes (2016, p. 702), the study findings in such periods are extremely significant for the determination of social priorities and policies for both functional and consequential crisis management and to minimize the risks for the future generations. In other words, social and scientific feedback (Barker, 2004) and crisis communication research are essential for the development of integrated crisis communication strategies. An integrated crisis communication strategy entails participatory communication practices such as distance education, work at home, and online healthcare that would contribute to the development of a democratic culture that integrates policies in health, education, economy, science, and culture based on sustainable development goals, instead of the adoption of simple, limited, stereotypical communicative policies as if these are valid in all periods and under all conditions.

In conclusion, the perception of the crisis managers that the negative developments experienced during the COVID-19 pandemic only affects today and the resulting messages are a serious indicator of significant normalization problems in education, employment, poverty, migration, healthcare, social-economic inequality, income distribution, taxation, and public services. Stokke (1991, p. 9) indicated that these problems would also negatively affect the satisfaction of the needs of the future generations and reduce their quality of life. Those affected by the crisis and those whose problems were not solved would transfer their problems to future generations traumatically. The factor that would double the dread of the situation is the fact that the miscommunication across the social stakeholders would reinforce the distrust for public authorities and even for the state as a whole, and spread to the whole society, which in turn would create a polarizing bias that would hinder social solidarity and the culture of symbiosis. It is clear that a strong communication infrastructure or the gradual closure of the digital divide between the social stakeholders could not change this adverse picture alone. This infrastructure should be integrated with a strong and inclusive goal: To fulfill the communication goals (SGD 18 on communication for all) that remain unfulfilled among the sustainable development goals. The joint will of the public authorities of the United Nations member states is more needed today for this action that would integrate the digital infrastructure and the governance superstructure.

The missing communication goals (SGD 18 on communication for all) among the sustainable development goals could inspire the development of a new crisis communication model. Based on the Turkish example, the development of an effective crisis communication strategy would depend on the development of a model that would integrate digital infrastructure and administrative superstructure. In this crisis communication model, it would be important to integrate the digital infrastructure and the administrative superstructure, in other words, the integration of the instruments with the goals. As the Turkish case demonstrated, it would be crucial for the governmental components to establish two-way communications both within the government and with the citizens affected by the crisis in the crisis communication model. This would be possible only with a robust digital infrastructure. A horizontal organization that would include all social components such as the local governments and civil society organizations would be possible based on the above-mentioned digital network infrastructure. Thus, crisis communication would allow the inclusion of all components in the government superstructure with a participatory approach and facilitate the government to overcome coordination challenges such as multi-headed administration.

The Turkish case also demonstrated that it was very important to include communication scientists, linguists, software developers, social scientists, psychologists, lawyers, and educators in crisis communication. This stemmed from the fact that these actors could assume roles that could eliminate the communication gaps between the crisis management and those affected by the crisis. These actors would not act as gatekeepers between those who manage the crisis and the citizens but as gate observers. These gate observers could establish an active dialogue between the parties by analyzing the message data that flow between those who manage the crisis and the citizens and the communicative reactions of the citizens in real time with scientific methods. The social knowledge that these actors would produce could lead to active implementation of the crisis management measures and allow the citizens to become the solution partners for the problem.

References

Barker, D. J. P. (2004). The developmental origins of adult disease. *Journal of the American College of Nutrition., 23*(6), 588–595.

Başaran, F. (2010). *İletişim Teknolojileri ve Toplumsal Gelişme [Communication Technologies and Social Development]*. Ütopya Yayınevi.

Beam, S. (1992). Surveying the territory: Re-examining MacBride and theories of development. *Gazette., 50*(2–3), 109–145.

Christensen, T., & Lægreid, P. (2020). The coronavirus crisis—Crisis communication, meaning-making, and reputation management. *International Public Management Journal, 23*(5), 713–729.

Duffy, B. E., & Chan, N. C. (2019). 'You never really know who's looking': Imagined surveillance across social media platforms. *New Media & Society., 21*(1), 119–138.

Fink, S. (1986). *Crisis management: Planning fort the inevitable*. American Management Ass.

Hudson, H. E. (1983). The role of telecommunications in development: A synthesis of current research. In O. H. Gandy, P. Espinosa, & J. A. Ordover (Eds.), *Proceedings from the tenth annual telecommunications policy research conference* (pp. 291–307). Ablex.

Hugill, P. J. (2003). Technology, its innovation and diffusion as the motor of capitalism. *Comparative Technology Transfer and Society, 1*(1), 89–113.

Jinqiu, Z., & Xiaoming, H. (2005). Modernization in the information age. *Media Asia, 32*(4), 191–196.

Liu, B. F., Fraustino, J. D., & Jin, Y. (2016). Social media use during disasters: How information form and source influence intended behavioral responses. *Communication Research, 43*(5), 626–646.

Mansell, R., & Wehn, U. (1998). *Knowledge societies: Information technology for sustainable development*. Oxford University Press.

Mattelart, A. (1994). *Mapping world communication: War, progress and culture*. University of Minnesota Press.

Merriam, S. B., & Tisdell, E. J. (2016). *Qualitative research: A guide to design and implementation* (4th ed.). Jossey-Bass.

Polk, E., & Servaes, J. (2015). Sustainability and participatory communication: A case study of the transition town Amherst. *Massachusetts. Management Communication Quarterly, 29*(1), 160–167.

Riaz, A. (1997). The role of telecommunications in economic growth: Proposal for an alternative framework of analysis. *Media, Culture & Society, 19*(4), 557–583.

Samarajiva, R., & Shields, P. (1990). Integration, telecommunication and development: Power in paradigms. *Journal of Communication, 40*(3), 84–105.

Servaes, J. (2000). Communication for development: Alive and kicking! *Communicato, 26*(1), 84–89.

Servaes, J. (2016). How 'sustainable' is development communication research? *The International Communication Gazette, 78*(7), 701–710.

Servaes, J. (Ed.). (2020). *Handbook of communication for development and social change*. Springer.

Servaes, J., & Lie, R. (2015). New challenges for communication for sustainable development and social change: A review essay. *The Journal of Multicultural Discourses, 10*(1), 124–148.

Servaes, J., & Malikhao, P. (2007). Communication and sustainable development. In FAO (Ed.), *Communication and sustainable development: Selected Papers from the 9th UN Roundtable on Communication for Development*. Food & Agriculture Org..

Stevenson, R. L. (2003). National development and communication. *Encyclopedia of International Media and Communications, 5*, 163–175.

Stokke, O. (1991). Sustainable development: A multi-challenge. *The European Journal of Development, 3*(1), 8–31.

World Commission on Environment and Development. (1987). *Our Common Future*. Oxford University Press.

CHAPTER 10

Conclusion: SDG18-Communication for All—Neither Too Late, Nor Too Early

Muhammad Jameel Yusha'u and Jan Servaes

Abstract The Sustainable Development Goals (SDGs) provide the most ambitious framework to address global development challenges. Yet, the framers of the 2030 Agenda missed the opportunity to add a dedicated goal to communication which has both independent and cross-cutting roles in the entire SDGs. This chapter argues that the United Nations must review the SDGs and include SDG18—Communication for all—if the SDGs are to achieve the desired results. The chapter provides current and real-life examples on how communication has transformed our society with real impact in media and communication, education, health, climate change, and so on. The COVID-19 pandemic has revealed the importance of communication as an important pillar because of how communication tools and instruments helped in containing the pandemic and

M. J. Yusha'u (✉)
Harvard Kennedy School, Cambridge, MA, USA

J. Servaes
KU Leuven, Leuven, Belgium

J. Servaes, M. J. Yusha'u (eds.), *SDG18 Communicaton for All, Volume 2*, Sustainable Development Goals Series,
https://doi.org/10.1007/978-3-031-19459-7_10

helped the global economy to survive. Examples have been provided on the role communication can play on each of the SDGs. The chapter recommends building a coalition of SDG18 champions and convening a major stakeholder conference that will help in setting the process to include SDG18—Communication for all—when the United Nations review the 2030 Agenda for Development.

Keywords SDGs • Communication • Development • 2030 Agenda • SDG18—Communication for all • COVID-19

Introduction

From the contributions so far in these two volumes on SDG18—Communication for all, the omission of SDG18 on communication for all couldn't be more glaring. It is clear that the transformations that took place in the last two to three decades have put communications for development at the centre of global development initiatives. The *Communication Initiative Network* highlighted this in a discussion on the role of communication in promoting the MDGs back in 2006. The organization brought forward the need to ensure effective citizen engagement in the implementation of the MDGs and provide more voice to global youth. The organization also highlighted how development experts have failed to understand the relevance of communication in development (Communication Initiative Network, 2006).

From the discussion in the preceding chapters, it is evident that lessons have not been learnt by development experts, especially those leading the policy realm to understand the need to integrate communication in the implementation of the SDGs. The fact that these two volumes, along with other recent studies on SDG18, have been brought forward indicates the apathy from policy makers to appreciate the role of communication in development.

Before delving into the key conclusion based on the insights from this book, let us provide a summary of the findings from the preceding chapters:

- The urgency and centrality of communication in achieving the SDGs. Since the 1990s, the global community has agreed to come up with a socio-economic framework that will guide socio-economic development. Communication for all is a necessity and people need it to achieve their full potential in life. To achieve each of the SDGs, communication must have a role to play.

- Development communication has a critical role to play in addressing global inequality. After at least seven decades of research and advocacy in communication for development, the SDGs provide an opportunity to draw from the power of communication to bridge the gap between communities and ensure an equitable society. Inequality is a major concern. In Latin America in particular, it has been a major source of concern due to rising poverty and income inequality. The role of civil society and effective government policies will be required to ensure a fair and just society.
- Public Service Media (PSM) should not only play a role as conveyer of information; it should also serve as a watchdog in the implementation of the SDGs. Public Service Broadcasting (PSB) as envisaged since the formation of the BBC World Service was intended to promote public interest. PSB has undergone a lot of changes in the past decades, but it has remained an important tool in development communication. Several governments have invested resources to promote PSB, although in recent years there are challenges with cuts and sometimes political interference. But it remains an indispensable tool if SDG18—Communication for all—is to be achieved. More dialogue can be conducted in relation to the SDGs. Policy makers can be held to account for using public service media. Even the UN which is the custodian of the SDGs can benefit from the reporting of the progress on the SDGs and work collectively with countries to address the gaps in financing, resource mobilization and implementation. Achieving sustainability towards 2030 needs the combined effect of public service media and the SDGs to form a united front.
- One of the key strengths of the SDGs is the diversity of the goals. Addressing the needs of at least seven billion people on the planet earth is a cumbersome undertaking. This is even more for minority communities such as indigenous people. Having a voice for communities facing racial discrimination requires a platform to amplify their voices. The case of indigenous people in Australia is a good example. By including SDG18—Communication for all—in the SDGs, such marginalized communities could discover their voices and find a footing in a world where inequality is growing by the day. Of relevance to the issue of minorities such as indigenous people in Australia are the utilization of the media to promote literacy and

access to information. In this case, SDG18—Communication for all—will play a cross-cutting role by strongly aiding the realization of SDGs 1, 2, 4, 10, 11 and 13 in particular. See Chap. 5 in this volume for key recommendations on how SDG18 could contribute in achieving sustainability for indigenous people.

- One of the key tenets of communication for development is social and behavioural change (Servaes & Malikhao, 2007; Servaes et al., 2012; Servaes, 2017, 2020). The extent to which the traditional media can influence social and behavioural change continues to be debated. While the debate is going on, a major source of concern called misinformation or fake news emerged. This was further heightened by the COVID-19 pandemic where social media sites delved into the debate about the pandemic and tried to influence public opinion resulting sometimes in resistance to the vaccine. A key contribution of this volume is how social media contributed to misinformation and fake news. A key lesson that emerged from this volume is that SDG18—Communication for all—is not just about promotion of the SDGs, empowering people and addressing inequality. It is also about tracking misinformation that could harm the public. In the case of COVID-19, fake news was a major setback on SDG3.
- An interesting perspective about the formulation of the SDGs is the role played by the global elites in formulating the 2030 Agenda for Development. Presidents, heads of government, prime ministers, ministers, top university professors, heads of multilateral institutions, and so on were very visible in the media. But what about the voices that may not have access to this group of elites? How can their voices count in the realization of the SDGs? This applies particularly to people with communication disabilities, children and people who do not speak the dominant languages. It is common to assume that people have easy access to English, Arabic, French, German, Spanish, Portuguese, Chinese, Urdu or any other dominant language in the world. But there are communities that are equally literate, yet do not have the luxury to express themselves in the dominant languages. So are children and people with communication disabilities. In 2017 a study group on language conducted a symposium on language and sustainable development at the United Nations. The symposium found that "the failure to account for language and language diversity

in formulating and implementing global policies have disproportionate effects on vulnerable populations, the primary stakeholders of the United Nations Sustainable Development Goals" (Centre for Applied Linguistics, 2017, para 1). This is a shortcoming that SDG18—Communication for all—could help address.

- The COVID-19 pandemic has highlighted the plight of several groups that might be suffering in silence. Among these are vulnerable groups of women that suffer from Intimate Partner Violence (IPV). The condition of these women is a major hindrance to the actualization of SDG5. SDG18—Communication for all—is one of the goals that could help identify and increase awareness on how to reduce the suffering of vulnerable women. This is even more difficult for immigrant populations who might be in a disadvantaged position due to language barriers or lack of awareness on how to stand-up for their right. That is why, as discussed by Servaes (2021), culture and communication, which are missing in the SDGs, have a vital role to play in achieving the global goals.
- Communication plays a pivotal role in many crises, especially during health emergencies like COVID-19. The case of Turkey is a good example. At the beginning the response of the ministry of health wasn't at par with the magnitude of the pandemic. This is a classic case on the absence of a clear communication goal in the SDGs. While governments and policy makers might have clarity about SDGs like poverty alleviation, ending hunger, ensuring healthcare for all and so on, what the framers of the SDGs failed to understand is that each of the SDGs can be affected by an emergency which requires a robust communication approach to tackle it. Applying the tools of crises communication with specific reference to the SDGs has been explored by Looser et al. (2019) where they suggested the adoption of the 7s Stakeholder paradigm, namely: Public Stakeholder Analysis (i.e., Policy Field Analysis and Crises Communication/Management), Stakeholder Identification, Stakeholder Prioritization, Stakeholder Interest Analysis, Stakeholder Response Strategies, Stakeholder Performance Gaps and Stakeholder Communication Strategies. If the 7s stakeholder paradigm had been applied on the SDGs prior to their adoption, perhaps SDG18—Communication for all—might would already be part of the global goals.

Why SDG18 Matters?

Yusha'u and Servaes (2021) have discussed the role of communication in supporting the global economy at the peak of the COVID-19 pandemic. Their argument remains valid looking at the reality on the ground. Let's take the journalism profession for example, which has been the traditional conveyer of information to billions of people across the globe. According to Mahon (2021), following the COVID-19 pandemic, smartphone or what is called mobile journalism is gradually taking over traditional journalism. Journalists around the world work remotely, file reports and organize interviews and discussions using digital communication tools. The way news is developed and consumed has been substantially transformed due to the effects of the pandemic.

Beckett (2020) has identified at least three impacts of COVID-19 on the global information ecosystem. First is the rise of online journalism which has increased substantially compared to 20 years ago. The second change is the move into social media. Third, journalism is going to be more diverse and much more distributed. In essence, we could argue that there would be more distribution of information.

These changes in the ecosystem of information and communication could benefit the implementation of the SDGs if harnessed effectively. People could become more aware of the dangers of poverty (SDG1), the threat of hunger (SDG2), why lack of access to health and vaccine could promote inequality (SDG3 and SDG10) and lack of attention to climate change (SDG13) could endanger the environment.

The health sector is another example of why SDG18, if harnessed properly, could be critical to the success of the SDGs (Malikhao, 2016). Following the COVID-19 pandemic, there was a surge in demand for digital health. In South-east Asia for instance a survey of 5302 university students found that 92% of the students refer to online sources such as Google and Bing to search for health information (Htay et al., 2022). In Saudi Arabia, COVID-19 resulted in the adoption of digital health applications to seek medical information in the country (Alhodaib & Alanzi, 2021). In South Africa, digital technologies such as SMS, WhatsApp, artificial intelligence, robotics and other applications were used for screening and diagnosing infections during COVID-19 (Mbunge et al., 2022). In Morocco, the government adopted legislations that gave room for the adoption of digital health technologies in the healthcare sector (Dehbi et al., 2022). A study published in one of the most authoritative health journals, *the Lancet,* found changes in attitude regarding perception about digital health during COVID-19. The study found that people stopped seeing digital health tools from being opportunities to necessities (Wong et al., 2022). Finally, Elias Mpofu (2020), applying a trans-disciplinary approach, provides a research-based guide to understanding and implementing sustainable community health in diverse international setting.

Education which is the main goal of SDG4 in the 2030 Agenda is one sector that is undergoing a massive transformation. Even before the COVID-19 pandemic, some scholars have envisaged the need to be more innovative and embrace new approaches using new technologies in the education system of countries. Christensen and Eyring (2011) have discussed the need for attitudinal change in higher education in more detail in their book, the *Innovative University*, where they warned tertiary institutions to be more vigilant before online education forces them to do so.

While the adoption of technology has been ongoing at various levels of the educational system in different parts of the world, COVID-19 could be the main game changer in mainstreaming digital education. Failure to understand digital technologies as communication, information and tools for social and behavioural change is a major bane in the attempt to achieve the SDGs. This perhaps explains why some countries came up with policies that quickly build the capacity of teachers in the learning of digital skills. A case in point is the case of 11 European countries that brought such policies. They are Germany, France, Portugal, Belgium, Cyprus, Denmark, Greece, Ireland, Italy, Malta and Spain (Zancajo et al., 2022).

These are a few examples that call for deeper reflection on the relevance of the missing SDG. The SDGs are meant to improve the lives of individuals, protect the planet and help ensure a prosperous future for all. In summary, the SDGs are meant to protect the interest of the public. The tenets of communication, journalism and information are nothing less than championing the interest of the public as we shall discuss in the following section.

SDG18, Communication and Public Interest

As championed by the United Nations since the adoption of the 2030 Agenda for development, the SDGs can be summarized into 5Ps (people, prosperity, planet, partnership and peace). The 5Ps can be grouped into three clusters of social inclusion, economic growth and environmental protection (United Nations Systems Staff College, 2017).

To further highlight the relevance of SDG18 for each of the global goals, we have highlighted in the table below, albeit not exhaustively, what role communication can play in the entire 2030 Agenda using the 5Ps as a framework, based on the lessons learned from the various chapters from these two volumes.

The examples highlighted in the third column on the role of communication in each of the SDGs highlights the linkage between communication, public interest and the SDGs. The SDGs cannot be operated in a vacuum. Some critics might argue that an independent goal may not be needed to implement the SDGs; rather the role of communication can be cascaded in each SDG as Table 10.1 highlights. That argument is implausible for the following reasons.

Firstly, having small targets in each of the goals about communication is a sign that the role of communication is still in the periphery. Poverty alleviation is taken seriously because there is a clear goal about poverty, same thing for health, education, energy, and so on. We can categorically state that the SDGs cannot be achieved without a role for communication, just like achieving any of the SDGs without alleviating poverty means the global agenda for development has failed. Any vision that is inevitable about sustainable development deserves a goal. Hence, the plea for the inclusion of SDG18.

Secondly, failure to have an SDG dedicated to communication means the lessons from COVID-19 have not been learned. We have argued proactively in our previous work (Yusha'u & Servaes, 2021; Servaes, 2021; Yusha'u, 2021) that if in 2015 communication didn't deserve a goal in the SDGs, COVID-19 pandemic has altered that situation. The examples highlighted earlier on how communications in its various forms changed the landscape of journalism, health and education further illustrate this point. We are living in a digital age where communication in its holistic sense is a pillar we have to live with in all our endeavours.

Thirdly, among the SDGs, there are goals that are fluid like communications. Almost all the SDGs from SDG8 to SDG17 are not targeting a single outcome compared to, for example, goals about poverty, hunger, education, health, women empowerment and water and sanitation. The rest of the SDGs from SDG8 to SDG17 were a mishmash of several development challenges clustered into a single goal. If 11 out of the 17 SDGs are hybrids of several development challenges, then adding SDG18—Communication for all—becomes even more tenable because it can aid the realization of each SDG in a more forceful and effective manner.

Table 10.1 Relevance of SDG18 for each of the SDGs

Category	*Cluster*	*Role of SDG18—Communication for all*	*Relevant SDG*
People	Social inclusion	• Awareness on SDGs to improve people's lives and generate public interest • Individual right • Digital inclusion • Highlighting inequality • Digital health • Digital education • Awareness on hygiene and sanitation • Women and economic empowerment	• SDG1 • SDG2 • SDG3 • SDG4 • SDG5 • SDG6
Prosperity	Economic growth	• Financial literacy • Public sensitization on alternative energy sources • Information about the rights of workers, good wages and decent living • Digital innovation and access to opportunity • Empowering communities through the power of information to address inequality	• SDG7 • SDG8 • SDG9 • SDG10
Planet	Environmental protection	• Advocacy to protect the planet • Awareness on the negative impact of waste • Public sensitization on protecting the environment • Mainstreaming media reporting on water conservation • Drawing public attention on the dangers of desertification	• SDG11 • SDG12 • SDG13 • SDG14 • SDG15
Partnership	Social inclusion, economic growth	• Promote partnership and strengthen resource mobilization to finance the goals	• SDG16
Peace	Social inclusion, economic growth, environmental protection	• Public awareness on the dangers of conflict • Supporting UN and the effort of regional organizations to ensure sustainable peace and stability • Sustaining multilateralism	• SDG16 • SDG17

Table 10.2 Ten peer-learning areas

Vision & strategy	
1.	Recognize the importance of public support
2.	Set goals for public awareness and track progress
3.	Adapt your narratives and campaigns to the SDGs
4.	Bring the SDGs into development education
People & partnerships	
5.	Understand and listen to your audiences
6.	Communicate "whole-government"
7.	Engage with non-state actors to broaden your reach
Tools, resources & innovation	
8.	Make effective use of new technologies
9.	Innovate in presenting results and performance data
10.	Mobilize resources for public engagement

Source: OECD

The Organisation for Economic Cooperation and Development (OECD) has conducted a detailed analysis which can easily be adopted on the alignment between SDGs, Communication and public interest (OECD, 2017). The report by the OECD through its Development Communication function identified ten peer-learning areas on the role of communication in the SDGs. The ten lessons could easily provide a road-map that can be synthesized along with other contributions such as Lee and Vargas (2020), Yusha'u and Servaes (2021) and Yusha'u (2021) to form a goal along with relevant targets for SDG18—Communication for all (Table 10.2).

The Next Steps

The role of communication in development is essential in achieving development objectives in the twenty-first century. The diversity of the contributions from the two volumes that we have covered has shown that SDG18—Communication for all—should be taken more seriously by the United Nations and all the stakeholders who have an influence in the formulation of the 2030 Agenda. As we noted in our previous book (Yusha'u & Servaes, 2021), the SDGs need to be reviewed. We stand by that position. Reviewing the SDGs to incorporate SDG18—Communication for all—can neither be too late in the current situation nor be too early had it been included in the SDGs ab initio.

The United Nations as the custodian of the SDGs should lead this effort. As we conclude this volume, we suggest the following steps in this important journey that aims to ensure sustainability for people, planet, prosperity, partnership and peace.

- Building a coalition of civil society, media proprietors, journalists and other public opinion leaders to lead the campaign on incorporating SDG18—Communication for all—in the SDGs.
- Researchers, academics and opinion leaders to publish more research on SDG18—Communication for all.
- Similar to the effort of OECD in drafting ten peer-learning lessons on the SDGs, a major stakeholder conference should be convened to discuss, review and advise the United Nations on how best to incorporate SDG18—Communication for all—to the 2030 Agenda for Development.
- Media and research organizations such as the International Association of Media and Communication Research (IAMCR), International Communication and Association (ICA), International Federation of Journalists (IFJ) and similar regional and (inter) national organizations, including professional bodies such as national union of journalists across countries, should take the lead in promoting SDG18—Communication for all. These organizations should take the campaign to the UN.
- These media and communication organizations should engage with UN member states proactively and highlight the role of communication for development in the reporting of the progress and challenges on SDGs to the High-Level Political Forum.
- As we noted in previous work, the UN should set a process for reviewing the SDGs to address the gaps identified especially in the aftermath of the challenges posed by the COVID-19 pandemic.

References

Alhodaib, H., & Alanzi, T. M. (2021). Understanding the impact of digital health strategies during the COVID-19 outbreak in Saudi Arabia. *Risk Management and Healthcare Policy*. Retrieved May 15, 2022, from https://www.dovepress.com/getfile.php?fileID=75779

Beckett, C. (2020). *The future of journalism post-Covid-19: Technology, diversity and collaboration*. London School of Economics. Retrieved May 11, 2022, from https://blogs.lse.ac.uk/polis/2020/06/12/the-future-of-journalism-post-covid19-technology-diversity-and-collaboration/

Centre for Applied Linguistics. (2017). *Language, the sustainable development goals, and vulnerable populations.* Retrieved May 14, 2022, from https://www.cal.org/resource-center/publications-products/language-sdg

Christensen, C. M., & Eyring, H. J. (2011). *The innovative university: Changing the DNA of higher education from the inside out.* Jossey-Bass.

Communication Initiative Network. (2006). *Communicating millennium development goals.* Retrieved May 11, 2022, from https://www.comminit.com/global/content/communicating-millennium-development-goals-mdgs

Dehbi, Z. E. O., Sedrati, H., Chaqsare, S., Azami, A. I., Merzouki, M., Raji, M., Rhalem, W., Idrissi, N. A., Nejjari. C., Amzazi, S., & Ghazal, H. (2022). Moroccan digital health response to the COVID-19 crisis. *Global Health Journal.* Retrieved May 15, 2022, from https://www.frontiersin.org/articles/10.3389/fpubh.2021.690462/full

Htay, M. N. U., Parial, L. L., Tolabing, M. C., Dadaczynski, K., Okan, O., Leung, A. Y. M., & Su, T. T. (2022). Digital health literacy, online information-seeking behaviour, and satisfaction of Covid-19 information among the university students of East and South-East Asia. *PLoS ONE, 17*(4), e0266276. https://doi.org/10.1371/journal.pone.0266276

Lee, P., & Vargas, L. (Eds.). (2020). *Expanding shrinking communication spaces.* Southbound.

Looser, S., Mohr, S., & Wehrmeyer, W. (2019). Crises communication vs. United Nation sustainable development goals: The 7S paradigm as feasible solution facilitator. *International Journal of Crisis Communication., 3*, 62–80.

Mahon, J. (2021). *How the Covid-19 pandemic changed digital journalism?* Retrieved May 11, 2022, from https://www.journalism.co.uk/news/how-the-coronavirus-pandemic-changed-digital-journalism/s2/a880580/

Malikhao, P. (2016). *Effective health communication for sustainable development. Public health in the 21st century.* Nova Publishers.

Mbunge, E., Batani, J., Gaobotse, G., & Muchemwa, B. (2022). Virtual healthcare services and digital health technologies deployed during coronavirus disease 2019 (COVID-19) pandemic in South Africa: A systematic review. *GlobalHealth Journal.* Retrieved May 15, 2022, from https://www.sciencedirect.com/science/article/pii/S2414644722000239

Mpofu, E. (Ed.). (2020). *Sustainable community health: Systems and practices in diverse settings.* Palgrave Macmillan.

OECD. (2017). 10 learning areas for SDGs communication. Presented at Global Festival for Ideas on Sustainable Development. Retrieved May 16, 2022, from https://www.oecd.org/dev/pgd/DevCom_10_Learning_Areas_SDG_Communications.pdf

Servaes, J. (2017). *Sustainable development goals in the Asian context.* Springer.

Servaes, J. (2020). *Handbook of communication for development and social change I & II*. Springer.

Servaes, J. (2021). The sustainable development goals: A major reboot or just another acronym? In M. J. Yusha'u & J. Servaes (Eds.), *The Palgrave handbook of international communication and sustainable development*. Palgrave Macmillan. https://doi.org/10.1007/978-3-030-69770-9_2

Servaes, J., & Malikhao P. (2007). Communication for sustainable development. In FAO (Eds). Communication and sustainable development. Selected papers from the 9th UN Roundtable on Communication for Development. Retrieved November 22, 2020, form http://www.fao.org/3/a-a1476e.pdf

Servaes, J., Polk, E., Shi, S., Reilly, D., & Yakupitijage, T. (2012). Towards a framework of sustainability indicators for 'communication for development and social change' projects. *International Communication Gazette., 74*(2), 99–123.

United Nations Systems Staff College. (2017). *United nations agenda for sustainable development*. Retrieved May 16, 2022, from https://www.un.org/development/desa/jpo/wp-content/uploads/sites/55/2017/02/2030-Agenda-for-Sustainable-Development-KCSD-Primer-new.pdf

Wong, B. L. H., Maaß, L., Vodden, A., Kessel, V. R., Sorbello, S., Buttigieg, S., Odone, A., and on behalf of the European Public Health Association (EUPHA) Digital Health Section. (2022). The dawn of digital public health in Europe: Implications for public health policy and practice. *The Lancet, 14*. Retrieved May 05, 2022, from https://www.thelancet.com/journals/lanepe/article/PIIS2666-7762(22)00009-6/fulltext

Yusha'u, M. J. (2021). SDG18—The missing ventilator: An introduction to the 2030 agenda for development. In M. J. Yusha'u & J. Servaes (Eds.), *The Palgrave handbook of international communication and sustainable development*. Palgrave Macmillan. https://doi.org/10.1007/978-3-030-69770-9_3

Yusha'u, M. J., & Servaes, J. (2021). *The Palgrave Handbook of international communication and sustainable development*. Palgrave Macmillan.

Zancajo, A., Verger, A., & Bolea, P. (2022, January). Digitalization and beyond: the effects of Covid-19 on post-pandemic educational policy and delivery in Europe. *Policy and Society, 41*(1), 111–128. https://doi.org/10.1093/polsoc/puab016

Index

J. Servaes, M. J. Yusha'u (eds.), *SDG18 Communicaton for All, Volume 2*, Sustainable Development Goals Series,
https://doi.org/10.1007/978-3-031-19459-7

Printed by Printforce, the Netherlands